Report on Medical School Faculty Salaries

2010–2011

Fan Zhang
Stefanie Wisniewski

AAMC Data Operations and Services
www.aamc.org

The contribution of Kavitha Sekar is gratefully acknowledged.

To order additional copies of this publication, please contact:

Association of American Medical Colleges
Customer Service/Order Fulfillment
2450 N Street, N.W.
Washington, D.C. 20037
T 202 828 0416
F 202 828 1123
www.aamc.org/publications

Price (shipping not included)

$124.00—AAMC Members
$238.00—Non-members, Non-profit
$409.00—Non-members, For-profit
(Product ID FACSAL12)

ISBN-978-1-57754-110-3
ISSN-1558-4968

Table of Contents

Compensation Tables (continued)

Faculty with a Ph.D. or Other Doctoral Degree – Basic Science Departments/Specialties

Faculty with a Ph.D. or Other Doctoral Degree – Clinical Science Departments/Specialties

Change in Mean and Median Total Compensation by Department/Specialty
2010-2011 through 2008-2009

Appendix: 2011 AAMC Faculty Salary Survey

Report on Medical School Faculty Salaries, 2010-2011

Overview

The *Report on Medical School Faculty Salaries, 2010-2011* is the AAMC's 47th review of full-time medical school faculty compensation. The report is based on data provided by 134 U.S. medical schools. All medical schools that were eligible to complete the survey throughout the entire survey administration participated. A list of participating institutions appears on page 4.

The report presents the total compensation attributable to teaching, patient care, and research for 95,643 full-time faculty. Medical schools provided data for an additional 2,653 faculty, but these faculty are not in the published tables for one or more of the following reasons:

1) The individuals earned income from the medical practice supplement component or from the bonus/incentive component of total compensation, but the institutions did not know the amounts of these components (578 faculty).

2) The individuals were non-doctoral faculty (2,051 faculty).

3) The individuals showed total compensations that were considered too low (below $33,000) to be the salaries of full-time faculty (28 faculty).

For the purposes of this report, faculty who hold both an M.D. or equivalent degree and a Ph.D. or other doctoral degree are included in the "M.D. or Equivalent Degree" tables, regardless of whether the degrees were earned simultaneously.

Data Collection

The survey collected data for the *prior* fiscal year – in this case, fiscal year 2010-2011. Respondents reported the total compensation for each full-time faculty member. The total compensation equaled the fixed/contractual salary component of total compensation plus the supplemental earnings components of total compensation (medical practice supplement, bonus/incentive pay, and uncontrolled outside earnings) for the 12-month period spanning 2010-2011. The survey, with definitions of the components of total compensation, is in the Appendix.

The AAMC deployed the survey as a Web-based application. The application required that submitted records include responses for both the fixed/contractual salary and the supplemental earnings components of total compensation. The application also tested whether or not total compensation fell within an expected range for a particular combination of degree, department/specialty, and rank. Respondents were prompted to confirm each record that fell outside the range.

Changes in the 2010-2011 Report

The following changes are reflected in the 2010-2011 Report:

Two new medical schools are among the Faculty Salary Survey participants for the first time this year: Charles E. Schmidt College of Medicine at Florida Atlantic University and Cooper Medical School of Rowan University.

Supplemental Earnings

In 2010-2011, 13,712 faculty (14.3 percent of all 95,643 faculty) were **not** eligible to receive supplemental earnings. A total of 81,931 faculty (85.7 percent) were eligible to receive supplemental earnings, although over one-quarter of this group (22,463 faculty) received no supplemental earnings.

Changes in Total Compensation since 2009-2010

For the combined ranks of assistant professor, associate professor, and professor, the mean total compensations for 2009-2010 and 2010-2011 are shown in the table below. The mean total compensation for M.D.'s in the clinical sciences was $254.9k in 2009-2010 and $262.4k in 2010-2011, an increase of 2.9 percent. Tables 32 and 33 show the change in mean total compensation for departments/specialties in the basic sciences and clinical sciences.

Total Compensation
Combined Assistant, Associate, and Professor Ranks
($1,000's)

		Basic Sciences		**Clinical Sciences**	
Degree	**Fiscal Year**	Mean Compensation	Sample Size	Mean Compensation	Sample Size
M.D.	*2009-2010*	$146.6	1,120	$254.9	56,782
	2010-2011	$150.6	1,145	$262.4	58,677
	Percent Change	2.7*	2.2*	2.9	3.3
Ph.D.	*2009-2010*	$122.3	11,202	$120.7	12,739
	2010-2011	$124.2	11,461	$123.4	12,928
	Percent Change	1.6	2.3	2.2	1.5

** Historically, the compensation and the counts for M.D. or equivalent faculty in basic science departments/specialties are more variable than the compensation and the counts for other faculty. Based on investigations of the data and conversations with participants, the pattern may be due to a variety of factors, such as changes in reporting practices, changes in organizational structures, as well as relatively small sample sizes.*

Although the percent change in mean total compensation for all faculty combined, regardless of degree, department/specialty, or rank, seems to have limited value in setting compensation policies, some organizations use this measure. The mean total compensation for the 95,643 faculty reported in 2010-2011 was $225.4k. The corresponding mean was $218.8k in 2009-2010 for 93,371 faculty. The difference amounts to a 2.9 percent increase in total compensation. During the fiscal year ending June 30, 2011, the Consumer Price Index-All Urban Consumers (CPI-U) increased by 3.6 percent.[1]

[1]Department of Labor, Bureau of Labor Statistics

List of Participating Medical Schools
AAMC Faculty Salary Survey, 2010-2011

Northeastern Region

Private (26)

Albany
Boston
Brown-Alpert
Columbia
Commonwealth
Cornell-Weill
Dartmouth
Drexel
Einstein
Georgetown
George Washington
Harvard
Hofstra North Shore-LIJ
Howard
Jefferson
Johns Hopkins
Mount Sinai
New York Medical
New York University
Penn State
Pennsylvania-Perelman
Pittsburgh
Rochester
Temple
Tufts
Yale

Public (12)

Buffalo
Connecticut
Cooper
Maryland
Massachusetts
Stony Brook
SUNY Downstate
SUNY Upstate
UMDNJ New Jersey
UMDNJ-RW Johnson
Uniformed Services-Hebert
Vermont

Southern Region

Private (13)

Baylor
Caribe
Duke
Emory
Meharry
Mercer
Miami-Miller
Morehouse
Ponce
Tulane
Vanderbilt
Virginia Tech Carilion
Wake Forest

Public (35)

Alabama
Arkansas
Central Florida
East Carolina-Brody
Eastern Virginia
East Tennessee-Quillen
FIU-Wertheim
Florida
Florida Atlantic-Schmidt
Florida State
Kentucky
Louisville
LSU New Orleans
LSU Shreveport
Marshall-Edwards
MC Georgia
Mississippi
MU South Carolina
North Carolina
Oklahoma
Puerto Rico
South Alabama
South Carolina
USF-Morsani
Tennessee
Texas A&M
Texas Tech
Texas Tech-Foster
UT Galveston
UT Houston
UT HSC San Antonio
UT Southwestern
Virginia
Virginia Commonwealth
West Virginia

Midwestern Region

Private (11)

Case Western
Chicago Med-Franklin
Chicago-Pritzker
Creighton
Loyola-Stritch
Mayo
MC Wisconsin
Northwestern-Feinberg
Rush
St Louis
Washington U St Louis

Public (21)

Cincinnati
Illinois
Indiana
Iowa-Carver
Kansas
Michigan
Michigan State
Minnesota
Missouri Columbia
Missouri Kansas City
Nebraska
North Dakota
Northeastern Ohio
Oakland Beaumont
Ohio State
South Dakota-Sanford
Southern Illinois
Toledo
Wayne State
Wisconsin
Wright State-Boonshoft

Western Region

Private (3)

Loma Linda
Southern Cal-Keck
Stanford

Public (13)

Arizona
Colorado
Hawaii-Burns
Nevada
New Mexico
Oregon
UC Davis
UC Irvine
UCLA-Geffen
UC San Diego
UC San Francisco
Utah
U Washington

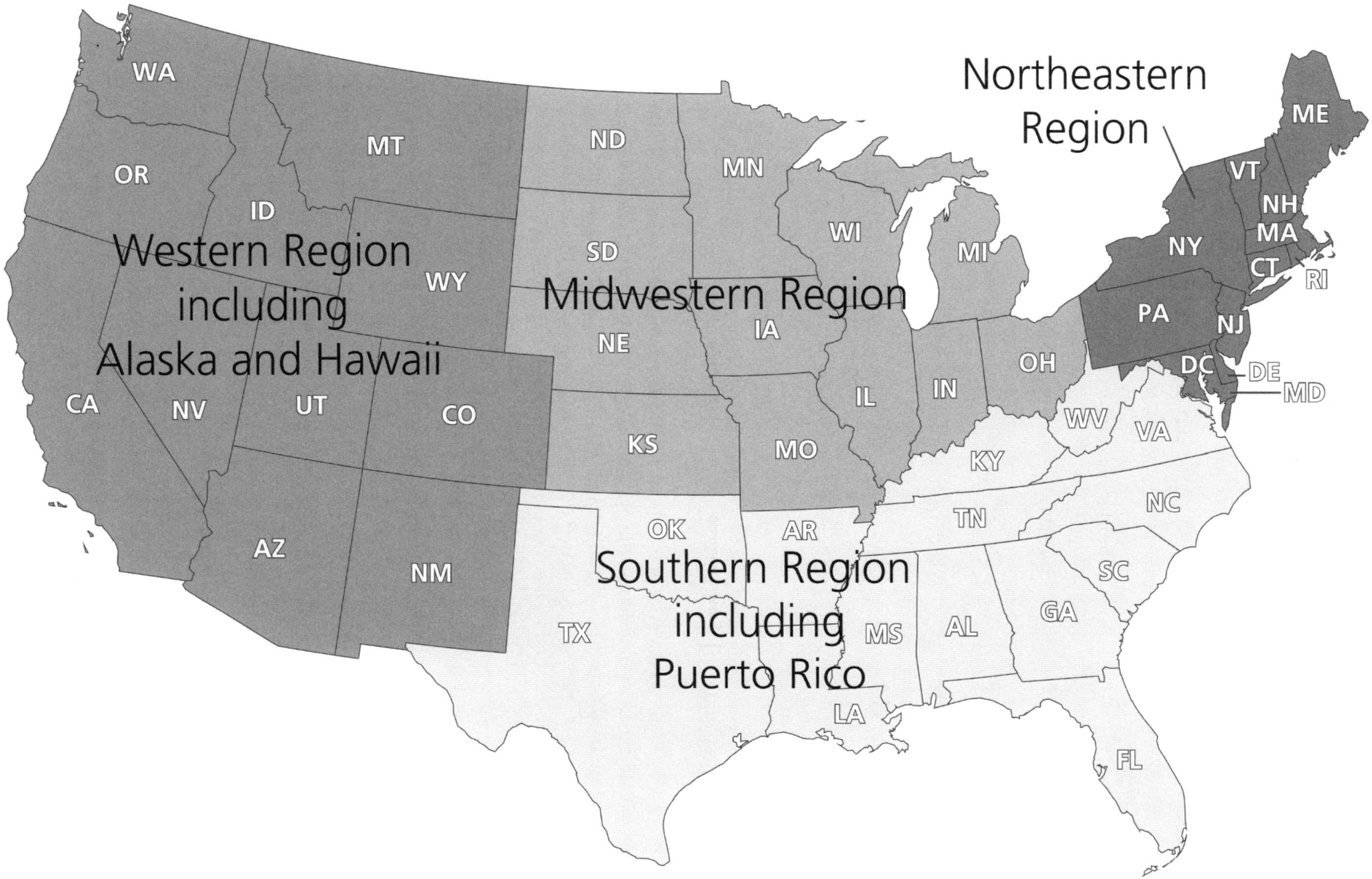
Northeastern Region
Midwestern Region
Western Region including Alaska and Hawaii
Southern Region including Puerto Rico
WA
OR
CA
ID
NV
MT
WY
UT
CO
AZ
NM
ND
SD
NE
KS
MN
IA
MO
WI
IL
MI
IN
OH
OK
TX
AR
LA
MS
AL
TN
KY
WV
VA
NC
SC
GA
FL
ME
VT
NH
MA
NY
CT
RI
PA
NJ
DC
DE
MD

Key to Compensation Tables

Sample Table Entry		Key
Associate Professor		The figures refer to associate professors.
Count:	**79**	Seventy-nine associate professors are in the sample.
25th:	**149**	The 25th percentile for total compensation is $149,000.
Median:	**191**	The median total compensation (50th percentile) is $191,000.
75th:	**259**	The 75th percentile for total compensation is $259,000.
Mean:	**216.1**	The mean (average) total compensation is $216,100.

Note on the Computation of Percentiles

Percentiles were produced when at least five faculty members were available for analysis. From a sorted array of salaries, the 50th percentile (the median) corresponded to the salaries below which 50 percent of the other salaries appeared. In the case of an even number of salaries, the 50th percentile equaled the average of the middlemost salaries. The 25th percentile corresponded to the median of the bottom half of salaries, and the 75th percentile corresponded to the median of the upper half of salaries.

TABLE 1 Survey Sample – Total Reported Faculty By Department/Specialty Type, Degree, and Institutional Control

	Total		Public		Private	
ALL DEPARTMENTS/SPECIALTIES	N	%	N	%	N	%
Total	95,643	100.0%	48,367	100.0%	47,276	100.0%
M.D. or Equivalent Degree	68,854	72.0%	33,878	70.0%	34,976	74.0%
Ph.D. or Other Doctoral Degree	26,789	28.0%	14,489	30.0%	12,300	26.0%
BASIC SCIENCE	N	%	N	%	N	%
Total	13,956	100.0%	7,707	100.0%	6,249	100.0%
M.D. or Equivalent Degree	1,324	9.5%	538	7.0%	786	12.6%
Ph.D. or Other Doctoral Degree	12,632	90.5%	7,169	93.0%	5,463	87.4%
CLINICAL SCIENCE	N	%	N	%	N	%
Total	81,687	100.0%	40,660	100.0%	41,027	100.0%
M.D. or Equivalent Degree	67,530	82.7%	33,340	82.0%	34,190	83.3%
Ph.D. or Other Doctoral Degree	14,157	17.3%	7,320	18.0%	6,837	16.7%

TABLE 2 Survey Sample – Total Reported Faculty
By Department/Specialty Type, Rank, and Institutional Control

	Total		Public		Private	
ALL DEPARTMENTS/SPECIALTIES	N	%	N	%	N	%
Total	95,643	100.0%	48,367	100.0%	47,276	100.0%
Chair	2,477	2.6%	1,450	3.0%	1,027	2.2%
Chief	2,745	2.9%	1,552	3.2%	1,193	2.5%
Professor	21,620	22.6%	12,055	24.9%	9,565	20.2%
Associate Professor	21,453	22.4%	11,372	23.5%	10,081	21.3%
Assistant Professor	41,138	43.0%	20,147	41.7%	20,991	44.4%
Instructor	6,210	6.5%	1,791	3.7%	4,419	9.3%
BASIC SCIENCE	N	%	N	%	N	%
Total	13,956	100.0%	7,707	100.0%	6,249	100.0%
Chair	648	4.6%	364	4.7%	284	4.5%
Chief	44	0.3%	27	0.4%	17	0.3%
Professor	4,761	34.1%	2,724	35.3%	2,037	32.6%
Associate Professor	3,477	24.9%	1,984	25.7%	1,493	23.9%
Assistant Professor	4,368	31.3%	2,309	30.0%	2,059	32.9%
Instructor	658	4.7%	299	3.9%	359	5.7%
CLINICAL SCIENCE	N	%	N	%	N	%
Total	81,687	100.0%	40,660	100.0%	41,027	100.0%
Chair	1,829	2.2%	1,086	2.7%	743	1.8%
Chief	2,701	3.3%	1,525	3.8%	1,176	2.9%
Professor	16,859	20.6%	9,331	22.9%	7,528	18.3%
Associate Professor	17,976	22.0%	9,388	23.1%	8,588	20.9%
Assistant Professor	36,770	45.0%	17,838	43.9%	18,932	46.1%
Instructor	5,552	6.8%	1,492	3.7%	4,060	9.9%

TABLE 3 Survey Sample – Total Reported Faculty
By Department/Specialty Type, Region, and Institutional Control

	Total		Public		Private	
ALL DEPARTMENTS/SPECIALTIES	N	%	N	%	N	%
Total	95,643	100.0%	48,367	100.0%	47,276	100.0%
Northeast	31,441	32.9%	6,915	14.3%	24,526	51.9%
Midwest	22,457	23.5%	12,038	24.9%	10,419	22.0%
South	27,860	29.1%	17,968	37.1%	9,892	20.9%
West	13,885	14.5%	11,446	23.7%	2,439	5.2%
BASIC SCIENCE	N	%	N	%	N	%
Total	13,956	100.0%	7,707	100.0%	6,249	100.0%
Northeast	4,299	30.8%	1,151	14.9%	3,148	50.4%
Midwest	3,256	23.3%	1,910	24.8%	1,346	21.5%
South	4,928	35.3%	3,415	44.3%	1,513	24.2%
West	1,473	10.6%	1,231	16.0%	242	3.9%
CLINICAL SCIENCE	N	%	N	%	N	%
Total	81,687	100.0%	40,660	100.0%	41,027	100.0%
Northeast	27,142	33.2%	5,764	14.2%	21,378	52.1%
Midwest	19,201	23.5%	10,128	24.9%	9,073	22.1%
South	22,932	28.1%	14,553	35.8%	8,379	20.4%
West	12,412	15.2%	10,215	25.1%	2,197	5.4%

TABLE 4

Summary Statistics on Medical School Faculty Compensation for All Schools
M.D. or Equivalent Degree, Basic Science Departments/Specialties
Total Compensation in Thousands of Dollars

BASIC SCIENCE - TOTAL ALL DEPARTMENTS/SPECIALTIES

	Instructor	Assistant Professor	Associate Professor	Professor	Chief	Chair
Count:	57	366	307	472	13	109
25th:	48	66	105	154	211	237
Median:	54	88	128	190	233	310
75th:	65	119	162	230	280	383
Mean:	60.6	97.7	137.4	200.4	243.5	326.8

Anatomy

	Instructor	Assistant Professor	Associate Professor	Professor	Chief	Chair
Count:	5	28	23	22	0	3
25th:	45	63	76	125		
Median:	58	70	94	154		
75th:	64	85	115	202		
Mean:	55.0	72.3	90.0	160.2		

Biochemistry

	Instructor	Assistant Professor	Associate Professor	Professor	Chief	Chair
Count:	3	31	21	31	0	9
25th:		54	103	148		241
Median:		78	113	165		328
75th:		101	129	236		365
Mean:		83.4	119.6	185.7		297.7

Bioethics/Medical Humanities

	Instructor	Assistant Professor	Associate Professor	Professor	Chief	Chair
Count:	0	2	2	6	0	5
25th:				189		222
Median:				199		233
75th:				210		275
Mean:				184.2		245.2

Biomedical Informatics

	Instructor	Assistant Professor	Associate Professor	Professor	Chief	Chair
Count:	0	15	19	8	2	3
25th:		132	148	185		
Median:		150	169	233		
75th:		191	219	278		
Mean:		162.6	184.4	246.0		

TABLE 4

Summary Statistics on Medical School Faculty Compensation for All Schools M.D. or Equivalent Degree, Basic Science Departments/Specialties Total Compensation in Thousands of Dollars (continued)

Biostatistics

	Instructor	Assistant Professor	Associate Professor	Professor	Chief	Chair
Count:	1	4	11	5	2	2
25th:			132	162		
Median:			156	200		
75th:			172	286		
Mean:			160.3	219.0		

Genetics

	Instructor	Assistant Professor	Associate Professor	Professor	Chief	Chair
Count:	4	62	34	48	4	15
25th:		88	136	174		262
Median:		112	153	210		363
75th:		140	163	243		439
Mean:		116.1	149.4	219.3		409.8

Microbiology

	Instructor	Assistant Professor	Associate Professor	Professor	Chief	Chair
Count:	5	28	26	59	0	14
25th:	45	68	107	149		277
Median:	48	82	126	179		338
75th:	62	111	138	225		384
Mean:	52.2	92.4	120.5	191.0		338.7

Molecular & Cellular Biology

	Instructor	Assistant Professor	Associate Professor	Professor	Chief	Chair
Count:	7	37	28	49	0	9
25th:	44	62	117	164		230
Median:	50	83	136	200		310
75th:	62	99	163	270		538
Mean:	55.0	87.1	143.9	227.1		401.1

Neurosciences

	Instructor	Assistant Professor	Associate Professor	Professor	Chief	Chair
Count:	5	27	30	33	1	10
25th:	56	70	100	158		272
Median:	60	93	120	197		303
75th:	78	122	181	232		334
Mean:	65.4	107.4	150.4	201.3		330.5

TABLE 4

Summary Statistics on Medical School Faculty Compensation for All Schools M.D. or Equivalent Degree, Basic Science Departments/Specialties Total Compensation in Thousands of Dollars (continued)

Pharmacology

	Instructor	Assistant Professor	Associate Professor	Professor	Chief	Chair
Count:	10	43	33	81	1	9
25th:	47	58	102	154		243
Median:	50	74	126	188		342
75th:	52	88	172	229		430
Mean:	53.0	79.8	136.9	197.7		338.6

Physiology

	Instructor	Assistant Professor	Associate Professor	Professor	Chief	Chair
Count:	7	27	31	68	2	12
25th:	41	67	103	142		246
Median:	46	75	113	166		280
75th:	62	93	144	213		345
Mean:	49.7	85.4	123.0	180.6		283.8

Other Basic Sciences

	Instructor	Assistant Professor	Associate Professor	Professor	Chief	Chair
Count:	10	62	49	62	1	18
25th:	54	65	114	159		192
Median:	67	100	130	201		236
75th:	90	130	183	233		336
Mean:	73.4	104.0	142.8	213.8		276.5

TABLE 5

Summary Statistics on Medical School Faculty Compensation for Public Schools M.D. or Equivalent Degree, Basic Science Departments/Specialties Total Compensation in Thousands of Dollars

BASIC SCIENCE - TOTAL ALL DEPARTMENTS/SPECIALTIES

	Instructor	Assistant Professor	Associate Professor	Professor	Chief	Chair
Count:	22	143	125	193	9	46
25th:	48	65	104	150	211	237
Median:	51	83	129	180	233	281
75th:	59	105	157	225	280	355
Mean:	54.8	90.7	135.5	196.6	243.3	308.3

Anatomy

	Instructor	Assistant Professor	Associate Professor	Professor	Chief	Chair
Count:	3	16	10	10	0	1
25th:		64	94	156		
Median:		70	106	192		
75th:		79	115	225		
Mean:		72.2	103.8	193.9		

Biochemistry

	Instructor	Assistant Professor	Associate Professor	Professor	Chief	Chair
Count:	0	11	12	10	0	3
25th:		53	108	148		
Median:		78	128	165		
75th:		93	148	242		
Mean:		77.2	128.2	184.5		

Bioethics/Medical Humanities

	Instructor	Assistant Professor	Associate Professor	Professor	Chief	Chair
Count:	0	1	1	2	0	3
25th:						
Median:						
75th:						
Mean:						

Biomedical Informatics

	Instructor	Assistant Professor	Associate Professor	Professor	Chief	Chair
Count:	0	2	9	4	0	1
25th:			141			
Median:			165			
75th:			200			
Mean:			168.4			

TABLE 5 Summary Statistics on Medical School Faculty Compensation for Public Schools
M.D. or Equivalent Degree, Basic Science Departments/Specialties
Total Compensation in Thousands of Dollars (continued)

Biostatistics

	Instructor	Assistant Professor	Associate Professor	Professor	Chief	Chair
Count:	1	1	6	2	2	1
25th:			133			
Median:			160			
75th:			173			
Mean:			170.5			

Genetics

	Instructor	Assistant Professor	Associate Professor	Professor	Chief	Chair
Count:	0	12	11	17	3	6
25th:		101	136	170		262
Median:		123	151	204		393
75th:		147	160	229		439
Mean:		117.7	143.3	199.8		391.5

Microbiology

	Instructor	Assistant Professor	Associate Professor	Professor	Chief	Chair
Count:	3	18	8	32	0	7
25th:		70	111	146		255
Median:		82	118	174		297
75th:		96	131	220		355
Mean:		88.4	117.9	187.4		349.9

Molecular & Cellular Biology

	Instructor	Assistant Professor	Associate Professor	Professor	Chief	Chair
Count:	4	21	9	21	0	3
25th:		58	95	173		
Median:		75	142	223		
75th:		96	163	343		
Mean:		79.0	141.7	257.3		

Neurosciences

	Instructor	Assistant Professor	Associate Professor	Professor	Chief	Chair
Count:	1	11	17	14	1	4
25th:		67	95	149		
Median:		101	107	178		
75th:		174	191	245		
Mean:		125.0	137.9	197.9		

TABLE 5

Summary Statistics on Medical School Faculty Compensation for Public Schools M.D. or Equivalent Degree, Basic Science Departments/Specialties Total Compensation in Thousands of Dollars (continued)

Pharmacology

	Instructor	Assistant Professor	Associate Professor	Professor	Chief	Chair
Count:	5	20	11	33	0	5
25th:	46	58	91	134		191
Median:	50	68	109	164		342
75th:	70	81	192	214		354
Mean:	56.2	68.8	140.2	178.0		286.2

Physiology

	Instructor	Assistant Professor	Associate Professor	Professor	Chief	Chair
Count:	3	12	12	31	2	5
25th:		66	105	143		233
Median:		77	113	163		275
75th:		94	142	212		334
Mean:		86.3	129.5	182.8		281.6

Other Basic Sciences

	Instructor	Assistant Professor	Associate Professor	Professor	Chief	Chair
Count:	2	18	19	17	1	7
25th:		97	95	121		146
Median:		119	129	187		236
75th:		127	156	224		384
Mean:		112.4	127.6	182.3		285.6

TABLE 6 Summary Statistics on Medical School Faculty Compensation for Private Schools
M.D. or Equivalent Degree, Basic Science Departments/Specialties
Total Compensation in Thousands of Dollars

BASIC SCIENCE - TOTAL ALL DEPARTMENTS/SPECIALTIES

	Instructor	Assistant Professor	Associate Professor	Professor	Chief	Chair
Count:	35	223	182	279	4	63
25th:	50	69	106	155		236
Median:	58	93	128	195		320
75th:	70	125	163	235		401
Mean:	64.2	102.1	138.7	203.0		340.3

Anatomy

	Instructor	Assistant Professor	Associate Professor	Professor	Chief	Chair
Count:	2	12	13	12	0	2
25th:		60	48	111		
Median:		70	85	134		
75th:		87	102	154		
Mean:		72.5	79.5	132.1		

Biochemistry

	Instructor	Assistant Professor	Associate Professor	Professor	Chief	Chair
Count:	3	20	9	21	0	6
25th:		57	99	146		219
Median:		78	104	165		328
75th:		108	119	232		328
Mean:		86.9	108.1	186.3		278.8

Bioethics/Medical Humanities

	Instructor	Assistant Professor	Associate Professor	Professor	Chief	Chair
Count:	0	1	1	4	0	2
25th:						
Median:						
75th:						
Mean:						

Biomedical Informatics

	Instructor	Assistant Professor	Associate Professor	Professor	Chief	Chair
Count:	0	13	10	4	2	2
25th:		130	168			
Median:		150	192			
75th:		198	219			
Mean:		164.9	198.7			

TABLE 6 **Summary Statistics on Medical School Faculty Compensation for Private Schools M.D. or Equivalent Degree, Basic Science Departments/Specialties Total Compensation in Thousands of Dollars (continued)**

Biostatistics

	Instructor	Assistant Professor	Associate Professor	Professor	Chief	Chair
Count:	0	3	5	3	0	1
25th:			126			
Median:			156			
75th:			166			
Mean:			148.0			

Genetics

	Instructor	Assistant Professor	Associate Professor	Professor	Chief	Chair
Count:	4	50	23	31	1	9
25th:		87	133	175		283
Median:		112	160	212		352
75th:		139	170	270		518
Mean:		115.7	152.3	229.9		422.0

Microbiology

	Instructor	Assistant Professor	Associate Professor	Professor	Chief	Chair
Count:	2	10	18	27	0	7
25th:		66	93	152		324
Median:		93	127	179		383
75th:		131	139	235		385
Mean:		99.5	121.6	195.2		327.6

Molecular & Cellular Biology

	Instructor	Assistant Professor	Associate Professor	Professor	Chief	Chair
Count:	3	16	19	28	0	6
25th:		64	117	142		309
Median:		90	129	192		464
75th:		113	163	242		605
Mean:		97.8	144.9	204.4		476.3

Neurosciences

	Instructor	Assistant Professor	Associate Professor	Professor	Chief	Chair
Count:	4	16	13	19	0	6
25th:		73	113	166		255
Median:		93	123	203		314
75th:		109	162	230		334
Mean:		95.3	166.9	203.8		352.3

TABLE 6 Summary Statistics on Medical School Faculty Compensation for Private Schools M.D. or Equivalent Degree, Basic Science Departments/Specialties Total Compensation in Thousands of Dollars (continued)

Pharmacology

	Instructor	Assistant Professor	Associate Professor	Professor	Chief	Chair
Count:	5	23	22	48	1	4
25th:	47	65	110	171		
Median:	50	76	129	201		
75th:	53	100	170	241		
Mean:	49.8	89.4	135.2	211.3		

Physiology

	Instructor	Assistant Professor	Associate Professor	Professor	Chief	Chair
Count:	4	15	19	37	0	7
25th:		67	93	141		244
Median:		75	113	173		280
75th:		84	144	214		360
Mean:		84.6	118.9	178.7		285.4

Other Basic Sciences

	Instructor	Assistant Professor	Associate Professor	Professor	Chief	Chair
Count:	8	44	30	45	0	11
25th:	64	62	119	163		192
Median:	72	88	134	205		236
75th:	97	133	192	266		315
Mean:	78.9	100.5	152.4	225.8		270.7

TABLE 7 Summary Statistics on Medical School Faculty Compensation for Northeastern Region
M.D. or Equivalent Degree, Basic Science Departments/Specialties
Total Compensation in Thousands of Dollars

BASIC SCIENCE - TOTAL ALL DEPARTMENTS/SPECIALTIES

	Instructor	Assistant Professor	Associate Professor	Professor	Chief	Chair
Count:	15	128	129	206	1	42
25th:	51	65	115	158		255
Median:	62	87	138	190		322
75th:	75	120	180	230		416
Mean:	66.3	99.1	148.8	200.9		367.0

Anatomy

	Instructor	Assistant Professor	Associate Professor	Professor	Chief	Chair
Count:	0	6	2	8	0	3
25th:		60		140		
Median:		70		187		
75th:		74		215		
Mean:		69.2		179.1		

Biochemistry

	Instructor	Assistant Professor	Associate Professor	Professor	Chief	Chair
Count:	0	11	8	15	0	1
25th:		56	99	138		
Median:		66	104	165		
75th:		98	111	236		
Mean:		74.1	106.0	189.2		

Bioethics/Medical Humanities

	Instructor	Assistant Professor	Associate Professor	Professor	Chief	Chair
Count:	0	0	1	3	0	2
25th:						
Median:						
75th:						
Mean:						

Biomedical Informatics

	Instructor	Assistant Professor	Associate Professor	Professor	Chief	Chair
Count:	0	4	9	1	0	2
25th:			152			
Median:			196			
75th:			244			
Mean:			201.8			

TABLE 7

Summary Statistics on Medical School Faculty Compensation for Northeastern Region M.D. or Equivalent Degree, Basic Science Departments/Specialties Total Compensation in Thousands of Dollars (continued)

Biostatistics

	Instructor	Assistant Professor	Associate Professor	Professor	Chief	Chair
Count:	0	1	3	3	0	1
25th:						
Median:						
75th:						
Mean:						

Genetics

	Instructor	Assistant Professor	Associate Professor	Professor	Chief	Chair
Count:	1	14	12	15	0	4
25th:		104	137	170		
Median:		128	148	190		
75th:		139	161	239		
Mean:		126.6	145.1	210.3		

Microbiology

	Instructor	Assistant Professor	Associate Professor	Professor	Chief	Chair
Count:	0	5	14	23	0	4
25th:		101	107	150		
Median:		131	128	179		
75th:		178	141	209		
Mean:		137.6	126.6	186.7		

Molecular & Cellular Biology

	Instructor	Assistant Professor	Associate Professor	Professor	Chief	Chair
Count:	4	17	12	21	0	5
25th:		65	125	167		310
Median:		83	142	192		457
75th:		113	179	285		695
Mean:		96.8	153.6	215.8		493.0

Neurosciences

	Instructor	Assistant Professor	Associate Professor	Professor	Chief	Chair
Count:	3	16	19	22	0	6
25th:		88	112	167		282
Median:		101	142	202		303
75th:		135	197	230		334
Mean:		119.8	170.1	206.7		354.7

TABLE 7 Summary Statistics on Medical School Faculty Compensation for Northeastern Region M.D. or Equivalent Degree, Basic Science Departments/Specialties Total Compensation in Thousands of Dollars (continued)

Pharmacology

	Instructor	Assistant Professor	Associate Professor	Professor	Chief	Chair
Count:	3	11	17	29	0	5
25th:		52	105	165		243
Median:		65	125	192		315
75th:		76	162	221		535
Mean:		66.0	133.4	190.1		374.2

Physiology

	Instructor	Assistant Professor	Associate Professor	Professor	Chief	Chair
Count:	0	8	5	37	1	4
25th:		68	83	151		
Median:		70	130	174		
75th:		78	159	234		
Mean:		87.3	122.8	186.3		

Other Basic Sciences

	Instructor	Assistant Professor	Associate Professor	Professor	Chief	Chair
Count:	4	35	27	29	0	5
25th:		55	126	177		195
Median:		85	156	203		265
75th:		121	202	307		469
Mean:		93.5	163.9	238.2		318.6

TABLE 8 Summary Statistics on Medical School Faculty Compensation for Southern Region
M.D. or Equivalent Degree, Basic Science Departments/Specialties
Total Compensation in Thousands of Dollars

BASIC SCIENCE - TOTAL ALL DEPARTMENTS/SPECIALTIES

	Instructor	Assistant Professor	Associate Professor	Professor	Chief	Chair
Count:	28	138	88	110	3	30
25th:	48	64	101	148		218
Median:	53	85	122	195		304
75th:	58	112	156	233		384
Mean:	52.7	91.7	131.0	201.3		301.7

Anatomy

	Instructor	Assistant Professor	Associate Professor	Professor	Chief	Chair
Count:	3	15	11	5	0	0
25th:		62	49	75		
Median:		69	90	130		
75th:		84	119	149		
Mean:		69.7	84.9	115.4		

Biochemistry

	Instructor	Assistant Professor	Associate Professor	Professor	Chief	Chair
Count:	2	10	7	5	0	2
25th:		53	128	93		
Median:		59	130	248		
75th:		90	148	257		
Mean:		68.4	140.1	189.2		

Bioethics/Medical Humanities

	Instructor	Assistant Professor	Associate Professor	Professor	Chief	Chair
Count:	0	1	1	2	0	1
25th:						
Median:						
75th:						
Mean:						

Biomedical Informatics

	Instructor	Assistant Professor	Associate Professor	Professor	Chief	Chair
Count:	0	6	3	2	0	0
25th:		138				
Median:		145				
75th:		190				
Mean:		157.3				

TABLE 8 Summary Statistics on Medical School Faculty Compensation for Southern Region M.D. or Equivalent Degree, Basic Science Departments/Specialties Total Compensation in Thousands of Dollars (continued)

Biostatistics

	Instructor	Assistant Professor	Associate Professor	Professor	Chief	Chair
Count:	1	3	2	1	0	0
25th:						
Median:						
75th:						
Mean:						

Genetics

	Instructor	Assistant Professor	Associate Professor	Professor	Chief	Chair
Count:	1	37	13	22	1	7
25th:		82	148	190		310
Median:		100	160	214		420
75th:		134	173	265		601
Mean:		106.8	161.2	231.1		422.3

Microbiology

	Instructor	Assistant Professor	Associate Professor	Professor	Chief	Chair
Count:	4	15	5	17	0	5
25th:		64	102	140		93
Median:		73	112	168		297
75th:		85	118	217		370
Mean:		77.1	110.0	175.2		244.6

Molecular & Cellular Biology

	Instructor	Assistant Professor	Associate Professor	Professor	Chief	Chair
Count:	2	13	12	16	0	3
25th:		50	101	164		
Median:		75	138	205		
75th:		96	160	297		
Mean:		72.7	139.6	239.8		

Neurosciences

	Instructor	Assistant Professor	Associate Professor	Professor	Chief	Chair
Count:	1	6	6	5	1	2
25th:		61	93	128		
Median:		65	103	150		
75th:		74	114	273		
Mean:		69.8	117.2	190.2		

TABLE 8 Summary Statistics on Medical School Faculty Compensation for Southern Region M.D. or Equivalent Degree, Basic Science Departments/Specialties Total Compensation in Thousands of Dollars (continued)

Pharmacology

	Instructor	Assistant Professor	Associate Professor	Professor	Chief	Chair
Count:	5	14	10	15	0	3
25th:	46	58	98	161		
Median:	50	71	120	190		
75th:	52	100	191	222		
Mean:	49.0	92.2	138.5	190.2		

Physiology

	Instructor	Assistant Professor	Associate Professor	Professor	Chief	Chair
Count:	6	7	10	10	1	5
25th:	44	64	105	120		163
Median:	51	84	106	145		275
75th:	62	106	122	188		283
Mean:	51.8	99.3	121.2	161.7		233.2

Other Basic Sciences

	Instructor	Assistant Professor	Associate Professor	Professor	Chief	Chair
Count:	3	11	8	10	0	2
25th:		77	103	166		
Median:		102	121	219		
75th:		124	128	226		
Mean:		102.3	117.4	203.1		

TABLE 9 Summary Statistics on Medical School Faculty Compensation for Midwestern Region
M.D. or Equivalent Degree, Basic Science Departments/Specialties
Total Compensation in Thousands of Dollars

BASIC SCIENCE - TOTAL ALL DEPARTMENTS/SPECIALTIES

	Instructor	Assistant Professor	Associate Professor	Professor	Chief	Chair
Count:	12	69	50	102	3	23
25th:	45	72	97	153		236
Median:	58	88	113	180		318
75th:	97	110	132	227		353
Mean:	71.6	95.6	119.4	195.2		319.2

Anatomy

	Instructor	Assistant Professor	Associate Professor	Professor	Chief	Chair
Count:	2	6	7	7	0	0
25th:		65	97	112		
Median:		77	105	143		
75th:		102	115	171		
Mean:		82.2	104.1	138.4		

Biochemistry

	Instructor	Assistant Professor	Associate Professor	Professor	Chief	Chair
Count:	1	6	4	5	0	3
25th:		54		150		
Median:		89		159		
75th:		100		177		
Mean:		87.8		162.2		

Bioethics/Medical Humanities

	Instructor	Assistant Professor	Associate Professor	Professor	Chief	Chair
Count:	0	0	0	1	0	1
25th:						
Median:						
75th:						
Mean:						

Biomedical Informatics

	Instructor	Assistant Professor	Associate Professor	Professor	Chief	Chair
Count:	0	0	1	2	0	0
25th:						
Median:						
75th:						
Mean:						

TABLE 9 Summary Statistics on Medical School Faculty Compensation for Midwestern Region
M.D. or Equivalent Degree, Basic Science Departments/Specialties
Total Compensation in Thousands of Dollars (continued)

Biostatistics

	Instructor	Assistant Professor	Associate Professor	Professor	Chief	Chair
Count:	0	0	2	0	0	0
25th:						
Median:						
75th:						
Mean:						

Genetics

	Instructor	Assistant Professor	Associate Professor	Professor	Chief	Chair
Count:	2	9	5	7	1	2
25th:		88	100	168		
Median:		127	113	209		
75th:		164	166	227		
Mean:		132.3	128.8	203.1		

Microbiology

	Instructor	Assistant Professor	Associate Professor	Professor	Chief	Chair
Count:	1	6	3	11	0	3
25th:		64		134		
Median:		89		173		
75th:		102		235		
Mean:		83.7		192.8		

Molecular & Cellular Biology

	Instructor	Assistant Professor	Associate Professor	Professor	Chief	Chair
Count:	1	2	3	8	0	0
25th:				142		
Median:				178		
75th:				224		
Mean:				183.9		

Neurosciences

	Instructor	Assistant Professor	Associate Professor	Professor	Chief	Chair
Count:	0	2	3	5	0	1
25th:				171		
Median:				184		
75th:				252		
Mean:				205.8		

TABLE 9 Summary Statistics on Medical School Faculty Compensation for Midwestern Region M.D. or Equivalent Degree, Basic Science Departments/Specialties Total Compensation in Thousands of Dollars (continued)

Pharmacology

	Instructor	Assistant Professor	Associate Professor	Professor	Chief	Chair
Count:	2	17	5	31	1	1
25th:		69	100	150		
Median:		75	129	182		
75th:		89	150	248		
Mean:		77.9	125.4	208.4		

Physiology

	Instructor	Assistant Professor	Associate Professor	Professor	Chief	Chair
Count:	1	10	12	10	0	3
25th:		71	98	161		
Median:		81	112	187		
75th:		93	126	211		
Mean:		80.5	113.6	185.9		

Other Basic Sciences

	Instructor	Assistant Professor	Associate Professor	Professor	Chief	Chair
Count:	2	11	5	15	1	9
25th:		97	91	157		169
Median:		127	116	204		236
75th:		160	169	248		343
Mean:		130.7	126.8	205.1		265.9

TABLE 10 **Summary Statistics on Medical School Faculty Compensation for Western Region M.D. or Equivalent Degree, Basic Science Departments/Specialties Total Compensation in Thousands of Dollars**

BASIC SCIENCE - TOTAL ALL DEPARTMENTS/SPECIALTIES

	Instructor	Assistant Professor	Associate Professor	Professor	Chief	Chair
Count:	2	31	40	54	6	14
25th:		88	111	143	233	232
Median:		122	140	192	257	257
75th:		151	162	237	282	279
Mean:		122.7	137.3	206.2	255.2	272.2

Anatomy

	Instructor	Assistant Professor	Associate Professor	Professor	Chief	Chair
Count:	0	1	3	2	0	0
25th:						
Median:						
75th:						
Mean:						

Biochemistry

	Instructor	Assistant Professor	Associate Professor	Professor	Chief	Chair
Count:	0	4	2	6	0	3
25th:				156		
Median:				195		
75th:				228		
Mean:				193.8		

Bioethics/Medical Humanities

	Instructor	Assistant Professor	Associate Professor	Professor	Chief	Chair
Count:	0	1	0	0	0	1
25th:						
Median:						
75th:						
Mean:						

Biomedical Informatics

	Instructor	Assistant Professor	Associate Professor	Professor	Chief	Chair
Count:	0	5	6	3	2	1
25th:		141	148			
Median:		163	164			
75th:		203	166			
Mean:		169.8	157.3			

TABLE 10 Summary Statistics on Medical School Faculty Compensation for Western Region M.D. or Equivalent Degree, Basic Science Departments/Specialties Total Compensation in Thousands of Dollars (continued)

Biostatistics

	Instructor	Assistant Professor	Associate Professor	Professor	Chief	Chair
Count:	0	0	4	1	2	1
25th:						
Median:						
75th:						
Mean:						

Genetics

	Instructor	Assistant Professor	Associate Professor	Professor	Chief	Chair
Count:	0	2	4	4	2	2
25th:						
Median:						
75th:						
Mean:						

Microbiology

	Instructor	Assistant Professor	Associate Professor	Professor	Chief	Chair
Count:	0	2	4	8	0	2
25th:				194		
Median:				218		
75th:				273		
Mean:				234.5		

Molecular & Cellular Biology

	Instructor	Assistant Professor	Associate Professor	Professor	Chief	Chair
Count:	0	5	1	4	0	1
25th:		62				
Median:		88				
75th:		127				
Mean:		93.0				

Neurosciences

	Instructor	Assistant Professor	Associate Professor	Professor	Chief	Chair
Count:	1	3	2	1	0	1
25th:						
Median:						
75th:						
Mean:						

TABLE 10 Summary Statistics on Medical School Faculty Compensation for Western Region M.D. or Equivalent Degree, Basic Science Departments/Specialties Total Compensation in Thousands of Dollars (continued)

Pharmacology

	Instructor	Assistant Professor	Associate Professor	Professor	Chief	Chair
Count:	0	1	1	6	0	0
25th:				137		
Median:				154		
75th:				294		
Mean:				198.0		

Physiology

	Instructor	Assistant Professor	Associate Professor	Professor	Chief	Chair
Count:	0	2	4	11	0	0
25th:				140		
Median:				156		
75th:				201		
Mean:				173.5		

Other Basic Sciences

	Instructor	Assistant Professor	Associate Professor	Professor	Chief	Chair
Count:	1	5	9	8	0	2
25th:		81	80	100		
Median:		122	114	173		
75th:		164	138	198		
Mean:		122.2	111.1	155.3		

TABLE 11 Summary Statistics on Medical School Faculty Compensation for All Schools
M.D. or Equivalent Degree, Clinical Science Departments/Specialties
Total Compensation in Thousands of Dollars

CLINICAL SCIENCE - TOTAL ALL DEPARTMENTS/SPECIALTIES

	Instructor	Assistant Professor	Associate Professor	Professor	Chief	Chair
Count:	4,512	30,665	14,577	13,435	2,562	1,779
25th:	107	155	181	213	234	356
Median:	155	204	236	273	308	475
75th:	222	286	329	368	417	611
Mean:	176.9	234.3	275.3	312.8	350.9	519.0

Total Anesthesiology

	Instructor	Assistant Professor	Associate Professor	Professor	Chief	Chair
Count:	351	2,532	927	612	96	95
25th:	224	270	299	313	316	456
Median:	285	308	337	355	361	515
75th:	332	354	387	404	390	603
Mean:	277.6	312.1	341.7	358.4	363.1	531.4

Anesthesiology: General

	Instructor	Assistant Professor	Associate Professor	Professor	Chief	Chair
Count:	326	2,106	782	511	72	90
25th:	226	270	299	312	324	457
Median:	287	308	335	354	362	513
75th:	334	355	385	404	390	603
Mean:	280.1	311.2	340.7	354.9	366.4	530.9

Anesthesiology: Pain Management

	Instructor	Assistant Professor	Associate Professor	Professor	Chief	Chair
Count:	14	142	50	29	11	3
25th:	207	260	291	314	312	
Median:	243	301	321	345	345	
75th:	304	331	360	370	392	
Mean:	268.1	312.1	326.4	339.7	366.9	

Anesthesiology: Pediatric

	Instructor	Assistant Professor	Associate Professor	Professor	Chief	Chair
Count:	11	284	95	72	13	2
25th:	200	278	305	324	291	
Median:	227	318	363	376	352	
75th:	268	356	406	439	381	
Mean:	215.4	318.2	358.7	390.6	341.2	

TABLE 11 Summary Statistics on Medical School Faculty Compensation for All Schools M.D. or Equivalent Degree, Clinical Science Departments/Specialties Total Compensation in Thousands of Dollars (continued)

Total Dermatology

	Instructor	Assistant Professor	Associate Professor	Professor	Chief	Chair
Count:	47	325	167	147	32	64
25th:	140	203	227	250	256	377
Median:	200	250	299	323	299	441
75th:	267	358	415	480	403	574
Mean:	228.9	292.5	353.1	444.0	330.3	488.1

Dermatology (excluding Mohs Surgery)

	Instructor	Assistant Professor	Associate Professor	Professor	Chief	Chair
Count:	42	274	152	127	26	60
25th:	140	200	226	245	243	377
Median:	200	235	293	310	278	438
75th:	250	334	388	393	400	540
Mean:	205.0	265.5	334.7	384.6	316.8	479.7

Dermatology: Mohs Surgery

	Instructor	Assistant Professor	Associate Professor	Professor	Chief	Chair
Count:	5	51	15	20	6	4
25th:	169	303	278	445	350	
Median:	319	385	522	578	379	
75th:	748	517	704	1,086	433	
Mean:	430.2	437.7	539.9	820.8	389.0	

Total Medicine

	Instructor	Assistant Professor	Associate Professor	Professor	Chief	Chair
Count:	1,546	8,077	4,155	4,125	655	164
25th:	116	146	171	208	226	312
Median:	155	180	209	254	278	433
75th:	196	231	270	326	350	546
Mean:	161.2	200.5	234.7	281.0	302.8	450.3

Allergy/Immunology-Med.

	Instructor	Assistant Professor	Associate Professor	Professor	Chief	Chair
Count:	15	62	30	54	17	2
25th:	60	125	138	176	204	
Median:	116	144	183	207	218	
75th:	197	190	224	250	248	
Mean:	124.4	160.2	191.3	232.1	232.1	

TABLE 11 Summary Statistics on Medical School Faculty Compensation for All Schools M.D. or Equivalent Degree, Clinical Science Departments/Specialties Total Compensation in Thousands of Dollars (continued)

Cardiology: Total

	Instructor	Assistant Professor	Associate Professor	Professor	Chief	Chair
Count:	125	1,108	666	770	59	25
25th:	108	210	231	254	374	453
Median:	174	266	289	312	431	533
75th:	242	350	383	411	509	653
Mean:	186.6	291.9	318.6	347.3	452.2	574.8

Cardiology: Invasive Interventional-Med.

	Instructor	Assistant Professor	Associate Professor	Professor	Chief	Chair
Count:	32	394	230	232	21	6
25th:	121	256	278	312	400	510
Median:	217	315	355	390	507	649
75th:	295	423	441	463	563	800
Mean:	242.1	351.4	375.1	430.0	493.5	639.3

Cardiology: Invasive Non-interventional-Med.

	Instructor	Assistant Professor	Associate Professor	Professor	Chief	Chair
Count:	11	119	81	66	12	0
25th:	75	237	237	262	382	
Median:	155	285	312	319	409	
75th:	250	375	406	411	525	
Mean:	163.4	312.9	344.8	337.9	460.5	

Cardiology: Non-invasive-Med.

	Instructor	Assistant Professor	Associate Professor	Professor	Chief	Chair
Count:	82	595	355	472	26	19
25th:	97	189	217	241	349	446
Median:	162	235	258	283	418	525
75th:	213	292	319	365	459	624
Mean:	168.0	248.4	276.1	307.9	415.0	554.5

Critical/Intensive Care-Med.

	Instructor	Assistant Professor	Associate Professor	Professor	Chief	Chair
Count:	16	112	67	37	2	2
25th:	171	170	181	220		
Median:	184	219	211	288		
75th:	201	297	272	365		
Mean:	194.6	238.8	239.4	299.1		

TABLE 11 Summary Statistics on Medical School Faculty Compensation for All Schools M.D. or Equivalent Degree, Clinical Science Departments/Specialties Total Compensation in Thousands of Dollars (continued)

Endocrinology-Med.

	Instructor	Assistant Professor	Associate Professor	Professor	Chief	Chair
Count:	55	373	213	298	57	10
25th:	93	128	148	184	197	373
Median:	116	144	171	215	241	422
75th:	144	173	203	266	290	451
Mean:	121.2	152.2	178.9	232.6	247.7	405.9

Gastroenterology-Med.

	Instructor	Assistant Professor	Associate Professor	Professor	Chief	Chair
Count:	57	621	358	374	61	9
25th:	85	200	234	245	316	365
Median:	150	240	285	307	359	407
75th:	213	302	371	399	411	437
Mean:	160.8	255.7	305.1	325.3	386.2	392.6

General Internal Medicine

	Instructor	Assistant Professor	Associate Professor	Professor	Chief	Chair
Count:	551	1,883	822	530	70	38
25th:	135	143	162	191	212	270
Median:	164	164	185	225	238	312
75th:	212	199	225	279	278	419
Mean:	173.7	176.6	200.8	249.5	268.2	373.2

Geriatrics-Med.

	Instructor	Assistant Professor	Associate Professor	Professor	Chief	Chair
Count:	30	248	134	87	26	10
25th:	120	134	164	192	239	241
Median:	138	151	180	219	263	270
75th:	166	172	202	260	329	355
Mean:	146.4	155.1	186.3	232.2	272.0	297.6

Hematology/Oncology-Med.

	Instructor	Assistant Professor	Associate Professor	Professor	Chief	Chair
Count:	139	953	513	612	83	14
25th:	88	163	194	233	260	472
Median:	140	191	231	290	321	531
75th:	185	238	281	344	389	609
Mean:	158.7	207.8	247.8	304.5	330.9	548.2

TABLE 11 Summary Statistics on Medical School Faculty Compensation for All Schools M.D. or Equivalent Degree, Clinical Science Departments/Specialties Total Compensation in Thousands of Dollars (continued)

Hospital Medicine

	Instructor	Assistant Professor	Associate Professor	Professor	Chief	Chair
Count:	248	562	69	23	17	0
25th:	147	165	180	210	211	
Median:	167	185	195	241	237	
75th:	195	207	231	301	313	
Mean:	172.1	189.2	205.9	255.4	262.3	

Infectious Disease-Med.

	Instructor	Assistant Professor	Associate Professor	Professor	Chief	Chair
Count:	78	536	339	331	66	14
25th:	85	123	149	188	202	309
Median:	107	138	166	217	243	484
75th:	139	162	196	251	280	547
Mean:	115.3	145.9	176.7	230.0	250.9	448.8

Nephrology-Med.

	Instructor	Assistant Professor	Associate Professor	Professor	Chief	Chair
Count:	52	500	272	305	56	9
25th:	81	140	173	211	253	343
Median:	127	163	199	245	296	429
75th:	160	197	249	280	337	475
Mean:	132.1	170.4	212.9	254.5	306.3	414.9

Pulmonary-Med.

	Instructor	Assistant Professor	Associate Professor	Professor	Chief	Chair
Count:	70	643	386	374	58	8
25th:	108	154	181	207	255	364
Median:	140	183	210	245	290	402
75th:	186	223	254	297	319	570
Mean:	152.4	194.5	224.4	257.4	297.7	452.9

Rheumatology-Med.

	Instructor	Assistant Professor	Associate Professor	Professor	Chief	Chair
Count:	36	232	146	159	52	1
25th:	74	126	149	185	198	
Median:	109	144	169	213	231	
75th:	134	172	199	258	263	
Mean:	106.8	149.7	183.4	229.8	234.1	

TABLE 11 Summary Statistics on Medical School Faculty Compensation for All Schools M.D. or Equivalent Degree, Clinical Science Departments/Specialties Total Compensation in Thousands of Dollars (continued)

Other Medicine

	Instructor	Assistant Professor	Associate Professor	Professor	Chief	Chair
Count:	74	244	140	171	31	22
25th:	84	125	161	193	217	355
Median:	124	171	211	244	268	541
75th:	168	235	268	317	314	601
Mean:	132.5	185.9	222.7	268.0	277.0	500.0

Total OB/GYN

	Instructor	Assistant Professor	Associate Professor	Professor	Chief	Chair
Count:	200	1,343	588	443	158	113
25th:	68	190	219	249	260	403
Median:	149	228	263	314	325	490
75th:	211	294	339	375	402	574
Mean:	157.4	253.7	308.9	339.4	351.0	541.5

OB/GYN: General

	Instructor	Assistant Professor	Associate Professor	Professor	Chief	Chair
Count:	101	783	290	156	51	34
25th:	151	187	210	205	236	294
Median:	186	219	246	272	266	450
75th:	226	277	292	337	324	529
Mean:	187.6	242.4	264.1	277.9	298.2	445.7

OB/GYN: Gynecologic Oncology

	Instructor	Assistant Professor	Associate Professor	Professor	Chief	Chair
Count:	21	127	75	61	31	15
25th:	62	225	263	305	305	404
Median:	67	260	339	375	365	497
75th:	183	302	462	456	457	619
Mean:	128.2	275.4	377.7	399.9	424.8	534.5

OB/GYN: Maternal & Fetal

	Instructor	Assistant Professor	Associate Professor	Professor	Chief	Chair
Count:	43	198	111	132	30	42
25th:	59	228	244	288	327	452
Median:	72	277	310	331	367	494
75th:	132	330	366	420	411	546
Mean:	124.3	286.1	318.4	379.3	383.6	519.0

Summary Statistics on Medical School Faculty Compensation for All Schools M.D. or Equivalent Degree, Clinical Science Departments/Specialties Total Compensation in Thousands of Dollars (continued)

OB/GYN: Reproductive Endocrinology

	Instructor	Assistant Professor	Associate Professor	Professor	Chief	Chair
Count:	8	79	63	52	22	16
25th:	68	197	223	231	271	400
Median:	254	230	274	300	318	485
75th:	393	297	352	417	403	665
Mean:	267.8	297.4	458.9	392.1	368.7	766.4

OB/GYN: Other OB/GYN

	Instructor	Assistant Professor	Associate Professor	Professor	Chief	Chair
Count:	27	156	49	42	24	6
25th:	60	167	192	215	220	579
Median:	69	204	249	273	309	655
75th:	105	268	295	326	400	804
Mean:	87.3	230.0	254.9	288.9	311.1	660.0

Total Pathology

	Instructor	Assistant Professor	Associate Professor	Professor	Chief	Chair
Count:	108	1,094	743	967	78	118
25th:	65	160	190	224	236	325
Median:	120	180	221	259	282	415
75th:	176	211	255	314	319	500
Mean:	136.3	190.7	230.2	274.7	292.7	432.9

Pathology: Anatomic

	Instructor	Assistant Professor	Associate Professor	Professor	Chief	Chair
Count:	59	551	381	429	34	52
25th:	79	164	200	239	240	325
Median:	161	184	229	270	297	403
75th:	221	223	264	323	319	468
Mean:	162.2	200.4	243.8	289.7	302.4	409.9

Pathology: Clinical

	Instructor	Assistant Professor	Associate Professor	Professor	Chief	Chair
Count:	21	295	213	308	31	32
25th:	78	158	189	223	217	362
Median:	100	178	216	255	271	413
75th:	148	207	253	312	315	510
Mean:	118.2	184.1	225.0	274.8	271.9	425.8

TABLE 11 Summary Statistics on Medical School Faculty Compensation for All Schools M.D. or Equivalent Degree, Clinical Science Departments/Specialties Total Compensation in Thousands of Dollars (continued)

Pathology: Other Pathology

	Instructor	Assistant Professor	Associate Professor	Professor	Chief	Chair
Count:	28	248	149	230	13	34
25th:	62	150	163	195	230	315
Median:	81	175	201	238	291	427
75th:	125	197	235	283	368	549
Mean:	95.4	176.7	202.9	246.4	317.0	474.9

Total Pediatrics

	Instructor	Assistant Professor	Associate Professor	Professor	Chief	Chair
Count:	626	4,715	2,207	1,889	581	116
25th:	99	134	160	190	194	321
Median:	120	156	190	227	229	392
75th:	149	189	229	278	276	496
Mean:	127.6	167.1	201.8	244.3	245.9	412.9

Adolescent Medicine

	Instructor	Assistant Professor	Associate Professor	Professor	Chief	Chair
Count:	7	61	36	25	16	1
25th:	56	119	146	161	163	
Median:	109	125	161	194	183	
75th:	138	138	176	236	225	
Mean:	100.1	129.1	163.8	207.7	192.3	

Allergy/Immunology-Peds.

	Instructor	Assistant Professor	Associate Professor	Professor	Chief	Chair
Count:	14	77	40	52	17	2
25th:	75	128	155	178	178	
Median:	95	140	177	215	227	
75th:	124	157	201	274	235	
Mean:	102.5	146.6	185.9	235.8	223.8	

Child & Adolescent Psychiatry

	Instructor	Assistant Professor	Associate Professor	Professor	Chief	Chair
Count:	11	83	45	39	16	2
25th:	120	150	163	195	197	
Median:	159	170	195	222	225	
75th:	176	189	229	264	259	
Mean:	156.6	175.7	201.6	231.0	241.1	

TABLE 11 Summary Statistics on Medical School Faculty Compensation for All Schools
M.D. or Equivalent Degree, Clinical Science Departments/Specialties
Total Compensation in Thousands of Dollars (continued)

Critical/Intensive Care-Peds.

	Instructor	Assistant Professor	Associate Professor	Professor	Chief	Chair
Count:	44	343	149	59	35	4
25th:	95	175	210	245	239	
Median:	152	194	240	275	257	
75th:	174	230	275	341	339	
Mean:	138.2	206.8	251.7	298.8	286.1	

Emergency Medicine-Peds.

	Instructor	Assistant Professor	Associate Professor	Professor	Chief	Chair
Count:	69	358	128	50	23	1
25th:	109	156	194	221	227	
Median:	136	178	215	237	267	
75th:	151	210	245	258	315	
Mean:	131.9	186.5	224.5	249.2	257.3	

Endocrinology-Peds.

	Instructor	Assistant Professor	Associate Professor	Professor	Chief	Chair
Count:	13	191	80	86	36	3
25th:	66	126	144	181	175	
Median:	101	134	164	198	200	
75th:	117	147	184	226	244	
Mean:	103.0	138.4	165.5	203.3	210.5	

Gastroenterology-Peds.

	Instructor	Assistant Professor	Associate Professor	Professor	Chief	Chair
Count:	23	216	105	92	33	6
25th:	59	153	179	210	211	280
Median:	120	166	202	232	251	531
75th:	193	185	222	279	281	646
Mean:	150.4	171.6	207.7	258.4	260.1	479.7

General Pediatrics

	Instructor	Assistant Professor	Associate Professor	Professor	Chief	Chair
Count:	117	1,030	397	300	56	40
25th:	108	128	145	172	191	252
Median:	124	142	161	205	221	325
75th:	150	170	190	254	264	411
Mean:	132.6	155.8	174.9	221.2	235.9	358.9

TABLE 11 Summary Statistics on Medical School Faculty Compensation for All Schools M.D. or Equivalent Degree, Clinical Science Departments/Specialties Total Compensation in Thousands of Dollars (continued)

Genetics-Peds.

	Instructor	Assistant Professor	Associate Professor	Professor	Chief	Chair
Count:	5	72	56	85	25	3
25th:	83	120	136	158	161	
Median:	110	130	149	180	187	
75th:	125	148	164	225	213	
Mean:	105.0	131.2	153.3	195.4	189.0	

Hematology/Oncology-Peds.

	Instructor	Assistant Professor	Associate Professor	Professor	Chief	Chair
Count:	37	352	197	171	43	4
25th:	78	131	161	201	190	
Median:	88	140	175	222	220	
75th:	115	155	200	258	270	
Mean:	94.9	146.2	184.3	240.9	229.1	

Hospital Medicine-Peds.

	Instructor	Assistant Professor	Associate Professor	Professor	Chief	Chair
Count:	86	201	38	11	13	0
25th:	114	133	153	174	165	
Median:	125	143	163	222	193	
75th:	141	174	188	253	215	
Mean:	128.0	154.5	172.8	218.9	193.5	

Infectious Disease-Peds.

	Instructor	Assistant Professor	Associate Professor	Professor	Chief	Chair
Count:	12	140	71	128	37	7
25th:	77	116	134	169	191	329
Median:	93	125	147	200	216	340
75th:	110	136	170	234	254	377
Mean:	91.8	127.0	153.1	210.5	223.0	362.1

Neonatology

	Instructor	Assistant Professor	Associate Professor	Professor	Chief	Chair
Count:	66	490	238	252	41	15
25th:	115	167	200	225	268	373
Median:	136	194	229	262	303	424
75th:	170	223	269	309	351	474
Mean:	146.1	201.7	241.3	275.2	319.1	471.8

TABLE 11 Summary Statistics on Medical School Faculty Compensation for All Schools
M.D. or Equivalent Degree, Clinical Science Departments/Specialties
Total Compensation in Thousands of Dollars (continued)

Nephrology-Peds.

	Instructor	Assistant Professor	Associate Professor	Professor	Chief	Chair
Count:	8	102	54	63	33	4
25th:	103	132	156	181	173	
Median:	123	138	171	207	208	
75th:	146	149	191	246	230	
Mean:	120.5	142.0	178.3	220.1	204.6	

Neurology-Peds.

	Instructor	Assistant Professor	Associate Professor	Professor	Chief	Chair
Count:	14	165	80	82	22	5
25th:	115	146	175	194	213	239
Median:	129	160	190	215	248	330
75th:	160	179	209	237	282	484
Mean:	133.4	163.6	197.1	217.1	242.8	355.0

Pediatric Cardiology

	Instructor	Assistant Professor	Associate Professor	Professor	Chief	Chair
Count:	30	311	222	145	36	3
25th:	88	172	214	258	269	
Median:	138	194	239	295	315	
75th:	178	217	284	357	423	
Mean:	134.7	200.7	251.2	314.9	349.2	

Pulmonary-Peds.

	Instructor	Assistant Professor	Associate Professor	Professor	Chief	Chair
Count:	20	158	98	76	28	3
25th:	66	137	163	186	206	
Median:	110	148	179	211	231	
75th:	155	164	203	245	266	
Mean:	114.5	154.7	191.4	222.8	240.9	

Rheumatology-Peds.

	Instructor	Assistant Professor	Associate Professor	Professor	Chief	Chair
Count:	9	52	21	17	19	0
25th:	71	133	145	194	175	
Median:	119	140	164	210	217	
75th:	130	158	174	235	276	
Mean:	103.4	143.2	160.5	226.9	229.3	

Summary Statistics on Medical School Faculty Compensation for All Schools
M.D. or Equivalent Degree, Clinical Science Departments/Specialties
Total Compensation in Thousands of Dollars (continued)

Other Pediatrics

	Instructor	Assistant Professor	Associate Professor	Professor	Chief	Chair
Count:	41	313	152	156	52	13
25th:	73	125	152	196	193	405
Median:	102	146	180	249	220	464
75th:	128	175	217	325	266	610
Mean:	113.8	154.5	192.2	273.8	243.1	485.8

Total Radiology

	Instructor	Assistant Professor	Associate Professor	Professor	Chief	Chair
Count:	359	2,121	867	886	163	163
25th:	110	282	310	327	341	511
Median:	272	328	360	380	402	582
75th:	360	387	429	445	469	653
Mean:	260.0	340.0	373.8	388.6	414.5	591.7

Diagnostic Radiology: Total

	Instructor	Assistant Professor	Associate Professor	Professor	Chief	Chair
Count:	258	1,545	575	612	135	79
25th:	120	285	308	328	343	491
Median:	286	328	353	375	404	568
75th:	371	387	430	438	464	661
Mean:	267.9	340.2	376.3	387.4	412.8	574.6

Diagnostic Radiology: Interventional

	Instructor	Assistant Professor	Associate Professor	Professor	Chief	Chair
Count:	63	327	146	113	23	19
25th:	250	317	364	357	405	486
Median:	337	372	439	420	459	560
75th:	460	439	515	495	525	647
Mean:	346.6	380.1	459.8	426.2	465.9	559.2

Diagnostic Radiology: Non-interventional

	Instructor	Assistant Professor	Associate Professor	Professor	Chief	Chair
Count:	195	1,218	429	499	112	60
25th:	76	276	299	327	335	497
Median:	263	320	339	365	393	574
75th:	355	373	402	428	443	670
Mean:	242.4	329.5	347.8	378.6	401.9	579.5

TABLE 11 Summary Statistics on Medical School Faculty Compensation for All Schools M.D. or Equivalent Degree, Clinical Science Departments/Specialties Total Compensation in Thousands of Dollars (continued)

Nuclear Medicine

	Instructor	Assistant Professor	Associate Professor	Professor	Chief	Chair
Count:	4	63	46	54	13	2
25th:		244	273	296	304	
Median:		302	311	335	392	
75th:		367	375	385	486	
Mean:		323.6	321.1	338.9	392.6	

Radiation Oncology

	Instructor	Assistant Professor	Associate Professor	Professor	Chief	Chair
Count:	56	292	154	131	8	70
25th:	230	269	322	349	339	541
Median:	293	316	378	418	401	620
75th:	341	370	432	498	546	662
Mean:	303.7	324.5	379.1	413.4	438.6	623.1

Other Radiology

	Instructor	Assistant Professor	Associate Professor	Professor	Chief	Chair
Count:	41	221	92	89	7	12
25th:	58	303	328	322	356	435
Median:	110	345	380	395	414	508
75th:	253	442	430	460	450	594
Mean:	155.1	363.6	376.1	390.5	459.7	564.7

Total Surgery

	Instructor	Assistant Professor	Associate Professor	Professor	Chief	Chair
Count:	285	3,689	2,008	1,885	537	355
25th:	69	247	301	321	385	545
Median:	149	308	390	419	475	651
75th:	295	410	505	549	614	841
Mean:	212.8	350.5	434.0	470.4	537.7	755.5

General Surgery

	Instructor	Assistant Professor	Associate Professor	Professor	Chief	Chair
Count:	39	611	302	354	61	52
25th:	60	220	262	277	359	514
Median:	96	262	316	358	454	630
75th:	235	334	387	440	582	741
Mean:	155.0	280.8	335.2	367.9	490.0	653.0

TABLE 11 Summary Statistics on Medical School Faculty Compensation for All Schools M.D. or Equivalent Degree, Clinical Science Departments/Specialties Total Compensation in Thousands of Dollars (continued)

Neurosurgery

	Instructor	Assistant Professor	Associate Professor	Professor	Chief	Chair
Count:	26	400	223	213	39	65
25th:	65	347	406	378	522	658
Median:	82	418	501	529	601	771
75th:	125	543	675	709	749	1,043
Mean:	167.1	479.0	585.8	626.9	686.0	968.5

Orthopaedic Surgery

	Instructor	Assistant Professor	Associate Professor	Professor	Chief	Chair
Count:	68	789	401	342	73	89
25th:	67	300	350	364	391	549
Median:	256	364	477	463	489	649
75th:	387	495	573	586	586	777
Mean:	304.5	416.8	501.9	499.7	504.7	697.2

Pediatric Surgery

	Instructor	Assistant Professor	Associate Professor	Professor	Chief	Chair
Count:	4	135	99	74	36	8
25th:		283	370	440	454	538
Median:		345	444	545	528	622
75th:		422	505	643	633	731
Mean:		343.6	442.8	539.7	551.0	654.8

Plastic Surgery

	Instructor	Assistant Professor	Associate Professor	Professor	Chief	Chair
Count:	15	212	103	89	41	14
25th:	120	244	283	342	363	563
Median:	220	300	378	436	475	751
75th:	372	424	491	534	683	1,270
Mean:	307.2	376.5	415.0	447.8	541.4	865.1

Surgical Oncology

	Instructor	Assistant Professor	Associate Professor	Professor	Chief	Chair
Count:	15	132	97	55	34	13
25th:	225	218	233	261	315	557
Median:	239	246	308	310	418	625
75th:	325	287	382	397	478	868
Mean:	260.6	261.2	324.1	350.9	408.4	721.5

TABLE 11 Summary Statistics on Medical School Faculty Compensation for All Schools M.D. or Equivalent Degree, Clinical Science Departments/Specialties Total Compensation in Thousands of Dollars (continued)

Thoracic & Cardiovascular Surgery

	Instructor	Assistant Professor	Associate Professor	Professor	Chief	Chair
Count:	32	314	180	191	68	23
25th:	80	275	368	412	449	600
Median:	174	342	465	530	623	866
75th:	316	468	616	717	849	1,226
Mean:	219.2	383.9	517.7	606.8	734.8	1,071.1

Transplant Surgery

	Instructor	Assistant Professor	Associate Professor	Professor	Chief	Chair
Count:	17	147	110	112	45	9
25th:	70	248	305	346	401	612
Median:	80	290	387	445	508	699
75th:	119	354	491	569	735	992
Mean:	116.8	296.0	400.2	485.8	573.0	883.1

Trauma/Critical Care Surgery

	Instructor	Assistant Professor	Associate Professor	Professor	Chief	Chair
Count:	15	256	112	85	37	8
25th:	150	248	296	322	362	468
Median:	254	281	351	369	425	586
75th:	316	326	418	435	481	637
Mean:	245.4	291.5	359.0	387.2	436.7	561.0

Urology

	Instructor	Assistant Professor	Associate Professor	Professor	Chief	Chair
Count:	31	360	205	206	34	57
25th:	65	235	286	310	388	416
Median:	80	281	351	382	463	545
75th:	132	336	426	467	566	633
Mean:	105.2	295.2	368.6	417.2	524.3	594.4

Vascular Surgery

	Instructor	Assistant Professor	Associate Professor	Professor	Chief	Chair
Count:	5	163	90	90	46	6
25th:	75	250	313	325	342	465
Median:	294	283	382	375	446	593
75th:	385	354	456	482	544	950
Mean:	242.8	308.7	407.6	407.5	469.7	663.3

TABLE 11 Summary Statistics on Medical School Faculty Compensation for All Schools M.D. or Equivalent Degree, Clinical Science Departments/Specialties Total Compensation in Thousands of Dollars (continued)

Other Surgery

	Instructor	Assistant Professor	Associate Professor	Professor	Chief	Chair
Count:	18	170	86	74	23	11
25th:	56	200	222	262	297	517
Median:	86	250	306	350	351	751
75th:	248	306	437	442	403	884
Mean:	163.9	263.9	356.1	366.7	348.5	689.6

Other Clinical Science

Community Health

	Instructor	Assistant Professor	Associate Professor	Professor	Chief	Chair
Count:	12	43	20	12	2	6
25th:	178	120	131	154		240
Median:	222	144	163	191		295
75th:	222	222	183	218		326
Mean:	191.3	172.7	165.1	195.1		318.0

Emergency Medicine

	Instructor	Assistant Professor	Associate Professor	Professor	Chief	Chair
Count:	255	1,416	451	185	34	66
25th:	173	207	230	245	267	371
Median:	204	229	252	271	304	433
75th:	241	261	283	318	347	497
Mean:	203.1	236.5	262.2	288.6	306.4	440.6

Family Medicine

	Instructor	Assistant Professor	Associate Professor	Professor	Chief	Chair
Count:	146	1,308	545	310	14	104
25th:	128	144	157	172	183	262
Median:	151	159	178	194	193	292
75th:	222	183	201	219	220	322
Mean:	171.3	166.0	180.5	202.1	220.9	295.1

Neurology

	Instructor	Assistant Professor	Associate Professor	Professor	Chief	Chair
Count:	121	1,110	569	667	68	92
25th:	69	136	165	191	193	326
Median:	121	155	189	226	218	378
75th:	155	188	224	261	267	436
Mean:	124.8	167.5	200.6	235.9	230.6	394.6

TABLE 11 Summary Statistics on Medical School Faculty Compensation for All Schools M.D. or Equivalent Degree, Clinical Science Departments/Specialties Total Compensation in Thousands of Dollars (continued)

Ophthalmology

	Instructor	Assistant Professor	Associate Professor	Professor	Chief	Chair
Count:	111	550	294	310	32	77
25th:	53	159	201	224	264	421
Median:	60	204	274	292	336	506
75th:	112	267	364	385	438	610
Mean:	95.3	224.4	303.4	331.1	397.2	524.3

Otolaryngology

	Instructor	Assistant Professor	Associate Professor	Professor	Chief	Chair
Count:	29	449	247	217	49	70
25th:	56	219	268	298	310	463
Median:	59	255	322	373	380	540
75th:	179	324	389	465	464	656
Mean:	120.0	287.2	356.7	403.1	412.7	602.8

Physical Medicine & Rehabilitation

	Instructor	Assistant Professor	Associate Professor	Professor	Chief	Chair
Count:	71	322	112	61	12	43
25th:	141	151	178	211	203	276
Median:	167	181	196	240	257	339
75th:	249	220	244	274	311	414
Mean:	211.8	193.9	215.4	255.0	263.6	347.0

Preventive Medicine

	Instructor	Assistant Professor	Associate Professor	Professor	Chief	Chair
Count:	17	70	39	40	2	12
25th:	120	121	140	200		226
Median:	141	137	184	223		240
75th:	236	157	235	266		292
Mean:	165.2	147.5	187.0	237.5		256.3

Psychiatry

	Instructor	Assistant Professor	Associate Professor	Professor	Chief	Chair
Count:	217	1,417	597	627	48	112
25th:	140	145	163	186	185	284
Median:	157	165	185	217	220	353
75th:	171	190	214	267	282	447
Mean:	154.5	171.6	193.2	232.6	240.2	365.8

TABLE 11

Summary Statistics on Medical School Faculty Compensation for All Schools M.D. or Equivalent Degree, Clinical Science Departments/Specialties Total Compensation in Thousands of Dollars (continued)

Other

	Instructor	Assistant Professor	Associate Professor	Professor	Chief	Chair
Count:	11	84	41	52	1	9
25th:	66	119	148	221		263
Median:	96	153	210	252		394
75th:	105	208	319	312		444
Mean:	96.5	170.1	262.4	262.0		368.2

TABLE 12 Summary Statistics on Medical School Faculty Compensation for Public Schools M.D. or Equivalent Degree, Clinical Science Departments/Specialties Total Compensation in Thousands of Dollars

CLINICAL SCIENCE - TOTAL ALL DEPARTMENTS/SPECIALTIES

	Instructor	Assistant Professor	Associate Professor	Professor	Chief	Chair
Count:	1,147	14,832	7,553	7,303	1,449	1,056
25th:	84	153	177	208	230	332
Median:	136	198	225	264	299	449
75th:	180	274	309	349	400	565
Mean:	142.5	224.7	258.7	295.1	332.5	473.6

Total Anesthesiology

	Instructor	Assistant Professor	Associate Professor	Professor	Chief	Chair
Count:	66	1,090	454	343	34	56
25th:	224	273	294	309	336	450
Median:	265	305	326	342	366	493
75th:	298	342	370	378	385	557
Mean:	252.2	310.4	333.7	343.1	366.8	505.1

Anesthesiology: General

	Instructor	Assistant Professor	Associate Professor	Professor	Chief	Chair
Count:	63	894	380	281	23	51
25th:	224	273	293	306	336	451
Median:	266	304	325	340	364	490
75th:	300	341	369	379	384	552
Mean:	256.0	308.2	331.5	340.2	369.6	501.8

Anesthesiology: Pain Management

	Instructor	Assistant Professor	Associate Professor	Professor	Chief	Chair
Count:	0	81	32	21	6	3
25th:		268	295	307	321	
Median:		305	312	334	364	
75th:		325	352	359	392	
Mean:		299.3	328.0	329.6	359.7	

Anesthesiology: Pediatric

	Instructor	Assistant Professor	Associate Professor	Professor	Chief	Chair
Count:	3	115	42	41	5	2
25th:		280	302	319	326	
Median:		319	351	358	366	
75th:		368	402	409	398	
Mean:		336.0	357.1	369.7	362.6	

TABLE 12 Summary Statistics on Medical School Faculty Compensation for Public Schools
M.D. or Equivalent Degree, Clinical Science Departments/Specialties
Total Compensation in Thousands of Dollars (continued)

Total Dermatology

	Instructor	Assistant Professor	Associate Professor	Professor	Chief	Chair
Count:	11	141	74	64	18	32
25th:	125	201	214	258	270	330
Median:	184	252	281	324	299	431
75th:	200	366	394	440	400	527
Mean:	175.6	297.7	336.3	391.2	324.9	447.3

Dermatology (excluding Mohs Surgery)

	Instructor	Assistant Professor	Associate Professor	Professor	Chief	Chair
Count:	8	114	62	55	15	30
25th:	102	193	197	247	261	316
Median:	184	237	270	299	282	430
75th:	200	350	326	371	400	508
Mean:	159.4	267.1	290.6	342.0	313.6	431.6

Dermatology: Mohs Surgery

	Instructor	Assistant Professor	Associate Professor	Professor	Chief	Chair
Count:	3	27	12	9	3	2
25th:		287	484	384		
Median:		368	559	494		
75th:		567	768	1,086		
Mean:		426.9	572.4	691.9		

Total Medicine

	Instructor	Assistant Professor	Associate Professor	Professor	Chief	Chair
Count:	358	3,595	1,998	2,152	386	96
25th:	91	144	167	204	225	298
Median:	137	174	197	244	272	394
75th:	171	221	251	306	345	492
Mean:	137.4	191.0	217.7	265.2	294.8	404.8

Allergy/Immunology-Med.

	Instructor	Assistant Professor	Associate Professor	Professor	Chief	Chair
Count:	4	27	14	31	10	2
25th:		128	117	176	204	
Median:		143	169	206	218	
75th:		185	213	257	235	
Mean:		165.5	180.4	239.6	241.5	

TABLE 12 Summary Statistics on Medical School Faculty Compensation for Public Schools M.D. or Equivalent Degree, Clinical Science Departments/Specialties Total Compensation in Thousands of Dollars (continued)

Cardiology: Total

	Instructor	Assistant Professor	Associate Professor	Professor	Chief	Chair
Count:	23	429	270	366	34	14
25th:	63	206	222	246	371	446
Median:	144	258	276	291	426	513
75th:	225	313	343	371	471	624
Mean:	154.1	272.2	288.1	318.2	437.4	568.2

Cardiology: Invasive Interventional-Med.

	Instructor	Assistant Professor	Associate Professor	Professor	Chief	Chair
Count:	3	132	82	87	12	2
25th:		253	280	286	377	
Median:		299	344	355	453	
75th:		354	396	420	519	
Mean:		320.0	342.9	373.9	452.3	

Cardiology: Invasive Non-interventional-Med.

	Instructor	Assistant Professor	Associate Professor	Professor	Chief	Chair
Count:	1	43	35	39	9	0
25th:		226	228	262	377	
Median:		263	297	302	385	
75th:		322	340	411	446	
Mean:		286.9	310.5	336.9	415.3	

Cardiology: Non-invasive-Med.

	Instructor	Assistant Professor	Associate Professor	Professor	Chief	Chair
Count:	19	254	153	240	13	12
25th:	60	190	210	239	343	453
Median:	124	237	243	272	426	513
75th:	185	285	292	334	467	591
Mean:	141.6	244.8	253.5	294.9	438.9	565.2

Critical/Intensive Care-Med.

	Instructor	Assistant Professor	Associate Professor	Professor	Chief	Chair
Count:	5	40	32	14	2	1
25th:	100	147	178	207		
Median:	175	177	185	220		
75th:	175	216	232	255		
Mean:	144.8	184.7	205.3	249.6		

TABLE 12 Summary Statistics on Medical School Faculty Compensation for Public Schools
M.D. or Equivalent Degree, Clinical Science Departments/Specialties
Total Compensation in Thousands of Dollars (continued)

Endocrinology-Med.

	Instructor	Assistant Professor	Associate Professor	Professor	Chief	Chair
Count:	13	172	105	151	36	10
25th:	54	122	146	181	195	373
Median:	105	139	168	215	238	422
75th:	125	165	198	266	280	451
Mean:	92.9	140.6	170.2	231.2	242.5	405.9

Gastroenterology-Med.

	Instructor	Assistant Professor	Associate Professor	Professor	Chief	Chair
Count:	8	276	169	188	36	2
25th:	74	206	222	233	300	
Median:	119	238	257	294	352	
75th:	186	290	346	354	408	
Mean:	135.6	252.4	284.7	311.9	365.9	

General Internal Medicine

	Instructor	Assistant Professor	Associate Professor	Professor	Chief	Chair
Count:	129	805	425	304	39	26
25th:	120	140	156	185	224	266
Median:	147	156	178	214	239	304
75th:	171	181	207	260	266	372
Mean:	149.1	165.3	187.2	229.1	263.9	317.2

Geriatrics-Med.

	Instructor	Assistant Professor	Associate Professor	Professor	Chief	Chair
Count:	11	117	82	56	16	9
25th:	105	135	164	193	213	236
Median:	130	152	178	219	253	265
75th:	188	172	197	262	281	325
Mean:	143.5	154.7	182.3	234.5	244.6	282.4

Hematology/Oncology-Med.

	Instructor	Assistant Professor	Associate Professor	Professor	Chief	Chair
Count:	31	421	239	289	43	3
25th:	81	162	187	225	260	
Median:	87	184	218	272	347	
75th:	107	221	256	336	409	
Mean:	100.7	199.8	233.5	291.5	340.1	

TABLE 12 Summary Statistics on Medical School Faculty Compensation for Public Schools
M.D. or Equivalent Degree, Clinical Science Departments/Specialties
Total Compensation in Thousands of Dollars (continued)

Hospital Medicine

	Instructor	Assistant Professor	Associate Professor	Professor	Chief	Chair
Count:	63	309	52	21	10	0
25th:	142	165	181	208	208	
Median:	163	181	196	236	229	
75th:	190	201	231	304	254	
Mean:	160.3	186.1	207.0	252.6	244.6	

Infectious Disease-Med.

	Instructor	Assistant Professor	Associate Professor	Professor	Chief	Chair
Count:	18	261	166	189	42	6
25th:	83	121	149	193	212	400
Median:	88	135	164	217	244	450
75th:	103	158	183	249	275	520
Mean:	95.3	140.6	169.8	229.3	253.4	431.2

Nephrology-Med.

	Instructor	Assistant Professor	Associate Professor	Professor	Chief	Chair
Count:	9	229	135	170	32	6
25th:	65	145	173	208	250	335
Median:	127	168	198	245	296	367
75th:	162	206	232	277	326	450
Mean:	118.8	176.0	211.7	252.8	291.5	384.7

Pulmonary-Med.

	Instructor	Assistant Professor	Associate Professor	Professor	Chief	Chair
Count:	12	276	189	213	34	7
25th:	79	159	182	207	257	363
Median:	129	185	209	240	297	392
75th:	164	230	252	290	315	637
Mean:	136.3	200.6	222.6	255.9	304.7	458.7

Rheumatology-Med.

	Instructor	Assistant Professor	Associate Professor	Professor	Chief	Chair
Count:	14	105	68	82	30	1
25th:	90	124	149	185	198	
Median:	105	143	166	207	224	
75th:	127	169	187	254	247	
Mean:	106.1	147.8	169.4	223.6	225.8	

TABLE 12 Summary Statistics on Medical School Faculty Compensation for Public Schools
M.D. or Equivalent Degree, Clinical Science Departments/Specialties
Total Compensation in Thousands of Dollars (continued)

Other Medicine

	Instructor	Assistant Professor	Associate Professor	Professor	Chief	Chair
Count:	18	128	52	78	22	9
25th:	82	137	150	173	217	285
Median:	85	173	182	218	247	405
75th:	136	237	269	280	288	559
Mean:	122.8	184.7	205.2	235.1	261.0	414.9

Total OB/GYN

	Instructor	Assistant Professor	Associate Professor	Professor	Chief	Chair
Count:	89	642	354	259	95	68
25th:	64	190	212	253	266	399
Median:	105	228	253	309	316	484
75th:	192	277	306	351	400	533
Mean:	133.4	239.8	269.3	316.4	332.4	476.2

OB/GYN: General

	Instructor	Assistant Professor	Associate Professor	Professor	Chief	Chair
Count:	41	397	193	97	36	18
25th:	145	185	207	216	237	289
Median:	178	214	238	275	267	409
75th:	225	252	268	322	315	494
Mean:	178.0	224.9	245.5	276.6	284.7	405.8

OB/GYN: Gynecologic Oncology

	Instructor	Assistant Professor	Associate Professor	Professor	Chief	Chair
Count:	14	59	47	35	20	6
25th:	62	225	262	311	327	495
Median:	68	257	318	358	365	516
75th:	180	284	385	447	417	566
Mean:	111.1	261.3	339.4	362.3	379.3	510.3

OB/GYN: Maternal & Fetal

	Instructor	Assistant Professor	Associate Professor	Professor	Chief	Chair
Count:	23	110	65	89	18	32
25th:	59	231	249	289	341	446
Median:	69	280	310	328	395	494
75th:	91	328	364	370	415	545
Mean:	92.9	286.0	306.5	363.0	396.8	509.4

TABLE 12 Summary Statistics on Medical School Faculty Compensation for Public Schools M.D. or Equivalent Degree, Clinical Science Departments/Specialties Total Compensation in Thousands of Dollars (continued)

OB/GYN: Reproductive Endocrinology

	Instructor	Assistant Professor	Associate Professor	Professor	Chief	Chair
Count:	0	34	27	24	13	12
25th:		187	212	226	260	395
Median:		219	238	284	300	456
75th:		270	283	327	384	549
Mean:		225.6	245.6	268.0	316.2	476.4

OB/GYN: Other OB/GYN

	Instructor	Assistant Professor	Associate Professor	Professor	Chief	Chair
Count:	11	42	22	14	8	0
25th:	60	192	182	201	239	
Median:	77	223	247	250	290	
75th:	105	287	286	326	376	
Mean:	79.7	241.4	246.5	265.4	311.0	

Total Pathology

	Instructor	Assistant Professor	Associate Professor	Professor	Chief	Chair
Count:	34	509	323	487	42	72
25th:	56	157	187	223	214	319
Median:	76	174	214	255	277	393
75th:	122	199	247	302	315	455
Mean:	95.8	178.9	220.0	267.2	273.0	401.4

Pathology: Anatomic

	Instructor	Assistant Professor	Associate Professor	Professor	Chief	Chair
Count:	21	261	185	228	19	35
25th:	56	161	190	238	236	311
Median:	65	178	221	265	278	392
75th:	108	200	250	313	315	450
Mean:	90.3	183.7	227.0	279.3	272.1	384.7

Pathology: Clinical

	Instructor	Assistant Professor	Associate Professor	Professor	Chief	Chair
Count:	6	164	94	178	22	19
25th:	59	154	187	217	204	354
Median:	109	173	211	251	274	423
75th:	162	202	241	294	319	484
Mean:	113.3	183.7	217.6	263.9	272.1	417.1

TABLE 12 Summary Statistics on Medical School Faculty Compensation for Public Schools M.D. or Equivalent Degree, Clinical Science Departments/Specialties Total Compensation in Thousands of Dollars (continued)

Pathology: Other Pathology

	Instructor	Assistant Professor	Associate Professor	Professor	Chief	Chair
Count:	7	84	44	81	1	18
25th:	46	103	165	186		315
Median:	64	165	192	234		395
75th:	148	185	222	273		433
Mean:	97.0	154.5	195.6	240.0		417.3

Total Pediatrics

	Instructor	Assistant Professor	Associate Professor	Professor	Chief	Chair
Count:	180	2,438	1,278	1,111	336	68
25th:	106	133	157	187	190	321
Median:	129	152	184	225	226	368
75th:	146	186	226	271	272	452
Mean:	128.3	164.3	198.0	237.3	240.6	380.3

Adolescent Medicine

	Instructor	Assistant Professor	Associate Professor	Professor	Chief	Chair
Count:	1	29	24	13	9	0
25th:		121	147	155	157	
Median:		127	160	194	177	
75th:		133	170	230	217	
Mean:		126.6	160.3	200.6	186.1	

Allergy/Immunology-Peds.

	Instructor	Assistant Professor	Associate Professor	Professor	Chief	Chair
Count:	3	29	19	31	7	1
25th:		126	148	183	171	
Median:		136	163	223	206	
75th:		147	190	261	234	
Mean:		144.3	174.8	232.0	214.4	

Child & Adolescent Psychiatry

	Instructor	Assistant Professor	Associate Professor	Professor	Chief	Chair
Count:	0	50	30	29	9	2
25th:		150	160	193	206	
Median:		165	190	222	221	
75th:		181	214	268	265	
Mean:		167.3	191.1	230.9	236.2	

TABLE 12 Summary Statistics on Medical School Faculty Compensation for Public Schools M.D. or Equivalent Degree, Clinical Science Departments/Specialties Total Compensation in Thousands of Dollars (continued)

Critical/Intensive Care-Peds.

	Instructor	Assistant Professor	Associate Professor	Professor	Chief	Chair
Count:	9	166	92	32	21	3
25th:	116	175	204	243	242	
Median:	154	192	237	269	257	
75th:	174	228	267	308	337	
Mean:	146.2	205.0	245.3	280.2	283.3	

Emergency Medicine-Peds.

	Instructor	Assistant Professor	Associate Professor	Professor	Chief	Chair
Count:	35	181	79	31	12	1
25th:	122	154	186	221	200	
Median:	143	176	208	232	262	
75th:	154	204	239	258	302	
Mean:	137.5	179.6	217.2	242.7	247.5	

Endocrinology-Peds.

	Instructor	Assistant Professor	Associate Professor	Professor	Chief	Chair
Count:	2	100	50	49	20	1
25th:		126	144	173	176	
Median:		136	161	194	190	
75th:		145	178	230	224	
Mean:		138.0	163.3	200.6	198.8	

Gastroenterology-Peds.

	Instructor	Assistant Professor	Associate Professor	Professor	Chief	Chair
Count:	2	100	51	56	19	3
25th:		150	171	199	217	
Median:		166	190	229	241	
75th:		179	210	271	278	
Mean:		166.6	190.8	241.3	250.9	

General Pediatrics

	Instructor	Assistant Professor	Associate Professor	Professor	Chief	Chair
Count:	33	596	257	200	39	23
25th:	95	129	145	170	188	244
Median:	124	141	160	201	218	320
75th:	135	166	185	252	259	365
Mean:	115.7	152.4	172.5	222.3	231.4	310.5

Summary Statistics on Medical School Faculty Compensation for Public Schools M.D. or Equivalent Degree, Clinical Science Departments/Specialties Total Compensation in Thousands of Dollars (continued)

Genetics-Peds.

	Instructor	Assistant Professor	Associate Professor	Professor	Chief	Chair
Count:	2	42	41	64	18	2
25th:		108	132	159	153	
Median:		126	145	179	170	
75th:		136	162	215	200	
Mean:		124.1	148.7	192.7	180.1	

Hematology/Oncology-Peds.

	Instructor	Assistant Professor	Associate Professor	Professor	Chief	Chair
Count:	12	171	101	81	21	3
25th:	75	132	161	193	187	
Median:	106	138	171	222	221	
75th:	118	150	190	246	263	
Mean:	95.8	143.7	181.4	235.3	225.1	

Hospital Medicine-Peds.

	Instructor	Assistant Professor	Associate Professor	Professor	Chief	Chair
Count:	30	120	23	7	7	0
25th:	115	132	150	174	167	
Median:	141	140	159	222	188	
75th:	141	152	190	247	223	
Mean:	129.0	144.1	171.7	212.6	195.3	

Infectious Disease-Peds.

	Instructor	Assistant Professor	Associate Professor	Professor	Chief	Chair
Count:	3	70	34	67	21	5
25th:		116	134	167	186	330
Median:		124	145	192	222	351
75th:		131	167	232	260	444
Mean:		126.4	150.5	200.0	225.6	379.8

Neonatology

	Instructor	Assistant Professor	Associate Professor	Professor	Chief	Chair
Count:	16	252	135	147	23	10
25th:	128	169	209	229	257	373
Median:	162	196	239	265	291	422
75th:	197	233	282	316	327	467
Mean:	183.1	207.2	252.6	281.9	311.4	436.7

TABLE 12 Summary Statistics on Medical School Faculty Compensation for Public Schools M.D. or Equivalent Degree, Clinical Science Departments/Specialties Total Compensation in Thousands of Dollars (continued)

Nephrology-Peds.

	Instructor	Assistant Professor	Associate Professor	Professor	Chief	Chair
Count:	1	67	35	38	18	2
25th:		132	157	194	166	
Median:		138	170	209	186	
75th:		145	182	255	213	
Mean:		142.0	172.8	226.8	194.1	

Neurology-Peds.

	Instructor	Assistant Professor	Associate Professor	Professor	Chief	Chair
Count:	10	89	38	45	13	4
25th:	115	145	164	192	204	
Median:	135	155	181	222	234	
75th:	160	176	200	239	267	
Mean:	138.1	160.7	184.1	218.6	223.5	

Pediatric Cardiology

	Instructor	Assistant Professor	Associate Professor	Professor	Chief	Chair
Count:	4	145	130	79	23	2
25th:		173	215	252	262	
Median:		194	236	291	325	
75th:		221	270	335	434	
Mean:		199.3	245.7	295.0	344.5	

Pulmonary-Peds.

	Instructor	Assistant Professor	Associate Professor	Professor	Chief	Chair
Count:	6	81	55	50	15	1
25th:	99	135	150	190	201	
Median:	128	146	172	212	229	
75th:	188	166	193	247	270	
Mean:	137.2	157.8	181.8	224.1	236.9	

Rheumatology-Peds.

	Instructor	Assistant Professor	Associate Professor	Professor	Chief	Chair
Count:	3	24	12	10	11	0
25th:		132	142	191	180	
Median:		141	152	201	221	
75th:		151	168	210	271	
Mean:		140.2	152.7	207.5	238.5	

TABLE 12 **Summary Statistics on Medical School Faculty Compensation for Public Schools M.D. or Equivalent Degree, Clinical Science Departments/Specialties Total Compensation in Thousands of Dollars (continued)**

Other Pediatrics

	Instructor	Assistant Professor	Associate Professor	Professor	Chief	Chair
Count:	8	126	72	82	30	5
25th:	91	131	154	193	192	329
Median:	107	150	182	225	220	407
75th:	123	180	219	287	265	580
Mean:	109.0	154.3	191.7	245.0	236.9	444.6

Total Radiology

	Instructor	Assistant Professor	Associate Professor	Professor	Chief	Chair
Count:	53	936	397	444	98	96
25th:	65	278	300	323	343	508
Median:	76	325	347	365	397	561
75th:	236	372	410	424	447	631
Mean:	150.8	329.1	356.0	374.7	405.5	570.1

Diagnostic Radiology: Total

	Instructor	Assistant Professor	Associate Professor	Professor	Chief	Chair
Count:	43	709	253	314	83	47
25th:	66	285	302	325	345	486
Median:	75	327	345	364	398	546
75th:	145	377	414	424	447	600
Mean:	141.6	333.4	360.1	377.7	410.5	550.6

Diagnostic Radiology: Interventional

	Instructor	Assistant Professor	Associate Professor	Professor	Chief	Chair
Count:	3	147	56	62	14	12
25th:		317	362	340	414	492
Median:		363	422	417	456	552
75th:		428	491	454	525	619
Mean:		369.0	435.2	407.9	462.1	557.6

Diagnostic Radiology: Non-interventional

	Instructor	Assistant Professor	Associate Professor	Professor	Chief	Chair
Count:	40	562	197	252	69	35
25th:	65	276	295	324	334	470
Median:	73	320	330	359	387	546
75th:	138	363	379	415	440	600
Mean:	135.8	324.2	338.8	370.3	400.0	548.2

TABLE 12 Summary Statistics on Medical School Faculty Compensation for Public Schools M.D. or Equivalent Degree, Clinical Science Departments/Specialties Total Compensation in Thousands of Dollars (continued)

Nuclear Medicine

	Instructor	Assistant Professor	Associate Professor	Professor	Chief	Chair
Count:	0	26	21	28	7	2
25th:		224	237	262	314	
Median:		283	288	327	402	
75th:		358	312	372	495	
Mean:		289.4	279.6	311.7	406.1	

Radiation Oncology

	Instructor	Assistant Professor	Associate Professor	Professor	Chief	Chair
Count:	3	129	75	64	4	41
25th:		262	322	327		531
Median:		307	364	382		611
75th:		362	424	438		658
Mean:		319.2	371.9	393.6		617.4

Other Radiology

	Instructor	Assistant Professor	Associate Professor	Professor	Chief	Chair
Count:	7	72	48	38	4	6
25th:	60	277	280	311		395
Median:	222	331	372	376		472
75th:	255	375	404	425		567
Mean:	177.6	318.8	342.8	364.7		479.8

Total Surgery

	Instructor	Assistant Professor	Associate Professor	Professor	Chief	Chair
Count:	81	1,838	1,017	989	296	202
25th:	56	245	299	312	370	538
Median:	75	302	375	394	457	624
75th:	125	390	486	519	570	750
Mean:	109.6	331.7	405.8	433.0	492.8	676.7

General Surgery

	Instructor	Assistant Professor	Associate Professor	Professor	Chief	Chair
Count:	14	328	173	216	32	33
25th:	55	225	260	264	365	488
Median:	60	260	309	330	467	612
75th:	130	321	371	402	569	685
Mean:	93.4	275.9	319.5	338.1	481.6	591.3

TABLE 12 Summary Statistics on Medical School Faculty Compensation for Public Schools M.D. or Equivalent Degree, Clinical Science Departments/Specialties Total Compensation in Thousands of Dollars (continued)

Neurosurgery

	Instructor	Assistant Professor	Associate Professor	Professor	Chief	Chair
Count:	9	222	97	118	16	37
25th:	57	333	404	377	481	642
Median:	88	402	478	502	538	706
75th:	94	500	575	635	651	908
Mean:	122.4	422.5	497.3	549.0	567.2	783.3

Orthopaedic Surgery

	Instructor	Assistant Professor	Associate Professor	Professor	Chief	Chair
Count:	12	395	223	166	42	54
25th:	54	300	338	361	387	547
Median:	55	363	444	428	526	618
75th:	93	473	552	540	640	749
Mean:	99.8	401.9	475.7	460.0	517.4	675.0

Pediatric Surgery

	Instructor	Assistant Professor	Associate Professor	Professor	Chief	Chair
Count:	0	50	51	38	22	3
25th:		294	370	467	417	
Median:		329	444	571	521	
75th:		410	510	658	633	
Mean:		338.5	454.8	544.8	547.1	

Plastic Surgery

	Instructor	Assistant Professor	Associate Professor	Professor	Chief	Chair
Count:	5	108	48	54	25	7
25th:	62	240	287	314	319	583
Median:	120	284	365	424	430	742
75th:	213	386	460	485	577	1,298
Mean:	133.8	326.0	380.5	414.2	476.0	1,010.0

Surgical Oncology

	Instructor	Assistant Professor	Associate Professor	Professor	Chief	Chair
Count:	2	58	44	23	24	7
25th:		228	207	261	301	554
Median:		245	273	298	403	571
75th:		272	323	360	453	641
Mean:		256.9	268.7	320.9	390.8	593.3

TABLE 12 Summary Statistics on Medical School Faculty Compensation for Public Schools M.D. or Equivalent Degree, Clinical Science Departments/Specialties Total Compensation in Thousands of Dollars (continued)

Thoracic & Cardiovascular Surgery

	Instructor	Assistant Professor	Associate Professor	Professor	Chief	Chair
Count:	4	129	85	85	34	9
25th:		275	351	412	436	667
Median:		319	432	517	515	850
75th:		416	591	673	770	995
Mean:		358.2	472.5	555.7	627.2	840.0

Transplant Surgery

	Instructor	Assistant Professor	Associate Professor	Professor	Chief	Chair
Count:	8	55	46	54	19	6
25th:	70	258	354	345	397	699
Median:	80	297	415	407	491	872
75th:	91	352	532	548	610	1,057
Mean:	81.8	309.4	468.9	450.8	536.2	1,019.8

Trauma/Critical Care Surgery

	Instructor	Assistant Professor	Associate Professor	Professor	Chief	Chair
Count:	4	143	77	56	25	7
25th:		239	294	321	368	480
Median:		278	350	363	437	600
75th:		320	425	419	483	641
Mean:		281.3	358.7	378.0	445.1	576.4

Urology

	Instructor	Assistant Professor	Associate Professor	Professor	Chief	Chair
Count:	15	188	100	97	19	29
25th:	60	234	285	311	354	403
Median:	71	271	325	371	423	497
75th:	115	318	400	455	498	588
Mean:	92.1	276.0	354.4	414.7	418.6	504.0

Vascular Surgery

	Instructor	Assistant Professor	Associate Professor	Professor	Chief	Chair
Count:	0	83	38	50	25	4
25th:		243	305	335	339	
Median:		279	350	371	433	
75th:		319	412	470	572	
Mean:		285.0	363.4	391.3	460.0	

TABLE 12 Summary Statistics on Medical School Faculty Compensation for Public Schools M.D. or Equivalent Degree, Clinical Science Departments/Specialties Total Compensation in Thousands of Dollars (continued)

Other Surgery

	Instructor	Assistant Professor	Associate Professor	Professor	Chief	Chair
Count:	8	79	35	32	13	6
25th:	51	205	194	267	287	475
Median:	67	249	311	331	345	539
75th:	235	303	400	438	383	751
Mean:	125.6	261.1	320.4	345.6	324.9	606.7

Other Clinical Science

Community Health

	Instructor	Assistant Professor	Associate Professor	Professor	Chief	Chair
Count:	1	12	8	6	1	3
25th:		112	131	136		
Median:		135	162	188		
75th:		147	175	231		
Mean:		134.8	158.3	190.3		

Emergency Medicine

	Instructor	Assistant Professor	Associate Professor	Professor	Chief	Chair
Count:	73	748	239	124	25	41
25th:	172	208	230	248	268	337
Median:	204	228	253	276	310	397
75th:	224	258	278	322	344	466
Mean:	188.5	235.8	257.5	290.8	305.4	412.7

Family Medicine

	Instructor	Assistant Professor	Associate Professor	Professor	Chief	Chair
Count:	54	907	429	253	6	75
25th:	115	145	160	171	179	259
Median:	139	160	179	192	212	292
75th:	149	183	203	216	257	315
Mean:	138.9	165.3	182.5	201.3	256.0	285.6

Neurology

	Instructor	Assistant Professor	Associate Professor	Professor	Chief	Chair
Count:	21	523	271	325	40	55
25th:	57	135	163	186	182	313
Median:	60	154	183	214	219	353
75th:	92	181	220	254	272	396
Mean:	74.8	163.2	193.0	230.3	232.1	362.7

TABLE 12 Summary Statistics on Medical School Faculty Compensation for Public Schools M.D. or Equivalent Degree, Clinical Science Departments/Specialties Total Compensation in Thousands of Dollars (continued)

Ophthalmology

	Instructor	Assistant Professor	Associate Professor	Professor	Chief	Chair
Count:	26	252	156	161	7	45
25th:	53	160	202	238	322	417
Median:	53	205	273	293	339	501
75th:	86	251	360	387	411	568
Mean:	81.7	226.4	306.5	333.7	351.0	512.9

Otolaryngology

	Instructor	Assistant Professor	Associate Professor	Professor	Chief	Chair
Count:	6	235	132	123	23	42
25th:	49	218	267	293	308	458
Median:	52	248	328	361	354	520
75th:	55	303	382	422	427	626
Mean:	51.5	272.2	333.9	380.1	388.2	538.9

Physical Medicine & Rehabilitation

	Instructor	Assistant Professor	Associate Professor	Professor	Chief	Chair
Count:	11	138	70	38	8	25
25th:	150	151	175	212	251	274
Median:	167	173	191	232	279	325
75th:	210	201	229	261	363	391
Mean:	170.4	181.5	214.3	242.6	298.4	330.0

Preventive Medicine

	Instructor	Assistant Professor	Associate Professor	Professor	Chief	Chair
Count:	2	23	19	25	1	5
25th:		116	136	197		219
Median:		125	168	219		235
75th:		137	199	251		253
Mean:		127.2	166.1	225.4		235.6

Psychiatry

	Instructor	Assistant Professor	Associate Professor	Professor	Chief	Chair
Count:	80	765	313	369	33	71
25th:	144	148	161	186	182	262
Median:	163	165	184	214	220	321
75th:	179	190	210	262	268	419
Mean:	162.4	172.7	188.6	229.1	232.0	342.4

TABLE 12

Summary Statistics on Medical School Faculty Compensation for Public Schools M.D. or Equivalent Degree, Clinical Science Departments/Specialties Total Compensation in Thousands of Dollars (continued)

Other

	Instructor	Assistant Professor	Associate Professor	Professor	Chief	Chair
Count:	1	40	21	30	0	4
25th:		141	189	229		
Median:		176	239	302		
75th:		224	476	333		
Mean:		194.2	327.5	284.4		

TABLE 13 Summary Statistics on Medical School Faculty Compensation for Private Schools
M.D. or Equivalent Degree, Clinical Science Departments/Specialties
Total Compensation in Thousands of Dollars

CLINICAL SCIENCE - TOTAL ALL DEPARTMENTS/SPECIALTIES

	Instructor	Assistant Professor	Associate Professor	Professor	Chief	Chair
Count:	3,365	15,833	7,024	6,132	1,113	723
25th:	115	158	188	220	239	400
Median:	164	210	249	286	319	522
75th:	238	300	351	399	434	668
Mean:	188.6	243.3	293.2	333.9	375.0	585.2

Total Anesthesiology

	Instructor	Assistant Professor	Associate Professor	Professor	Chief	Chair
Count:	285	1,442	473	269	62	39
25th:	224	266	306	323	304	485
Median:	288	313	351	376	354	537
75th:	344	364	398	419	392	617
Mean:	283.5	313.3	349.5	377.9	361.0	569.1

Anesthesiology: General

	Instructor	Assistant Professor	Associate Professor	Professor	Chief	Chair
Count:	263	1,212	402	230	49	39
25th:	226	266	306	322	320	485
Median:	291	313	348	372	361	537
75th:	347	365	396	416	399	617
Mean:	285.9	313.5	349.3	372.8	365.0	569.1

Anesthesiology: Pain Management

	Instructor	Assistant Professor	Associate Professor	Professor	Chief	Chair
Count:	14	61	18	8	5	0
25th:	207	256	267	329	297	
Median:	243	297	350	376	325	
75th:	304	393	380	409	480	
Mean:	268.1	329.2	323.6	366.3	375.6	

Anesthesiology: Pediatric

	Instructor	Assistant Professor	Associate Professor	Professor	Chief	Chair
Count:	8	169	53	31	8	0
25th:	214	271	306	327	289	
Median:	243	317	382	422	321	
75th:	277	350	406	458	357	
Mean:	231.1	306.2	360.0	418.2	327.8	

TABLE 13 Summary Statistics on Medical School Faculty Compensation for Private Schools M.D. or Equivalent Degree, Clinical Science Departments/Specialties Total Compensation in Thousands of Dollars (continued)

Total Dermatology

	Instructor	Assistant Professor	Associate Professor	Professor	Chief	Chair
Count:	36	184	93	83	14	32
25th:	150	208	244	250	243	403
Median:	208	250	309	319	306	455
75th:	300	351	424	529	405	677
Mean:	245.2	288.4	366.5	484.7	337.3	528.8

Dermatology (excluding Mohs Surgery)

	Instructor	Assistant Professor	Associate Professor	Professor	Chief	Chair
Count:	34	160	90	72	11	30
25th:	145	201	240	244	230	404
Median:	204	235	309	311	270	455
75th:	267	316	423	416	405	666
Mean:	215.7	264.3	365.0	417.2	321.1	527.8

Dermatology: Mohs Surgery

	Instructor	Assistant Professor	Associate Professor	Professor	Chief	Chair
Count:	2	24	3	11	3	2
25th:		338		529		
Median:		388		616		
75th:		504		1,656		
Mean:		449.7		926.2		

Total Medicine

	Instructor	Assistant Professor	Associate Professor	Professor	Chief	Chair
Count:	1,188	4,482	2,157	1,973	269	68
25th:	120	149	176	214	234	394
Median:	160	184	225	268	284	509
75th:	205	240	296	351	362	619
Mean:	168.3	208.1	250.4	298.2	314.2	514.6

Allergy/Immunology-Med.

	Instructor	Assistant Professor	Associate Professor	Professor	Chief	Chair
Count:	11	35	16	23	7	0
25th:	60	115	142	172	199	
Median:	116	144	195	220	220	
75th:	197	202	238	243	261	
Mean:	125.3	156.1	200.8	222.0	218.7	

TABLE 13 Summary Statistics on Medical School Faculty Compensation for Private Schools M.D. or Equivalent Degree, Clinical Science Departments/Specialties Total Compensation in Thousands of Dollars (continued)

Cardiology: Total

	Instructor	Assistant Professor	Associate Professor	Professor	Chief	Chair
Count:	102	679	396	404	25	11
25th:	115	210	239	266	377	501
Median:	175	275	306	338	443	596
75th:	243	379	405	436	549	665
Mean:	193.9	304.4	339.5	373.6	472.4	583.3

Cardiology: Invasive Interventional-Med.

	Instructor	Assistant Professor	Associate Professor	Professor	Chief	Chair
Count:	29	262	148	145	9	4
25th:	121	258	278	325	450	
Median:	215	349	369	423	537	
75th:	311	443	454	470	647	
Mean:	246.3	367.1	392.9	463.7	548.4	

Cardiology: Invasive Non-interventional-Med.

	Instructor	Assistant Professor	Associate Professor	Professor	Chief	Chair
Count:	10	76	46	27	3	0
25th:	75	245	240	245		
Median:	147	303	343	338		
75th:	208	402	423	421		
Mean:	154.7	327.6	370.9	339.3		

Cardiology: Non-invasive-Med.

	Instructor	Assistant Professor	Associate Professor	Professor	Chief	Chair
Count:	63	341	202	232	13	7
25th:	129	189	221	245	344	368
Median:	167	231	271	296	380	596
75th:	231	298	346	387	451	640
Mean:	176.0	251.0	293.2	321.3	391.2	536.1

Critical/Intensive Care-Med.

	Instructor	Assistant Professor	Associate Professor	Professor	Chief	Chair
Count:	11	72	35	23	0	1
25th:	183	197	196	277		
Median:	197	256	261	321		
75th:	243	337	293	379		
Mean:	217.2	268.8	270.5	329.2		

TABLE 13 Summary Statistics on Medical School Faculty Compensation for Private Schools M.D. or Equivalent Degree, Clinical Science Departments/Specialties Total Compensation in Thousands of Dollars (continued)

Endocrinology-Med.

	Instructor	Assistant Professor	Associate Professor	Professor	Chief	Chair
Count:	42	201	108	147	21	0
25th:	100	132	149	186	200	
Median:	117	149	176	215	261	
75th:	150	176	213	266	298	
Mean:	129.9	162.1	187.4	234.0	256.6	

Gastroenterology-Med.

	Instructor	Assistant Professor	Associate Professor	Professor	Chief	Chair
Count:	49	345	189	186	25	7
25th:	92	190	244	252	327	350
Median:	150	245	310	328	390	407
75th:	216	316	402	410	462	443
Mean:	164.9	258.4	323.3	338.9	415.4	388.4

General Internal Medicine

	Instructor	Assistant Professor	Associate Professor	Professor	Chief	Chair
Count:	422	1,078	397	226	31	12
25th:	140	146	167	200	207	288
Median:	171	172	197	239	237	431
75th:	222	212	245	314	282	695
Mean:	181.2	185.0	215.5	276.8	273.7	494.6

Geriatrics-Med.

	Instructor	Assistant Professor	Associate Professor	Professor	Chief	Chair
Count:	19	131	52	31	10	1
25th:	125	133	164	192	249	
Median:	144	149	187	219	310	
75th:	166	172	207	255	364	
Mean:	148.1	155.5	192.7	228.2	315.8	

Hematology/Oncology-Med.

	Instructor	Assistant Professor	Associate Professor	Professor	Chief	Chair
Count:	108	532	274	323	40	11
25th:	120	166	198	244	259	435
Median:	155	201	250	297	306	530
75th:	214	251	309	357	380	609
Mean:	175.4	214.1	260.3	316.1	321.1	533.3

TABLE 13 Summary Statistics on Medical School Faculty Compensation for Private Schools M.D. or Equivalent Degree, Clinical Science Departments/Specialties Total Compensation in Thousands of Dollars (continued)

Hospital Medicine

	Instructor	Assistant Professor	Associate Professor	Professor	Chief	Chair
Count:	185	253	17	2	7	0
25th:	154	167	178		214	
Median:	171	194	188		311	
75th:	200	217	234		344	
Mean:	176.2	193.0	202.7		287.6	

Infectious Disease-Med.

	Instructor	Assistant Professor	Associate Professor	Professor	Chief	Chair
Count:	60	275	173	142	24	8
25th:	90	125	150	186	198	296
Median:	115	140	170	218	224	488
75th:	144	168	209	252	297	568
Mean:	121.3	151.0	183.2	231.0	246.5	462.0

Nephrology-Med.

	Instructor	Assistant Professor	Associate Professor	Professor	Chief	Chair
Count:	43	271	137	135	24	3
25th:	81	134	173	211	268	
Median:	127	158	200	248	295	
75th:	160	188	254	287	347	
Mean:	134.9	165.7	214.2	256.7	326.2	

Pulmonary-Med.

	Instructor	Assistant Professor	Associate Professor	Professor	Chief	Chair
Count:	58	367	197	161	24	1
25th:	108	151	180	205	246	
Median:	144	180	213	247	280	
75th:	201	218	256	306	321	
Mean:	155.7	189.9	226.2	259.4	287.8	

Rheumatology-Med.

	Instructor	Assistant Professor	Associate Professor	Professor	Chief	Chair
Count:	22	127	78	77	22	0
25th:	62	128	149	185	197	
Median:	109	144	182	220	241	
75th:	145	173	236	272	277	
Mean:	107.1	151.3	195.7	236.5	245.5	

TABLE 13 Summary Statistics on Medical School Faculty Compensation for Private Schools M.D. or Equivalent Degree, Clinical Science Departments/Specialties Total Compensation in Thousands of Dollars (continued)

Other Medicine

	Instructor	Assistant Professor	Associate Professor	Professor	Chief	Chair
Count:	56	116	88	93	9	13
25th:	90	118	170	206	214	449
Median:	129	165	225	270	297	546
75th:	170	226	267	360	398	663
Mean:	135.6	187.2	233.0	295.5	316.2	558.9

Total OB/GYN

	Instructor	Assistant Professor	Associate Professor	Professor	Chief	Chair
Count:	111	701	234	184	63	45
25th:	69	189	231	239	252	439
Median:	168	232	292	326	334	522
75th:	228	308	417	448	426	731
Mean:	176.7	266.5	368.9	371.6	379.1	640.1

OB/GYN: General

	Instructor	Assistant Professor	Associate Professor	Professor	Chief	Chair
Count:	60	386	97	59	15	16
25th:	163	188	221	182	230	318
Median:	189	225	277	264	261	486
75th:	234	313	373	361	337	564
Mean:	194.1	260.4	300.9	280.0	330.5	490.6

OB/GYN: Gynecologic Oncology

	Instructor	Assistant Professor	Associate Professor	Professor	Chief	Chair
Count:	7	68	28	26	11	9
25th:	61	223	267	267	305	402
Median:	67	262	454	420	453	466
75th:	349	313	549	595	537	696
Mean:	162.4	287.7	442.1	450.5	507.6	550.7

OB/GYN: Maternal & Fetal

	Instructor	Assistant Professor	Associate Professor	Professor	Chief	Chair
Count:	20	88	46	43	12	10
25th:	68	216	239	285	301	467
Median:	85	272	316	369	348	487
75th:	263	350	388	481	369	560
Mean:	160.3	286.2	335.1	413.2	363.8	549.5

TABLE 13 Summary Statistics on Medical School Faculty Compensation for Private Schools M.D. or Equivalent Degree, Clinical Science Departments/Specialties Total Compensation in Thousands of Dollars (continued)

OB/GYN: Reproductive Endocrinology

	Instructor	Assistant Professor	Associate Professor	Professor	Chief	Chair
Count:	8	45	36	28	9	4
25th:	68	206	240	267	283	
Median:	254	250	305	388	377	
75th:	393	329	551	516	591	
Mean:	267.8	351.7	618.9	498.5	444.4	

OB/GYN: Other OB/GYN

	Instructor	Assistant Professor	Associate Professor	Professor	Chief	Chair
Count:	16	114	27	28	16	6
25th:	60	165	212	223	220	579
Median:	65	189	249	280	332	655
75th:	105	264	302	327	400	804
Mean:	92.4	225.8	261.8	300.6	311.2	660.0

Total Pathology

	Instructor	Assistant Professor	Associate Professor	Professor	Chief	Chair
Count:	74	585	420	480	36	46
25th:	80	164	197	224	237	378
Median:	135	186	228	264	293	474
75th:	198	225	266	326	358	550
Mean:	155.0	200.9	238.1	282.3	315.8	482.3

Pathology: Anatomic

	Instructor	Assistant Professor	Associate Professor	Professor	Chief	Chair
Count:	38	290	196	201	15	17
25th:	158	167	211	241	243	381
Median:	177	194	238	276	304	434
75th:	241	255	307	350	378	517
Mean:	201.9	215.5	259.7	301.5	340.8	461.9

Pathology: Clinical

	Instructor	Assistant Professor	Associate Professor	Professor	Chief	Chair
Count:	15	131	119	130	9	13
25th:	80	161	190	226	236	373
Median:	100	182	225	270	249	402
75th:	134	211	262	340	296	565
Mean:	120.2	184.6	230.8	289.8	271.4	438.4

TABLE 13 Summary Statistics on Medical School Faculty Compensation for Private Schools
M.D. or Equivalent Degree, Clinical Science Departments/Specialties
Total Compensation in Thousands of Dollars (continued)

Pathology: Other Pathology

	Instructor	Assistant Professor	Associate Professor	Professor	Chief	Chair
Count:	21	164	105	149	12	16
25th:	63	155	162	201	230	383
Median:	98	181	204	240	278	529
75th:	125	205	236	286	368	612
Mean:	94.8	188.1	205.9	249.8	317.8	539.6

Total Pediatrics

	Instructor	Assistant Professor	Associate Professor	Professor	Chief	Chair
Count:	446	2,277	929	778	245	48
25th:	94	135	165	195	200	312
Median:	119	160	196	230	233	435
75th:	151	194	232	289	287	590
Mean:	127.4	170.2	207.0	254.3	253.3	459.0

Adolescent Medicine

	Instructor	Assistant Professor	Associate Professor	Professor	Chief	Chair
Count:	6	32	12	12	7	1
25th:	56	117	143	168	158	
Median:	96	125	162	185	194	
75th:	138	141	200	236	236	
Mean:	97.5	131.3	170.8	215.4	200.1	

Allergy/Immunology-Peds.

	Instructor	Assistant Professor	Associate Professor	Professor	Chief	Chair
Count:	11	48	21	21	10	1
25th:	59	131	156	175	185	
Median:	85	145	189	214	229	
75th:	132	164	204	301	236	
Mean:	99.9	148.0	195.8	241.3	230.3	

Child & Adolescent Psychiatry

	Instructor	Assistant Professor	Associate Professor	Professor	Chief	Chair
Count:	11	33	15	10	7	0
25th:	120	151	178	195	182	
Median:	159	172	206	223	228	
75th:	176	220	232	227	257	
Mean:	156.6	188.3	222.5	231.2	247.3	

TABLE 13 Summary Statistics on Medical School Faculty Compensation for Private Schools M.D. or Equivalent Degree, Clinical Science Departments/Specialties Total Compensation in Thousands of Dollars (continued)

Critical/Intensive Care-Peds.

	Instructor	Assistant Professor	Associate Professor	Professor	Chief	Chair
Count:	35	177	57	27	14	1
25th:	78	175	223	262	235	
Median:	151	195	256	276	256	
75th:	174	232	288	380	339	
Mean:	136.1	208.5	262.0	320.8	290.4	

Emergency Medicine-Peds.

	Instructor	Assistant Professor	Associate Professor	Professor	Chief	Chair
Count:	34	177	49	19	11	0
25th:	76	162	203	220	230	
Median:	128	181	223	243	267	
75th:	144	225	267	290	316	
Mean:	126.3	193.5	236.2	259.8	268.0	

Endocrinology-Peds.

	Instructor	Assistant Professor	Associate Professor	Professor	Chief	Chair
Count:	11	91	30	37	16	2
25th:	61	125	144	185	174	
Median:	102	134	169	200	222	
75th:	126	149	185	230	246	
Mean:	106.1	138.9	169.2	206.8	225.3	

Gastroenterology-Peds.

	Instructor	Assistant Professor	Associate Professor	Professor	Chief	Chair
Count:	21	116	54	36	14	3
25th:	61	156	190	224	209	
Median:	122	167	207	242	257	
75th:	196	189	235	305	283	
Mean:	159.8	175.8	223.5	285.0	272.6	

General Pediatrics

	Instructor	Assistant Professor	Associate Professor	Professor	Chief	Chair
Count:	84	434	140	100	17	17
25th:	109	126	145	175	194	267
Median:	125	143	166	210	239	353
75th:	155	174	199	257	271	604
Mean:	139.2	160.4	179.1	219.1	246.3	424.3

Genetics-Peds.

	Instructor	Assistant Professor	Associate Professor	Professor	Chief	Chair
Count:	3	30	15	21	7	1
25th:		124	140	155	199	
Median:		148	155	180	219	
75th:		155	172	230	224	
Mean:		141.1	165.9	203.6	212.0	

Hematology/Oncology-Peds.

	Instructor	Assistant Professor	Associate Professor	Professor	Chief	Chair
Count:	25	181	96	90	22	1
25th:	84	130	164	202	197	
Median:	88	142	180	224	215	
75th:	114	160	204	265	270	
Mean:	94.4	148.6	187.3	245.8	233.1	

Hospital Medicine-Peds.

	Instructor	Assistant Professor	Associate Professor	Professor	Chief	Chair
Count:	56	81	15	4	6	0
25th:	113	139	158		162	
Median:	120	165	165		200	
75th:	128	194	182		207	
Mean:	127.5	169.9	174.5		191.3	

Infectious Disease-Peds.

	Instructor	Assistant Professor	Associate Professor	Professor	Chief	Chair
Count:	9	70	37	61	16	2
25th:	77	115	135	177	192	
Median:	99	126	147	206	215	
75th:	110	137	182	240	238	
Mean:	92.4	127.6	155.5	222.0	219.6	

Neonatology

	Instructor	Assistant Professor	Associate Professor	Professor	Chief	Chair
Count:	50	238	103	105	18	5
25th:	109	165	195	216	296	362
Median:	133	189	216	258	335	469
75th:	164	214	255	307	356	759
Mean:	134.2	195.9	226.3	265.7	328.9	542.0

TABLE 13

Summary Statistics on Medical School Faculty Compensation for Private Schools M.D. or Equivalent Degree, Clinical Science Departments/Specialties Total Compensation in Thousands of Dollars (continued)

Nephrology-Peds.

	Instructor	Assistant Professor	Associate Professor	Professor	Chief	Chair
Count:	7	35	19	25	15	2
25th:	110	124	151	175	195	
Median:	126	143	191	200	213	
75th:	159	164	214	232	244	
Mean:	124.0	142.0	188.4	209.8	217.3	

Neurology-Peds.

	Instructor	Assistant Professor	Associate Professor	Professor	Chief	Chair
Count:	4	76	42	37	9	1
25th:		150	185	195	220	
Median:		169	199	211	282	
75th:		182	223	237	309	
Mean:		167.0	208.8	215.2	270.7	

Pediatric Cardiology

	Instructor	Assistant Professor	Associate Professor	Professor	Chief	Chair
Count:	26	166	92	66	13	1
25th:	88	171	208	263	270	
Median:	138	195	247	297	311	
75th:	180	210	296	389	432	
Mean:	136.0	201.9	258.9	338.7	357.5	

Pulmonary-Peds.

	Instructor	Assistant Professor	Associate Professor	Professor	Chief	Chair
Count:	14	77	43	26	13	2
25th:	59	140	172	181	215	
Median:	110	150	182	203	231	
75th:	151	164	209	239	271	
Mean:	104.7	151.4	203.7	220.2	245.5	

Rheumatology-Peds.

	Instructor	Assistant Professor	Associate Professor	Professor	Chief	Chair
Count:	6	28	9	7	8	0
25th:	61	133	152	216	161	
Median:	105	140	166	234	186	
75th:	120	163	189	252	308	
Mean:	95.2	145.7	170.9	254.6	216.8	

TABLE 13

Summary Statistics on Medical School Faculty Compensation for Private Schools M.D. or Equivalent Degree, Clinical Science Departments/Specialties Total Compensation in Thousands of Dollars (continued)

Other Pediatrics

	Instructor	Assistant Professor	Associate Professor	Professor	Chief	Chair
Count:	33	187	80	74	22	8
25th:	69	115	143	196	198	447
Median:	96	143	178	279	215	469
75th:	128	170	216	396	300	610
Mean:	114.9	154.7	192.7	305.7	251.5	511.5

Total Radiology

	Instructor	Assistant Professor	Associate Professor	Professor	Chief	Chair
Count:	306	1,185	470	442	65	67
25th:	182	285	323	334	338	530
Median:	290	332	370	401	414	626
75th:	371	400	447	475	477	709
Mean:	278.9	348.6	388.9	402.6	428.0	622.7

Diagnostic Radiology: Total

	Instructor	Assistant Professor	Associate Professor	Professor	Chief	Chair
Count:	215	836	322	298	52	32
25th:	233	285	320	335	338	506
Median:	303	330	364	396	410	617
75th:	383	400	443	459	472	711
Mean:	293.1	345.9	389.0	397.6	416.6	609.9

Diagnostic Radiology: Interventional

	Instructor	Assistant Professor	Associate Professor	Professor	Chief	Chair
Count:	60	180	90	51	9	7
25th:	259	318	364	384	341	400
Median:	346	376	453	432	459	568
75th:	469	453	540	525	537	692
Mean:	353.0	389.2	475.1	448.3	471.9	562.0

Diagnostic Radiology: Non-interventional

	Instructor	Assistant Professor	Associate Professor	Professor	Chief	Chair
Count:	155	656	232	247	43	25
25th:	158	276	302	328	335	511
Median:	295	321	347	381	396	630
75th:	365	380	415	442	469	716
Mean:	269.9	334.0	355.5	387.2	405.1	623.3

TABLE 13 Summary Statistics on Medical School Faculty Compensation for Private Schools M.D. or Equivalent Degree, Clinical Science Departments/Specialties Total Compensation in Thousands of Dollars (continued)

Nuclear Medicine

	Instructor	Assistant Professor	Associate Professor	Professor	Chief	Chair
Count:	4	37	25	26	6	0
25th:		259	305	308	291	
Median:		303	337	352	342	
75th:		540	393	412	477	
Mean:		347.7	355.9	368.2	376.8	

Radiation Oncology

	Instructor	Assistant Professor	Associate Professor	Professor	Chief	Chair
Count:	53	163	79	67	4	29
25th:	230	276	330	363		569
Median:	297	320	387	471		630
75th:	347	380	457	505		682
Mean:	308.4	328.8	385.9	432.3		631.2

Other Radiology

	Instructor	Assistant Professor	Associate Professor	Professor	Chief	Chair
Count:	34	149	44	51	3	6
25th:	58	313	356	322		500
Median:	88	360	396	402		554
75th:	240	511	540	528		885
Mean:	150.4	385.3	412.6	409.7		649.5

Total Surgery

	Instructor	Assistant Professor	Associate Professor	Professor	Chief	Chair
Count:	204	1,851	991	896	241	153
25th:	80	250	305	336	409	559
Median:	225	320	412	447	508	731
75th:	329	434	530	621	700	976
Mean:	253.8	369.1	462.9	511.7	593.0	859.6

General Surgery

	Instructor	Assistant Professor	Associate Professor	Professor	Chief	Chair
Count:	25	283	129	138	29	19
25th:	70	215	271	315	357	609
Median:	193	265	331	415	445	731
75th:	256	350	416	495	609	966
Mean:	189.4	286.6	356.2	414.7	499.2	760.1

TABLE 13 Summary Statistics on Medical School Faculty Compensation for Private Schools M.D. or Equivalent Degree, Clinical Science Departments/Specialties Total Compensation in Thousands of Dollars (continued)

Neurosurgery

	Instructor	Assistant Professor	Associate Professor	Professor	Chief	Chair
Count:	17	178	126	95	23	28
25th:	66	360	408	385	534	738
Median:	75	457	534	650	672	890
75th:	250	628	703	785	774	1,522
Mean:	190.8	549.5	654.0	723.6	768.6	1,213.3

Orthopaedic Surgery

	Instructor	Assistant Professor	Associate Professor	Professor	Chief	Chair
Count:	56	394	178	176	31	35
25th:	169	292	362	383	392	555
Median:	286	368	505	505	464	682
75th:	447	505	609	652	560	943
Mean:	348.4	431.7	534.8	537.1	487.4	731.5

Pediatric Surgery

	Instructor	Assistant Professor	Associate Professor	Professor	Chief	Chair
Count:	4	85	48	36	14	5
25th:		278	370	423	496	471
Median:		350	441	530	549	647
75th:		427	505	599	605	873
Mean:		346.5	430.1	534.2	557.2	667.0

Plastic Surgery

	Instructor	Assistant Professor	Associate Professor	Professor	Chief	Chair
Count:	10	104	55	35	16	7
25th:	220	250	283	397	444	527
Median:	365	313	407	474	594	760
75th:	550	480	515	646	790	900
Mean:	393.9	429.0	445.1	499.7	643.7	720.3

Surgical Oncology

	Instructor	Assistant Professor	Associate Professor	Professor	Chief	Chair
Count:	13	74	53	32	10	6
25th:	227	214	278	255	367	625
Median:	284	250	341	314	458	868
75th:	344	301	428	410	554	991
Mean:	278.9	264.5	370.1	372.5	450.5	871.2

TABLE 13 Summary Statistics on Medical School Faculty Compensation for Private Schools M.D. or Equivalent Degree, Clinical Science Departments/Specialties Total Compensation in Thousands of Dollars (continued)

Thoracic & Cardiovascular Surgery

	Instructor	Assistant Professor	Associate Professor	Professor	Chief	Chair
Count:	28	185	95	106	34	14
25th:	86	278	386	413	460	600
Median:	200	374	471	555	732	996
75th:	327	502	689	762	1,177	1,917
Mean:	237.2	401.9	558.2	647.9	842.4	1,219.7

Transplant Surgery

	Instructor	Assistant Professor	Associate Professor	Professor	Chief	Chair
Count:	9	92	64	58	26	3
25th:	55	243	264	352	420	
Median:	101	288	338	477	530	
75th:	240	355	467	675	770	
Mean:	147.9	288.1	350.9	518.3	600.0	

Trauma/Critical Care Surgery

	Instructor	Assistant Professor	Associate Professor	Professor	Chief	Chair
Count:	11	113	35	29	12	1
25th:	189	250	301	326	349	
Median:	254	295	353	381	421	
75th:	316	368	397	452	471	
Mean:	252.7	304.5	359.5	404.9	419.0	

Urology

	Instructor	Assistant Professor	Associate Professor	Professor	Chief	Chair
Count:	16	172	105	109	15	28
25th:	68	240	286	305	466	514
Median:	102	292	371	383	613	560
75th:	142	371	434	470	812	766
Mean:	117.4	316.2	382.1	419.5	658.1	688.1

Vascular Surgery

	Instructor	Assistant Professor	Associate Professor	Professor	Chief	Chair
Count:	5	80	52	40	21	2
25th:	75	258	323	315	371	
Median:	294	297	408	401	460	
75th:	385	369	496	532	558	
Mean:	242.8	333.3	439.9	427.7	481.2	

TABLE 13 Summary Statistics on Medical School Faculty Compensation for Private Schools M.D. or Equivalent Degree, Clinical Science Departments/Specialties Total Compensation in Thousands of Dollars (continued)

Other Surgery

	Instructor	Assistant Professor	Associate Professor	Professor	Chief	Chair
Count:	10	91	51	42	10	5
25th:	58	180	222	258	297	670
Median:	101	250	305	366	367	814
75th:	325	319	530	450	427	896
Mean:	194.6	266.3	380.5	382.7	379.2	789.0

Other Clinical Science

Community Health

	Instructor	Assistant Professor	Associate Professor	Professor	Chief	Chair
Count:	11	31	12	6	1	3
25th:	178	120	129	171		
Median:	222	161	167	191		
75th:	222	222	190	204		
Mean:	192.3	187.5	169.6	199.8		

Emergency Medicine

	Instructor	Assistant Professor	Associate Professor	Professor	Chief	Chair
Count:	182	668	212	61	9	25
25th:	173	206	230	240	261	431
Median:	203	230	250	267	289	472
75th:	253	265	292	314	363	548
Mean:	208.9	237.3	267.5	284.1	309.3	486.3

Family Medicine

	Instructor	Assistant Professor	Associate Professor	Professor	Chief	Chair
Count:	92	401	116	57	8	29
25th:	138	140	149	182	185	265
Median:	178	156	174	198	189	292
75th:	222	187	196	226	198	380
Mean:	190.3	167.6	173.3	205.8	194.6	319.6

Neurology

	Instructor	Assistant Professor	Associate Professor	Professor	Chief	Chair
Count:	100	587	298	342	28	37
25th:	84	136	168	200	199	355
Median:	128	158	193	241	217	432
75th:	160	196	230	270	262	479
Mean:	135.3	171.2	207.4	241.2	228.5	442.2

TABLE 13 Summary Statistics on Medical School Faculty Compensation for Private Schools M.D. or Equivalent Degree, Clinical Science Departments/Specialties Total Compensation in Thousands of Dollars (continued)

Ophthalmology

	Instructor	Assistant Professor	Associate Professor	Professor	Chief	Chair
Count:	85	298	138	149	25	32
25th:	47	154	201	215	251	428
Median:	65	203	274	288	333	545
75th:	116	271	367	388	446	634
Mean:	99.5	222.8	299.9	328.4	410.2	540.4

Otolaryngology

	Instructor	Assistant Professor	Associate Professor	Professor	Chief	Chair
Count:	23	214	115	94	26	28
25th:	58	219	268	308	311	508
Median:	63	266	313	388	408	612
75th:	261	364	399	501	488	757
Mean:	137.8	303.7	382.8	433.2	434.4	698.6

Physical Medicine & Rehabilitation

	Instructor	Assistant Professor	Associate Professor	Professor	Chief	Chair
Count:	60	184	42	23	4	18
25th:	137	150	185	203		277
Median:	173	191	205	243		384
75th:	252	249	248	307		450
Mean:	219.4	203.2	217.2	275.6		370.7

Preventive Medicine

	Instructor	Assistant Professor	Associate Professor	Professor	Chief	Chair
Count:	15	47	20	15	1	7
25th:	130	132	160	203		226
Median:	141	143	209	238		243
75th:	236	176	236	317		363
Mean:	171.5	157.4	206.8	257.7		271.1

Psychiatry

	Instructor	Assistant Professor	Associate Professor	Professor	Chief	Chair
Count:	137	652	284	258	15	41
25th:	131	142	167	186	195	313
Median:	154	164	188	225	220	421
75th:	167	190	219	272	307	496
Mean:	149.8	170.4	198.3	237.6	258.2	406.2

TABLE 13

Summary Statistics on Medical School Faculty Compensation for Private Schools M.D. or Equivalent Degree, Clinical Science Departments/Specialties Total Compensation in Thousands of Dollars (continued)

Other

	Instructor	Assistant Professor	Associate Professor	Professor	Chief	Chair
Count:	10	44	20	22	1	5
25th:	90	106	138	209		270
Median:	98	134	177	232		394
75th:	105	171	230	256		444
Mean:	100.1	148.2	194.1	231.6		364.4

TABLE 14

Summary Statistics on Medical School Faculty Compensation for Northeastern Region M.D. or Equivalent Degree, Clinical Science Departments/Specialties Total Compensation in Thousands of Dollars

CLINICAL SCIENCE - TOTAL ALL DEPARTMENTS/SPECIALTIES

	Instructor	Assistant Professor	Associate Professor	Professor	Chief	Chair
Count:	2,199	10,833	4,668	3,756	801	534
25th:	129	158	186	213	238	390
Median:	176	208	246	272	315	503
75th:	254	297	350	378	431	657
Mean:	203.4	242.8	298.6	330.7	370.2	586.9

Total Anesthesiology

	Instructor	Assistant Professor	Associate Professor	Professor	Chief	Chair
Count:	211	977	331	161	34	30
25th:	237	273	303	313	323	463
Median:	291	315	344	363	348	539
75th:	347	361	393	422	388	618
Mean:	292.9	314.3	347.2	374.3	355.6	561.2

Anesthesiology: General

	Instructor	Assistant Professor	Associate Professor	Professor	Chief	Chair
Count:	195	807	281	136	25	28
25th:	238	277	304	314	324	474
Median:	293	316	342	361	350	539
75th:	351	365	391	417	410	634
Mean:	294.7	317.3	347.5	371.6	361.9	565.4

Anesthesiology: Pain Management

	Instructor	Assistant Professor	Associate Professor	Professor	Chief	Chair
Count:	13	60	14	5	4	1
25th:	210	254	267	307		
Median:	243	299	350	400		
75th:	331	336	372	427		
Mean:	272.9	302.4	331.2	373.4		

Anesthesiology: Pediatric

	Instructor	Assistant Professor	Associate Professor	Professor	Chief	Chair
Count:	3	110	36	20	5	1
25th:		250	282	307	288	
Median:		310	381	381	304	
75th:		346	406	451	359	
Mean:		298.7	351.6	392.9	319.6	

TABLE 14 Summary Statistics on Medical School Faculty Compensation for Northeastern Region
M.D. or Equivalent Degree, Clinical Science Departments/Specialties
Total Compensation in Thousands of Dollars (continued)

Total Dermatology

	Instructor	Assistant Professor	Associate Professor	Professor	Chief	Chair
Count:	31	121	56	47	8	23
25th:	145	210	248	243	212	401
Median:	203	261	320	323	230	458
75th:	294	370	433	490	263	738
Mean:	242.2	297.9	399.2	512.0	241.9	544.4

Dermatology (excluding Mohs Surgery)

	Instructor	Assistant Professor	Associate Professor	Professor	Chief	Chair
Count:	30	107	54	41	7	22
25th:	145	209	247	228	210	401
Median:	201	250	315	317	230	452
75th:	248	364	427	451	243	708
Mean:	213.3	279.7	382.5	457.0	225.4	533.5

Dermatology: Mohs Surgery

	Instructor	Assistant Professor	Associate Professor	Professor	Chief	Chair
Count:	1	14	2	6	1	1
25th:		333		437		
Median:		365		624		
75th:		517		1,656		
Mean:		437.0		888.2		

Total Medicine

	Instructor	Assistant Professor	Associate Professor	Professor	Chief	Chair
Count:	825	3,102	1,485	1,231	202	50
25th:	126	148	175	209	234	425
Median:	164	180	219	259	279	533
75th:	211	234	282	331	373	640
Mean:	175.4	203.5	248.1	290.2	318.7	553.9

Allergy/Immunology-Med.

	Instructor	Assistant Professor	Associate Professor	Professor	Chief	Chair
Count:	9	24	13	15	6	1
25th:	63	116	115	157	204	
Median:	142	144	167	202	226	
75th:	200	193	255	240	261	
Mean:	138.1	160.0	184.3	227.5	232.0	

TABLE 14 Summary Statistics on Medical School Faculty Compensation for Northeastern Region
M.D. or Equivalent Degree, Clinical Science Departments/Specialties
Total Compensation in Thousands of Dollars (continued)

Cardiology: Total

	Instructor	Assistant Professor	Associate Professor	Professor	Chief	Chair
Count:	76	444	254	228	18	10
25th:	139	209	244	257	368	459
Median:	190	273	300	313	414	579
75th:	251	343	400	387	500	640
Mean:	208.3	294.6	343.9	365.6	451.5	613.0

Cardiology: Invasive Interventional-Med.

	Instructor	Assistant Professor	Associate Professor	Professor	Chief	Chair
Count:	20	138	83	63	3	2
25th:	148	275	279	310		
Median:	219	320	384	385		
75th:	375	412	497	513		
Mean:	270.7	371.6	417.7	506.1		

Cardiology: Invasive Non-interventional-Med.

	Instructor	Assistant Professor	Associate Professor	Professor	Chief	Chair
Count:	8	47	26	17	3	0
25th:	95	240	300	251		
Median:	178	295	343	352		
75th:	234	400	439	413		
Mean:	168.8	315.9	411.1	351.0		

Cardiology: Non-invasive-Med.

	Instructor	Assistant Professor	Associate Professor	Professor	Chief	Chair
Count:	48	259	145	148	12	8
25th:	139	190	224	247	344	442
Median:	186	230	270	289	377	563
75th:	241	296	328	359	435	632
Mean:	188.9	249.7	289.7	307.4	394.9	597.1

Critical/Intensive Care-Med.

	Instructor	Assistant Professor	Associate Professor	Professor	Chief	Chair
Count:	9	58	32	19	0	2
25th:	175	197	203	285		
Median:	195	231	256	323		
75th:	201	318	289	398		
Mean:	193.2	262.7	263.6	351.0		

TABLE 14 Summary Statistics on Medical School Faculty Compensation for Northeastern Region
M.D. or Equivalent Degree, Clinical Science Departments/Specialties
Total Compensation in Thousands of Dollars (continued)

Endocrinology-Med.

	Instructor	Assistant Professor	Associate Professor	Professor	Chief	Chair
Count:	27	130	83	90	15	1
25th:	100	134	152	186	190	
Median:	125	154	178	220	242	
75th:	165	176	212	297	295	
Mean:	133.6	163.7	190.2	243.6	259.6	

Gastroenterology-Med.

	Instructor	Assistant Professor	Associate Professor	Professor	Chief	Chair
Count:	36	243	116	104	18	4
25th:	121	190	236	242	300	
Median:	184	230	307	292	407	
75th:	235	306	382	386	504	
Mean:	190.0	255.3	332.5	324.9	433.1	

General Internal Medicine

	Instructor	Assistant Professor	Associate Professor	Professor	Chief	Chair
Count:	323	754	288	148	25	6
25th:	140	145	168	199	216	408
Median:	167	165	197	238	230	584
75th:	222	200	252	324	277	884
Mean:	184.0	182.2	220.4	283.9	276.6	631.8

Geriatrics-Med.

	Instructor	Assistant Professor	Associate Professor	Professor	Chief	Chair
Count:	13	102	36	24	9	2
25th:	130	136	178	196	249	
Median:	145	157	196	230	270	
75th:	185	172	212	262	382	
Mean:	160.3	157.8	200.3	227.0	293.1	

Hematology/Oncology-Med.

	Instructor	Assistant Professor	Associate Professor	Professor	Chief	Chair
Count:	76	328	162	186	32	6
25th:	126	158	193	227	257	472
Median:	159	192	233	282	282	562
75th:	236	237	286	364	355	609
Mean:	190.1	201.3	254.4	307.5	311.9	565.8

TABLE 14 Summary Statistics on Medical School Faculty Compensation for Northeastern Region M.D. or Equivalent Degree, Clinical Science Departments/Specialties Total Compensation in Thousands of Dollars (continued)

Hospital Medicine

	Instructor	Assistant Professor	Associate Professor	Professor	Chief	Chair
Count:	77	157	14	3	3	0
25th:	150	164	182			
Median:	167	179	198			
75th:	196	202	231			
Mean:	171.8	186.3	202.9			

Infectious Disease-Med.

	Instructor	Assistant Professor	Associate Professor	Professor	Chief	Chair
Count:	45	220	137	96	18	4
25th:	99	130	153	193	202	
Median:	120	146	169	235	273	
75th:	150	165	206	276	313	
Mean:	130.2	153.5	182.9	245.8	279.0	

Nephrology-Med.

	Instructor	Assistant Professor	Associate Professor	Professor	Chief	Chair
Count:	31	174	95	80	16	1
25th:	93	132	171	203	247	
Median:	144	156	197	242	279	
75th:	176	185	247	278	332	
Mean:	152.9	164.1	208.9	251.5	315.3	

Pulmonary-Med.

	Instructor	Assistant Professor	Associate Professor	Professor	Chief	Chair
Count:	42	279	148	104	16	0
25th:	122	152	185	204	242	
Median:	164	183	218	239	283	
75th:	213	225	261	292	324	
Mean:	174.9	195.5	231.1	253.7	318.4	

Rheumatology-Med.

	Instructor	Assistant Professor	Associate Professor	Professor	Chief	Chair
Count:	18	84	52	53	16	0
25th:	72	126	150	188	196	
Median:	122	143	171	221	246	
75th:	150	185	195	279	284	
Mean:	117.4	151.6	183.5	240.7	248.6	

TABLE 14 Summary Statistics on Medical School Faculty Compensation for Northeastern Region M.D. or Equivalent Degree, Clinical Science Departments/Specialties Total Compensation in Thousands of Dollars (continued)

Other Medicine

	Instructor	Assistant Professor	Associate Professor	Professor	Chief	Chair
Count:	43	105	55	81	10	13
25th:	114	137	167	198	297	426
Median:	131	171	218	225	377	574
75th:	174	237	271	298	463	663
Mean:	143.6	186.7	225.5	244.2	375.9	560.5

Total OB/GYN

	Instructor	Assistant Professor	Associate Professor	Professor	Chief	Chair
Count:	88	497	159	120	50	33
25th:	71	198	233	226	252	451
Median:	184	240	302	328	356	500
75th:	248	311	446	458	454	706
Mean:	186.2	275.4	403.7	382.2	404.0	680.1

OB/GYN: General

	Instructor	Assistant Professor	Associate Professor	Professor	Chief	Chair
Count:	45	230	51	34	18	9
25th:	175	189	214	170	230	426
Median:	200	213	248	239	257	500
75th:	248	290	338	350	355	708
Mean:	202.0	253.3	285.0	259.2	327.1	565.1

OB/GYN: Gynecologic Oncology

	Instructor	Assistant Professor	Associate Professor	Professor	Chief	Chair
Count:	5	59	23	17	9	4
25th:	65	226	385	352	321	
Median:	69	264	482	539	453	
75th:	409	335	600	616	641	
Mean:	203.4	294.3	499.0	509.2	543.7	

OB/GYN: Maternal & Fetal

	Instructor	Assistant Professor	Associate Professor	Professor	Chief	Chair
Count:	14	86	37	34	9	11
25th:	70	242	239	275	310	386
Median:	117	280	328	370	365	471
75th:	307	338	385	458	430	560
Mean:	196.4	297.3	334.5	393.7	387.6	524.9

TABLE 14 Summary Statistics on Medical School Faculty Compensation for Northeastern Region M.D. or Equivalent Degree, Clinical Science Departments/Specialties Total Compensation in Thousands of Dollars (continued)

OB/GYN: Reproductive Endocrinology

	Instructor	Assistant Professor	Associate Professor	Professor	Chief	Chair
Count:	8	36	30	22	8	5
25th:	68	211	271	234	247	424
Median:	254	243	343	359	411	504
75th:	393	369	715	622	596	2,655
Mean:	267.8	372.5	690.1	506.0	451.6	1,332.2

OB/GYN: Other OB/GYN

	Instructor	Assistant Professor	Associate Professor	Professor	Chief	Chair
Count:	16	86	18	13	6	4
25th:	62	166	190	148	343	
Median:	68	215	264	231	390	
75th:	105	313	340	424	429	
Mean:	86.6	258.9	283.2	298.5	386.7	

Total Pathology

	Instructor	Assistant Professor	Associate Professor	Professor	Chief	Chair
Count:	49	395	272	298	41	36
25th:	122	163	196	224	234	373
Median:	161	184	225	265	294	446
75th:	211	215	259	317	327	527
Mean:	172.5	189.3	235.6	280.0	298.7	466.4

Pathology: Anatomic

	Instructor	Assistant Professor	Associate Professor	Professor	Chief	Chair
Count:	32	201	132	132	15	14
25th:	159	165	209	240	240	378
Median:	174	190	235	275	300	446
75th:	234	225	276	317	349	498
Mean:	203.2	196.2	252.3	293.0	315.9	444.9

Pathology: Clinical

	Instructor	Assistant Professor	Associate Professor	Professor	Chief	Chair
Count:	6	98	71	71	15	9
25th:	100	165	184	226	217	364
Median:	131	183	220	270	284	390
75th:	134	219	253	345	319	484
Mean:	139.0	195.1	231.2	296.0	284.0	413.0

Summary Statistics on Medical School Faculty Compensation for Northeastern Region M.D. or Equivalent Degree, Clinical Science Departments/Specialties Total Compensation in Thousands of Dollars (continued)

Pathology: Other Pathology

	Instructor	Assistant Professor	Associate Professor	Professor	Chief	Chair
Count:	11	96	69	95	11	13
25th:	60	155	180	210	228	370
Median:	98	180	212	232	291	493
75th:	132	199	236	288	367	579
Mean:	101.5	168.8	208.1	250.2	295.2	526.5

Total Pediatrics

	Instructor	Assistant Professor	Associate Professor	Professor	Chief	Chair
Count:	178	1,310	529	472	146	36
25th:	110	134	162	192	197	330
Median:	134	158	195	226	234	425
75th:	173	190	232	282	282	531
Mean:	150.8	168.8	208.1	252.8	250.9	451.5

Adolescent Medicine

	Instructor	Assistant Professor	Associate Professor	Professor	Chief	Chair
Count:	3	29	10	12	4	1
25th:		115	133	161		
Median:		125	143	175		
75th:		140	154	215		
Mean:		130.2	144.7	207.8		

Allergy/Immunology-Peds.

	Instructor	Assistant Professor	Associate Professor	Professor	Chief	Chair
Count:	3	25	12	11	3	1
25th:		130	155	173		
Median:		141	199	225		
75th:		171	222	289		
Mean:		151.8	209.2	246.6		

Child & Adolescent Psychiatry

	Instructor	Assistant Professor	Associate Professor	Professor	Chief	Chair
Count:	8	26	9	8	4	0
25th:	127	149	179	202		
Median:	151	166	206	221		
75th:	167	189	285	271		
Mean:	151.1	184.3	239.7	236.5		

TABLE 14 Summary Statistics on Medical School Faculty Compensation for Northeastern Region
M.D. or Equivalent Degree, Clinical Science Departments/Specialties
Total Compensation in Thousands of Dollars (continued)

Critical/Intensive Care-Peds.

	Instructor	Assistant Professor	Associate Professor	Professor	Chief	Chair
Count:	6	87	25	12	8	1
25th:	110	173	201	225	226	
Median:	156	191	228	272	247	
75th:	199	230	312	413	266	
Mean:	156.0	207.9	257.4	307.8	268.5	

Emergency Medicine-Peds.

	Instructor	Assistant Professor	Associate Professor	Professor	Chief	Chair
Count:	16	107	28	5	6	0
25th:	124	150	204	233	230	
Median:	140	180	223	248	274	
75th:	158	200	245	349	316	
Mean:	144.6	179.4	227.5	282.4	277.7	

Endocrinology-Peds.

	Instructor	Assistant Professor	Associate Professor	Professor	Chief	Chair
Count:	3	60	25	25	11	2
25th:		122	153	184	175	
Median:		134	165	200	201	
75th:		155	185	231	257	
Mean:		143.4	168.4	207.7	230.0	

Gastroenterology-Peds.

	Instructor	Assistant Professor	Associate Professor	Professor	Chief	Chair
Count:	10	66	24	23	11	4
25th:	189	160	191	230	183	
Median:	196	173	224	269	268	
75th:	274	200	283	328	286	
Mean:	237.2	186.2	251.3	310.0	271.1	

General Pediatrics

	Instructor	Assistant Professor	Associate Professor	Professor	Chief	Chair
Count:	54	269	90	64	10	12
25th:	110	125	139	178	200	279
Median:	126	140	159	214	227	346
75th:	172	165	195	259	259	586
Mean:	147.2	156.3	175.5	222.7	259.6	436.8

TABLE 14 Summary Statistics on Medical School Faculty Compensation for Northeastern Region
M.D. or Equivalent Degree, Clinical Science Departments/Specialties
Total Compensation in Thousands of Dollars (continued)

Genetics-Peds.

	Instructor	Assistant Professor	Associate Professor	Professor	Chief	Chair
Count:	0	15	7	20	4	2
25th:		125	155	133		
Median:		145	176	169		
75th:		155	197	230		
Mean:		145.1	184.9	187.7		

Hematology/Oncology-Peds.

	Instructor	Assistant Professor	Associate Professor	Professor	Chief	Chair
Count:	5	80	48	43	13	0
25th:	82	134	166	204	177	
Median:	85	145	180	225	220	
75th:	98	160	204	266	284	
Mean:	88.6	146.4	182.1	251.7	230.1	

Hospital Medicine-Peds.

	Instructor	Assistant Professor	Associate Professor	Professor	Chief	Chair
Count:	7	42	12	5	3	0
25th:	124	130	147	161		
Median:	142	136	163	204		
75th:	188	147	176	279		
Mean:	156.4	141.3	165.4	216.8		

Infectious Disease-Peds.

	Instructor	Assistant Professor	Associate Professor	Professor	Chief	Chair
Count:	4	48	17	33	10	1
25th:		112	136	157	177	
Median:		125	148	203	223	
75th:		137	182	230	274	
Mean:		126.7	162.3	218.9	226.3	

Neonatology

	Instructor	Assistant Professor	Associate Professor	Professor	Chief	Chair
Count:	22	129	67	61	11	2
25th:	128	171	198	202	259	
Median:	157	192	220	236	301	
75th:	191	222	270	292	347	
Mean:	160.2	203.4	237.5	256.2	311.0	

Summary Statistics on Medical School Faculty Compensation for Northeastern Region M.D. or Equivalent Degree, Clinical Science Departments/Specialties Total Compensation in Thousands of Dollars (continued)

Nephrology-Peds.

	Instructor	Assistant Professor	Associate Professor	Professor	Chief	Chair
Count:	5	28	14	12	8	1
25th:	118	128	156	214	169	
Median:	132	143	189	228	201	
75th:	162	152	232	247	232	
Mean:	138.2	142.6	197.6	232.7	205.3	

Neurology-Peds.

	Instructor	Assistant Professor	Associate Professor	Professor	Chief	Chair
Count:	5	41	16	25	6	2
25th:	98	146	190	195	225	
Median:	126	163	202	211	273	
75th:	172	183	229	234	293	
Mean:	133.2	165.6	219.9	208.6	262.5	

Pediatric Cardiology

	Instructor	Assistant Professor	Associate Professor	Professor	Chief	Chair
Count:	7	85	42	32	7	0
25th:	133	161	202	268	245	
Median:	151	188	259	310	311	
75th:	219	211	301	406	522	
Mean:	171.3	195.6	269.4	352.5	357.6	

Pulmonary-Peds.

	Instructor	Assistant Professor	Associate Professor	Professor	Chief	Chair
Count:	6	46	20	14	8	1
25th:	112	132	166	190	205	
Median:	153	145	191	195	235	
75th:	170	162	224	260	263	
Mean:	143.5	156.2	212.4	232.6	241.9	

Rheumatology-Peds.

	Instructor	Assistant Professor	Associate Professor	Professor	Chief	Chair
Count:	0	17	4	5	2	0
25th:		133		208		
Median:		140		236		
75th:		163		328		
Mean:		145.7		261.6		

TABLE 14 Summary Statistics on Medical School Faculty Compensation for Northeastern Region
M.D. or Equivalent Degree, Clinical Science Departments/Specialties
Total Compensation in Thousands of Dollars (continued)

Other Pediatrics

	Instructor	Assistant Professor	Associate Professor	Professor	Chief	Chair
Count:	14	110	59	62	17	6
25th:	85	131	161	196	196	393
Median:	110	161	184	253	222	438
75th:	151	190	237	362	259	492
Mean:	148.1	175.9	202.4	293.0	236.2	439.8

Total Radiology

	Instructor	Assistant Professor	Associate Professor	Professor	Chief	Chair
Count:	214	802	301	241	63	48
25th:	216	277	316	327	356	527
Median:	289	323	360	390	421	582
75th:	351	378	424	449	469	686
Mean:	273.0	327.1	378.0	388.7	417.7	614.4

Diagnostic Radiology: Total

	Instructor	Assistant Professor	Associate Professor	Professor	Chief	Chair
Count:	164	650	217	178	49	24
25th:	191	283	325	341	358	534
Median:	290	328	364	400	422	591
75th:	354	380	434	445	459	686
Mean:	269.6	332.3	390.7	394.2	417.5	609.7

Diagnostic Radiology: Interventional

	Instructor	Assistant Professor	Associate Professor	Professor	Chief	Chair
Count:	40	118	66	26	10	9
25th:	241	308	364	400	405	449
Median:	277	359	410	443	459	568
75th:	373	400	495	521	481	677
Mean:	292.4	362.7	473.6	462.4	435.1	557.0

Diagnostic Radiology: Non-interventional

	Instructor	Assistant Professor	Associate Professor	Professor	Chief	Chair
Count:	124	532	151	152	39	15
25th:	160	278	305	330	358	546
Median:	290	322	347	384	421	601
75th:	349	370	405	437	447	763
Mean:	262.2	325.5	354.4	382.6	413.0	641.3

TABLE 14 Summary Statistics on Medical School Faculty Compensation for Northeastern Region M.D. or Equivalent Degree, Clinical Science Departments/Specialties Total Compensation in Thousands of Dollars (continued)

Nuclear Medicine

	Instructor	Assistant Professor	Associate Professor	Professor	Chief	Chair
Count:	4	18	19	16	6	0
25th:		224	237	300	291	
Median:		259	300	322	458	
75th:		273	388	358	524	
Mean:		242.0	307.8	321.0	423.3	

Radiation Oncology

	Instructor	Assistant Professor	Associate Professor	Professor	Chief	Chair
Count:	33	99	47	32	5	19
25th:	231	280	330	322	240	546
Median:	307	311	365	408	363	588
75th:	352	361	452	503	655	709
Mean:	314.0	317.5	382.5	427.9	430.4	628.9

Other Radiology

	Instructor	Assistant Professor	Associate Professor	Professor	Chief	Chair
Count:	13	35	18	15	3	5
25th:	159	241	224	207		435
Median:	239	301	318	321		504
75th:	297	391	367	390		768
Mean:	229.5	301.3	287.6	311.5		581.6

Total Surgery

	Instructor	Assistant Professor	Associate Professor	Professor	Chief	Chair
Count:	142	1,317	663	501	170	103
25th:	125	250	309	323	389	558
Median:	257	318	415	465	461	721
75th:	362	442	575	668	633	1,034
Mean:	299.7	380.5	492.0	557.3	567.0	887.0

General Surgery

	Instructor	Assistant Professor	Associate Professor	Professor	Chief	Chair
Count:	23	202	70	66	28	15
25th:	90	228	259	243	351	609
Median:	200	281	336	364	457	721
75th:	261	356	409	517	604	1,068
Mean:	200.5	301.3	372.9	413.5	483.6	807.9

TABLE 14 Summary Statistics on Medical School Faculty Compensation for Northeastern Region M.D. or Equivalent Degree, Clinical Science Departments/Specialties Total Compensation in Thousands of Dollars (continued)

Neurosurgery

	Instructor	Assistant Professor	Associate Professor	Professor	Chief	Chair
Count:	8	139	79	57	12	20
25th:	70	350	440	437	663	709
Median:	100	485	575	666	762	960
75th:	446	659	801	1,123	945	1,611
Mean:	275.1	583.3	734.1	936.8	925.8	1,276.6

Orthopaedic Surgery

	Instructor	Assistant Professor	Associate Professor	Professor	Chief	Chair
Count:	36	261	138	91	18	28
25th:	253	284	382	375	319	512
Median:	340	371	515	540	417	674
75th:	579	548	700	724	534	925
Mean:	435.3	455.4	574.2	574.8	439.2	727.3

Pediatric Surgery

	Instructor	Assistant Professor	Associate Professor	Professor	Chief	Chair
Count:	2	47	26	24	7	2
25th:		262	330	388	413	
Median:		345	409	536	451	
75th:		425	467	643	499	
Mean:		336.4	403.9	523.2	463.4	

Plastic Surgery

	Instructor	Assistant Professor	Associate Professor	Professor	Chief	Chair
Count:	8	62	35	21	10	2
25th:	177	245	284	339	389	
Median:	365	308	380	474	463	
75th:	594	593	491	655	814	
Mean:	411.6	441.2	449.2	492.1	615.7	

Surgical Oncology

	Instructor	Assistant Professor	Associate Professor	Professor	Chief	Chair
Count:	14	59	32	16	10	1
25th:	229	225	303	233	367	
Median:	262	262	353	299	429	
75th:	325	340	435	401	511	
Mean:	275.8	280.6	393.8	391.1	431.0	

Summary Statistics on Medical School Faculty Compensation for Northeastern Region M.D. or Equivalent Degree, Clinical Science Departments/Specialties Total Compensation in Thousands of Dollars (continued)

Thoracic & Cardiovascular Surgery

	Instructor	Assistant Professor	Associate Professor	Professor	Chief	Chair
Count:	19	129	65	62	25	8
25th:	100	287	372	472	437	820
Median:	260	375	470	549	503	1,446
75th:	340	505	801	841	1,235	2,002
Mean:	260.0	408.4	583.0	705.3	785.9	1,417.3

Transplant Surgery

	Instructor	Assistant Professor	Associate Professor	Professor	Chief	Chair
Count:	6	51	40	30	15	1
25th:	101	235	269	400	364	
Median:	180	275	345	487	482	
75th:	255	325	432	770	792	
Mean:	190.2	270.1	363.4	584.4	566.4	

Trauma/Critical Care Surgery

	Instructor	Assistant Professor	Associate Professor	Professor	Chief	Chair
Count:	10	87	33	18	10	3
25th:	248	250	292	350	368	
Median:	282	289	365	439	428	
75th:	316	349	421	577	486	
Mean:	272.1	302.2	364.6	445.3	446.6	

Urology

	Instructor	Assistant Professor	Associate Professor	Professor	Chief	Chair
Count:	8	121	52	56	12	18
25th:	64	240	281	281	451	512
Median:	68	295	344	352	505	560
75th:	97	370	465	468	681	715
Mean:	82.4	323.7	405.2	407.7	565.6	688.7

Vascular Surgery

	Instructor	Assistant Professor	Associate Professor	Professor	Chief	Chair
Count:	3	74	47	23	14	1
25th:		250	327	353	401	
Median:		301	424	456	504	
75th:		386	497	613	600	
Mean:		330.9	460.0	478.4	529.3	

TABLE 14 Summary Statistics on Medical School Faculty Compensation for Northeastern Region M.D. or Equivalent Degree, Clinical Science Departments/Specialties Total Compensation in Thousands of Dollars (continued)

Other Surgery

	Instructor	Assistant Professor	Associate Professor	Professor	Chief	Chair
Count:	5	85	46	37	9	4
25th:	229	215	218	205	316	
Median:	257	257	305	336	369	
75th:	434	353	493	520	439	
Mean:	316.4	284.0	366.7	377.4	367.9	

Other Clinical Science

Community Health

	Instructor	Assistant Professor	Associate Professor	Professor	Chief	Chair
Count:	1	12	7	8	0	4
25th:		123	155	176		
Median:		134	162	191		
75th:		153	225	199		
Mean:		186.8	193.9	196.8		

Emergency Medicine

	Instructor	Assistant Professor	Associate Professor	Professor	Chief	Chair
Count:	130	626	168	48	14	24
25th:	176	208	236	246	256	430
Median:	207	230	257	272	269	482
75th:	246	255	285	327	288	555
Mean:	209.5	235.3	270.6	295.4	272.6	496.0

Family Medicine

	Instructor	Assistant Professor	Associate Professor	Professor	Chief	Chair
Count:	55	275	96	45	2	22
25th:	128	140	157	175		285
Median:	143	155	178	193		314
75th:	213	179	196	214		355
Mean:	177.1	164.1	178.9	192.6		338.1

Neurology

	Instructor	Assistant Professor	Associate Professor	Professor	Chief	Chair
Count:	64	384	190	222	22	30
25th:	122	135	166	195	203	329
Median:	148	154	189	227	214	403
75th:	172	184	220	257	237	460
Mean:	151.9	163.5	204.7	236.9	220.7	412.7

TABLE 14 Summary Statistics on Medical School Faculty Compensation for Northeastern Region
M.D. or Equivalent Degree, Clinical Science Departments/Specialties
Total Compensation in Thousands of Dollars (continued)

Ophthalmology

	Instructor	Assistant Professor	Associate Professor	Professor	Chief	Chair
Count:	21	154	68	61	14	22
25th:	60	140	198	205	235	358
Median:	70	203	258	250	324	545
75th:	146	249	365	343	440	630
Mean:	119.1	208.2	306.0	278.5	418.2	535.0

Otolaryngology

	Instructor	Assistant Professor	Associate Professor	Professor	Chief	Chair
Count:	10	128	72	55	16	19
25th:	58	212	264	274	276	400
Median:	63	270	319	399	319	627
75th:	267	396	468	550	411	1,075
Mean:	162.8	325.2	423.9	463.1	400.6	748.1

Physical Medicine & Rehabilitation

	Instructor	Assistant Professor	Associate Professor	Professor	Chief	Chair
Count:	41	82	23	11	3	14
25th:	140	162	177	237		254
Median:	180	192	194	267		335
75th:	250	235	243	568		450
Mean:	231.9	218.8	217.7	361.1		362.3

Preventive Medicine

	Instructor	Assistant Professor	Associate Professor	Professor	Chief	Chair
Count:	5	35	11	16	1	4
25th:	101	125	130	191		
Median:	131	140	168	206		
75th:	137	157	187	247		
Mean:	121.2	149.0	160.8	226.9		

Psychiatry

	Instructor	Assistant Professor	Associate Professor	Professor	Chief	Chair
Count:	124	577	211	191	14	31
25th:	132	147	164	188	182	310
Median:	155	166	182	220	199	408
75th:	167	189	214	270	304	487
Mean:	149.4	171.6	195.1	234.3	240.9	409.0

TABLE 14 Summary Statistics on Medical School Faculty Compensation for Northeastern Region M.D. or Equivalent Degree, Clinical Science Departments/Specialties Total Compensation in Thousands of Dollars (continued)

Other

	Instructor	Assistant Professor	Associate Professor	Professor	Chief	Chair
Count:	10	39	26	28	1	5
25th:	90	102	155	215		300
Median:	98	140	258	242		410
75th:	105	227	458	306		521
Mean:	100.1	173.2	304.0	256.4		410.2

TABLE 15 Summary Statistics on Medical School Faculty Compensation for Southern Region M.D. or Equivalent Degree, Clinical Science Departments/Specialties Total Compensation in Thousands of Dollars

CLINICAL SCIENCE - TOTAL ALL DEPARTMENTS/SPECIALTIES

	Instructor	Assistant Professor	Associate Professor	Professor	Chief	Chair
Count:	685	8,813	4,144	3,566	858	591
25th:	64	152	178	208	228	341
Median:	115	200	228	268	308	457
75th:	165	273	314	357	398	580
Mean:	127.1	223.6	258.5	298.6	334.6	480.7

Total Anesthesiology

	Instructor	Assistant Professor	Associate Professor	Professor	Chief	Chair
Count:	41	703	259	162	51	31
25th:	94	259	302	326	308	465
Median:	239	294	329	358	362	519
75th:	265	340	378	399	385	587
Mean:	209.9	298.0	336.1	361.0	363.2	534.5

Anesthesiology: General

	Instructor	Assistant Professor	Associate Professor	Professor	Chief	Chair
Count:	40	600	226	131	40	30
25th:	94	257	302	325	312	465
Median:	240	292	328	355	367	517
75th:	265	335	371	394	386	587
Mean:	209.5	294.2	331.6	353.3	369.3	533.8

Anesthesiology: Pain Management

	Instructor	Assistant Professor	Associate Professor	Professor	Chief	Chair
Count:	0	20	13	10	5	0
25th:		249	292	312	297	
Median:		259	310	357	312	
75th:		279	370	366	352	
Mean:		264.9	326.3	344.3	321.6	

Anesthesiology: Pediatric

	Instructor	Assistant Professor	Associate Professor	Professor	Chief	Chair
Count:	1	83	20	21	6	1
25th:		295	348	338	337	
Median:		325	399	376	364	
75th:		363	423	501	395	
Mean:		334.1	392.7	417.3	357.2	

TABLE 15 Summary Statistics on Medical School Faculty Compensation for Southern Region M.D. or Equivalent Degree, Clinical Science Departments/Specialties Total Compensation in Thousands of Dollars (continued)

Total Dermatology

	Instructor	Assistant Professor	Associate Professor	Professor	Chief	Chair
Count:	2	60	40	36	11	19
25th:		180	215	240	270	381
Median:		247	273	275	350	438
75th:		353	351	501	461	527
Mean:		271.2	312.9	430.1	358.4	480.9

Dermatology (excluding Mohs Surgery)

	Instructor	Assistant Professor	Associate Professor	Professor	Chief	Chair
Count:	2	51	35	30	8	18
25th:		170	211	225	260	381
Median:		232	258	267	319	435
75th:		345	350	307	471	510
Mean:		253.3	296.0	310.5	359.3	475.2

Dermatology: Mohs Surgery

	Instructor	Assistant Professor	Associate Professor	Professor	Chief	Chair
Count:	0	9	5	6	3	1
25th:		275	252	449		
Median:		350	472	855		
75th:		499	590	1,107		
Mean:		373.0	431.0	1,028.0		

Total Medicine

	Instructor	Assistant Professor	Associate Professor	Professor	Chief	Chair
Count:	228	2,150	1,034	1,063	217	60
25th:	85	142	166	203	217	307
Median:	134	180	200	252	268	427
75th:	190	227	256	317	340	507
Mean:	138.5	196.6	220.7	270.5	284.3	413.2

Allergy/Immunology-Med.

	Instructor	Assistant Professor	Associate Professor	Professor	Chief	Chair
Count:	2	10	4	11	7	1
25th:		130		149	189	
Median:		135		191	208	
75th:		149		222	235	
Mean:		131.4		186.9	219.1	

TABLE 15

Summary Statistics on Medical School Faculty Compensation for Southern Region M.D. or Equivalent Degree, Clinical Science Departments/Specialties Total Compensation in Thousands of Dollars (continued)

Cardiology: Total

	Instructor	Assistant Professor	Associate Professor	Professor	Chief	Chair
Count:	14	292	158	206	21	8
25th:	56	210	215	245	382	461
Median:	63	263	284	302	432	530
75th:	202	360	359	388	491	655
Mean:	125.8	299.8	295.4	332.3	447.1	557.9

Cardiology: Invasive Interventional-Med.

	Instructor	Assistant Professor	Associate Professor	Professor	Chief	Chair
Count:	3	123	50	75	7	2
25th:		256	293	275	435	
Median:		323	358	351	507	
75th:		425	401	447	528	
Mean:		361.2	356.6	382.3	488.7	

Cardiology: Invasive Non-interventional-Med.

	Instructor	Assistant Professor	Associate Professor	Professor	Chief	Chair
Count:	1	37	17	20	6	0
25th:		245	247	265	371	
Median:		305	314	300	382	
75th:		418	407	378	385	
Mean:		327.0	328.1	320.7	383.5	

Cardiology: Non-invasive-Med.

	Instructor	Assistant Professor	Associate Professor	Professor	Chief	Chair
Count:	10	132	91	111	8	6
25th:	55	184	203	232	370	475
Median:	61	224	238	266	429	530
75th:	64	263	297	345	472	596
Mean:	84.3	235.0	255.7	300.7	458.5	548.3

Critical/Intensive Care-Med.

	Instructor	Assistant Professor	Associate Professor	Professor	Chief	Chair
Count:	1	15	6	1	1	0
25th:		185	230			
Median:		227	234			
75th:		287	269			
Mean:		226.5	259.5			

TABLE 15 Summary Statistics on Medical School Faculty Compensation for Southern Region
M.D. or Equivalent Degree, Clinical Science Departments/Specialties
Total Compensation in Thousands of Dollars (continued)

Endocrinology-Med.

	Instructor	Assistant Professor	Associate Professor	Professor	Chief	Chair
Count:	12	108	46	72	24	6
25th:	54	125	150	183	193	406
Median:	98	139	170	214	216	448
75th:	107	165	200	249	298	490
Mean:	87.4	143.4	173.9	226.5	240.9	427.0

Gastroenterology-Med.

	Instructor	Assistant Professor	Associate Professor	Professor	Chief	Chair
Count:	7	162	80	94	19	1
25th:	75	200	220	232	295	
Median:	85	240	257	282	351	
75th:	158	298	310	338	393	
Mean:	110.0	245.4	267.5	291.8	340.0	

General Internal Medicine

	Instructor	Assistant Professor	Associate Professor	Professor	Chief	Chair
Count:	70	511	227	110	24	14
25th:	118	140	160	180	200	270
Median:	139	163	181	212	221	309
75th:	194	200	212	268	265	372
Mean:	154.8	173.5	188.9	230.3	247.5	317.6

Geriatrics-Med.

	Instructor	Assistant Professor	Associate Professor	Professor	Chief	Chair
Count:	6	72	44	32	8	4
25th:	120	134	157	200	230	
Median:	135	150	173	224	261	
75th:	148	165	191	265	292	
Mean:	134.3	151.6	173.8	246.7	249.3	

Hematology/Oncology-Med.

	Instructor	Assistant Professor	Associate Professor	Professor	Chief	Chair
Count:	14	231	121	137	19	7
25th:	113	174	198	253	243	435
Median:	145	196	246	300	325	530
75th:	165	233	282	354	381	709
Mean:	136.2	209.3	249.8	301.5	322.3	538.0

TABLE 15 Summary Statistics on Medical School Faculty Compensation for Southern Region M.D. or Equivalent Degree, Clinical Science Departments/Specialties Total Compensation in Thousands of Dollars (continued)

Hospital Medicine

	Instructor	Assistant Professor	Associate Professor	Professor	Chief	Chair
Count:	51	167	13	4	3	0
25th:	164	177	180			
Median:	190	195	195			
75th:	197	216	243			
Mean:	186.0	196.5	209.8			

Infectious Disease-Med.

	Instructor	Assistant Professor	Associate Professor	Professor	Chief	Chair
Count:	14	157	90	99	21	4
25th:	75	120	149	193	197	
Median:	96	132	163	218	241	
75th:	108	149	183	254	272	
Mean:	89.7	137.1	165.3	230.2	235.3	

Nephrology-Med.

	Instructor	Assistant Professor	Associate Professor	Professor	Chief	Chair
Count:	11	154	71	105	22	7
25th:	55	140	173	208	242	335
Median:	63	162	189	244	309	450
75th:	138	201	234	290	341	486
Mean:	88.5	170.8	212.7	256.1	304.8	417.3

Pulmonary-Med.

	Instructor	Assistant Professor	Associate Professor	Professor	Chief	Chair
Count:	9	165	102	112	22	3
25th:	57	149	184	203	251	
Median:	87	181	210	245	286	
75th:	125	221	245	291	309	
Mean:	91.6	190.1	218.8	254.8	280.6	

Rheumatology-Med.

	Instructor	Assistant Professor	Associate Professor	Professor	Chief	Chair
Count:	3	52	35	42	17	0
25th:		127	152	178	187	
Median:		142	169	196	222	
75th:		164	190	252	242	
Mean:		144.1	181.0	211.4	213.1	

TABLE 15 Summary Statistics on Medical School Faculty Compensation for Southern Region M.D. or Equivalent Degree, Clinical Science Departments/Specialties Total Compensation in Thousands of Dollars (continued)

Other Medicine

	Instructor	Assistant Professor	Associate Professor	Professor	Chief	Chair
Count:	14	54	37	38	9	5
25th:	59	86	158	148	118	280
Median:	85	139	187	238	229	536
75th:	90	194	253	340	286	548
Mean:	82.4	142.3	203.7	267.3	209.3	438.2

Total OB/GYN

	Instructor	Assistant Professor	Associate Professor	Professor	Chief	Chair
Count:	54	431	222	149	56	39
25th:	59	189	226	259	259	397
Median:	107	226	259	311	316	494
75th:	185	275	306	359	376	554
Mean:	127.4	238.5	270.0	314.3	317.0	490.0

OB/GYN: General

	Instructor	Assistant Professor	Associate Professor	Professor	Chief	Chair
Count:	28	299	118	51	18	13
25th:	97	185	223	204	257	280
Median:	177	222	253	279	274	397
75th:	215	266	287	348	337	516
Mean:	163.4	235.8	260.1	276.9	292.1	408.5

OB/GYN: Gynecologic Oncology

	Instructor	Assistant Professor	Associate Professor	Professor	Chief	Chair
Count:	9	33	29	21	10	6
25th:	58	225	238	305	305	369
Median:	145	249	277	374	365	501
75th:	188	280	344	445	409	566
Mean:	126.8	254.8	291.5	368.2	355.3	479.5

OB/GYN: Maternal & Fetal

	Instructor	Assistant Professor	Associate Professor	Professor	Chief	Chair
Count:	14	46	40	51	13	17
25th:	54	251	265	287	318	456
Median:	59	294	296	325	350	512
75th:	81	344	360	359	407	598
Mean:	65.8	295.6	311.9	340.2	360.3	535.7

TABLE 15 Summary Statistics on Medical School Faculty Compensation for Southern Region M.D. or Equivalent Degree, Clinical Science Departments/Specialties Total Compensation in Thousands of Dollars (continued)

OB/GYN: Reproductive Endocrinology

	Instructor	Assistant Professor	Associate Professor	Professor	Chief	Chair
Count:	0	13	18	13	8	3
25th:		186	212	234	274	
Median:		200	237	323	308	
75th:		247	283	351	361	
Mean:		199.4	246.9	303.9	319.1	

OB/GYN: Other OB/GYN

	Instructor	Assistant Professor	Associate Professor	Professor	Chief	Chair
Count:	3	40	17	13	7	0
25th:		167	181	232	198	
Median:		195	227	309	226	
75th:		229	274	339	321	
Mean:		192.1	228.0	282.8	243.1	

Total Pathology

	Instructor	Assistant Professor	Associate Professor	Professor	Chief	Chair
Count:	10	309	198	250	12	37
25th:	48	154	181	214	272	318
Median:	59	173	210	244	317	415
75th:	93	197	233	285	366	475
Mean:	83.4	181.3	209.9	254.3	347.5	409.6

Pathology: Anatomic

	Instructor	Assistant Professor	Associate Professor	Professor	Chief	Chair
Count:	3	125	104	114	6	18
25th:		157	187	235	278	311
Median:		173	211	258	317	399
75th:		192	233	296	376	442
Mean:		177.0	213.1	268.8	346.3	398.9

Pathology: Clinical

	Instructor	Assistant Professor	Associate Professor	Professor	Chief	Chair
Count:	2	82	52	85	5	9
25th:		150	188	207	255	294
Median:		171	213	234	276	425
75th:		196	236	259	349	502
Mean:		172.9	210.7	237.7	296.4	399.6

TABLE 15 Summary Statistics on Medical School Faculty Compensation for Southern Region M.D. or Equivalent Degree, Clinical Science Departments/Specialties Total Compensation in Thousands of Dollars (continued)

Pathology: Other Pathology

	Instructor	Assistant Professor	Associate Professor	Professor	Chief	Chair
Count:	5	102	42	51	1	10
25th:	45	152	171	172		341
Median:	52	176	197	241		418
75th:	157	235	228	318		478
Mean:	91.2	193.2	201.1	249.8		437.8

Total Pediatrics

	Instructor	Assistant Professor	Associate Professor	Professor	Chief	Chair
Count:	129	1,553	722	559	181	41
25th:	92	132	157	184	186	284
Median:	119	154	188	225	223	368
75th:	139	190	229	277	272	435
Mean:	115.9	166.1	198.6	238.7	238.7	366.1

Adolescent Medicine

	Instructor	Assistant Professor	Associate Professor	Professor	Chief	Chair
Count:	1	8	16	8	3	0
25th:		114	152	162		
Median:		132	162	190		
75th:		139	188	229		
Mean:		125.8	171.5	193.8		

Allergy/Immunology-Peds.

	Instructor	Assistant Professor	Associate Professor	Professor	Chief	Chair
Count:	2	22	13	17	6	1
25th:		120	138	171	162	
Median:		130	163	199	186	
75th:		141	188	333	206	
Mean:		127.1	165.0	249.1	186.7	

Child & Adolescent Psychiatry

	Instructor	Assistant Professor	Associate Professor	Professor	Chief	Chair
Count:	0	17	13	9	3	2
25th:		146	162	188		
Median:		157	186	220		
75th:		189	212	278		
Mean:		167.1	186.2	232.1		

TABLE 15 Summary Statistics on Medical School Faculty Compensation for Southern Region M.D. or Equivalent Degree, Clinical Science Departments/Specialties Total Compensation in Thousands of Dollars (continued)

Critical/Intensive Care-Peds.

	Instructor	Assistant Professor	Associate Professor	Professor	Chief	Chair
Count:	6	100	53	18	13	2
25th:	107	182	210	242	244	
Median:	135	196	247	251	257	
75th:	183	238	275	281	307	
Mean:	139.5	214.0	253.8	279.6	280.5	

Emergency Medicine-Peds.

	Instructor	Assistant Professor	Associate Professor	Professor	Chief	Chair
Count:	9	122	38	14	9	1
25th:	116	156	191	221	150	
Median:	131	193	215	232	239	
75th:	173	244	247	250	282	
Mean:	138.2	200.7	224.3	251.1	212.1	

Endocrinology-Peds.

	Instructor	Assistant Professor	Associate Professor	Professor	Chief	Chair
Count:	3	59	26	26	9	1
25th:		127	144	161	165	
Median:		136	159	192	176	
75th:		144	193	235	201	
Mean:		136.5	167.9	198.9	183.9	

Gastroenterology-Peds.

	Instructor	Assistant Professor	Associate Professor	Professor	Chief	Chair
Count:	2	71	31	24	11	0
25th:		148	158	190	202	
Median:		165	185	226	236	
75th:		175	221	252	274	
Mean:		160.4	187.7	228.4	252.6	

General Pediatrics

	Instructor	Assistant Professor	Associate Professor	Professor	Chief	Chair
Count:	25	322	131	94	24	13
25th:	92	125	145	164	187	226
Median:	115	136	159	196	216	275
75th:	131	158	187	242	276	411
Mean:	113.0	147.0	172.3	210.7	240.6	286.1

TABLE 15 Summary Statistics on Medical School Faculty Compensation for Southern Region M.D. or Equivalent Degree, Clinical Science Departments/Specialties Total Compensation in Thousands of Dollars (continued)

Genetics-Peds.

	Instructor	Assistant Professor	Associate Professor	Professor	Chief	Chair
Count:	2	20	22	21	7	1
25th:		120	130	150	132	
Median:		138	140	171	167	
75th:		153	150	200	199	
Mean:		132.9	143.2	177.6	168.9	

Hematology/Oncology-Peds.

	Instructor	Assistant Professor	Associate Professor	Professor	Chief	Chair
Count:	10	134	58	49	12	0
25th:	85	130	156	185	187	
Median:	114	139	174	211	214	
75th:	117	160	190	234	255	
Mean:	103.7	146.6	178.2	218.9	227.7	

Hospital Medicine-Peds.

	Instructor	Assistant Professor	Associate Professor	Professor	Chief	Chair
Count:	19	72	11	1	5	0
25th:	141	143	155		153	
Median:	141	167	173		178	
75th:	141	194	206		213	
Mean:	135.6	172.7	183.9		181.6	

Infectious Disease-Peds.

	Instructor	Assistant Professor	Associate Professor	Professor	Chief	Chair
Count:	5	49	25	45	11	3
25th:	67	115	130	166	179	
Median:	100	123	147	185	204	
75th:	115	137	163	231	265	
Mean:	92.6	127.3	148.8	202.4	219.4	

Neonatology

	Instructor	Assistant Professor	Associate Professor	Professor	Chief	Chair
Count:	15	186	82	82	13	7
25th:	120	158	205	239	266	351
Median:	135	198	240	279	291	416
75th:	161	224	270	318	329	461
Mean:	141.1	199.5	239.3	286.1	308.1	398.9

TABLE 15 Summary Statistics on Medical School Faculty Compensation for Southern Region M.D. or Equivalent Degree, Clinical Science Departments/Specialties Total Compensation in Thousands of Dollars (continued)

Nephrology-Peds.

	Instructor	Assistant Professor	Associate Professor	Professor	Chief	Chair
Count:	0	35	18	16	10	2
25th:		133	162	180	185	
Median:		138	173	204	209	
75th:		155	188	249	212	
Mean:		144.3	173.1	218.3	202.3	

Neurology-Peds.

	Instructor	Assistant Professor	Associate Professor	Professor	Chief	Chair
Count:	3	59	25	18	9	2
25th:		153	179	190	184	
Median:		170	190	218	234	
75th:		183	217	260	274	
Mean:		169.1	197.0	229.5	220.2	

Pediatric Cardiology

	Instructor	Assistant Professor	Associate Professor	Professor	Chief	Chair
Count:	7	104	80	43	14	1
25th:	60	181	212	253	276	
Median:	104	201	240	300	307	
75th:	130	229	271	350	342	
Mean:	105.7	212.3	249.5	308.5	337.2	

Pulmonary-Peds.

	Instructor	Assistant Professor	Associate Professor	Professor	Chief	Chair
Count:	3	53	29	19	7	1
25th:		136	165	184	207	
Median:		148	179	200	231	
75th:		164	212	241	261	
Mean:		152.6	190.8	208.8	237.3	

Rheumatology-Peds.

	Instructor	Assistant Professor	Associate Professor	Professor	Chief	Chair
Count:	1	13	7	5	6	0
25th:		122	136	181	168	
Median:		138	151	196	199	
75th:		144	178	220	226	
Mean:		131.7	150.7	199.4	195.0	

TABLE 15 Summary Statistics on Medical School Faculty Compensation for Southern Region M.D. or Equivalent Degree, Clinical Science Departments/Specialties Total Compensation in Thousands of Dollars (continued)

Other Pediatrics

	Instructor	Assistant Professor	Associate Professor	Professor	Chief	Chair
Count:	16	107	44	50	9	4
25th:	62	97	141	198	170	
Median:	85	131	165	235	207	
75th:	127	147	203	306	326	
Mean:	92.4	128.3	180.5	270.1	266.6	

Total Radiology

	Instructor	Assistant Professor	Associate Professor	Professor	Chief	Chair
Count:	39	536	233	194	63	50
25th:	58	290	303	326	330	505
Median:	70	325	349	383	375	556
75th:	277	368	408	430	445	632
Mean:	164.0	327.6	355.0	384.7	401.4	559.6

Diagnostic Radiology: Total

	Instructor	Assistant Professor	Associate Professor	Professor	Chief	Chair
Count:	15	352	144	123	55	25
25th:	70	291	305	328	332	448
Median:	250	325	346	377	375	530
75th:	396	365	408	425	445	584
Mean:	236.7	325.0	354.0	388.6	401.8	531.3

Diagnostic Radiology: Interventional

	Instructor	Assistant Professor	Associate Professor	Professor	Chief	Chair
Count:	3	78	24	19	10	5
25th:		320	372	293	396	437
Median:		361	423	442	434	544
75th:		405	460	540	525	604
Mean:		358.1	411.8	427.3	486.0	525.0

Diagnostic Radiology: Non-interventional

	Instructor	Assistant Professor	Associate Professor	Professor	Chief	Chair
Count:	12	274	120	104	45	20
25th:	70	280	302	330	326	461
Median:	154	315	336	365	374	529
75th:	344	353	386	414	423	584
Mean:	205.7	315.6	342.4	381.5	383.0	532.9

TABLE 15 **Summary Statistics on Medical School Faculty Compensation for Southern Region M.D. or Equivalent Degree, Clinical Science Departments/Specialties Total Compensation in Thousands of Dollars (continued)**

Nuclear Medicine

	Instructor	Assistant Professor	Associate Professor	Professor	Chief	Chair
Count:	0	14	11	8	5	2
25th:		224	257	321	305	
Median:		275	305	345	371	
75th:		367	393	414	440	
Mean:		287.4	318.1	340.8	371.8	

Radiation Oncology

	Instructor	Assistant Professor	Associate Professor	Professor	Chief	Chair
Count:	4	77	49	35	1	19
25th:		264	312	320		541
Median:		346	364	421		630
75th:		384	428	506		662
Mean:		328.1	371.8	414.0		633.4

Other Radiology

	Instructor	Assistant Professor	Associate Professor	Professor	Chief	Chair
Count:	20	93	29	28	2	4
25th:	58	300	269	311		
Median:	59	326	363	351		
75th:	64	375	399	413		
Mean:	83.4	342.8	346.2	343.7		

Total Surgery

	Instructor	Assistant Professor	Associate Professor	Professor	Chief	Chair
Count:	59	1,068	579	563	169	120
25th:	55	242	297	303	366	545
Median:	63	300	362	391	464	622
75th:	90	382	475	498	587	755
Mean:	82.0	326.8	395.2	418.8	504.7	682.4

General Surgery

	Instructor	Assistant Professor	Associate Professor	Professor	Chief	Chair
Count:	9	184	103	117	15	15
25th:	56	220	266	247	360	452
Median:	60	263	312	327	425	594
75th:	130	309	378	405	582	660
Mean:	96.3	275.9	321.3	328.1	497.9	573.9

TABLE 15 Summary Statistics on Medical School Faculty Compensation for Southern Region M.D. or Equivalent Degree, Clinical Science Departments/Specialties Total Compensation in Thousands of Dollars (continued)

Neurosurgery

	Instructor	Assistant Professor	Associate Professor	Professor	Chief	Chair
Count:	6	111	60	60	18	21
25th:	60	341	397	375	493	651
Median:	66	401	486	488	581	706
75th:	69	500	590	643	672	988
Mean:	66.8	423.3	501.5	493.9	613.0	808.7

Orthopaedic Surgery

	Instructor	Assistant Professor	Associate Professor	Professor	Chief	Chair
Count:	14	230	101	85	28	29
25th:	55	297	331	349	444	549
Median:	55	353	412	401	531	594
75th:	75	450	507	498	590	711
Mean:	77.6	385.8	444.1	443.1	530.9	640.9

Pediatric Surgery

	Instructor	Assistant Professor	Associate Professor	Professor	Chief	Chair
Count:	0	48	33	26	12	5
25th:		299	345	447	483	530
Median:		350	475	544	509	596
75th:		408	508	599	567	679
Mean:		350.1	435.9	530.0	547.3	602.6

Plastic Surgery

	Instructor	Assistant Professor	Associate Professor	Professor	Chief	Chair
Count:	1	73	34	29	11	5
25th:		233	268	278	311	653
Median:		266	351	400	360	760
75th:		362	509	503	534	1,658
Mean:		341.5	390.6	408.6	416.9	1,076.0

Surgical Oncology

	Instructor	Assistant Professor	Associate Professor	Professor	Chief	Chair
Count:	1	40	38	19	13	6
25th:		219	222	265	294	554
Median:		245	302	302	340	670
75th:		258	354	345	452	845
Mean:		243.8	295.5	325.6	372.6	787.8

TABLE 15 Summary Statistics on Medical School Faculty Compensation for Southern Region
M.D. or Equivalent Degree, Clinical Science Departments/Specialties
Total Compensation in Thousands of Dollars (continued)

Thoracic & Cardiovascular Surgery

	Instructor	Assistant Professor	Associate Professor	Professor	Chief	Chair
Count:	3	85	52	62	17	7
25th:		258	351	374	432	733
Median:		330	451	454	689	866
75th:		450	601	665	826	1,000
Mean:		359.5	500.8	543.7	627.0	883.7

Transplant Surgery

	Instructor	Assistant Professor	Associate Professor	Professor	Chief	Chair
Count:	3	42	22	39	16	4
25th:		231	300	345	449	
Median:		294	335	417	501	
75th:		328	413	513	595	
Mean:		293.9	346.6	453.3	534.7	

Trauma/Critical Care Surgery

	Instructor	Assistant Professor	Associate Professor	Professor	Chief	Chair
Count:	2	78	43	33	14	3
25th:		233	292	322	341	
Median:		270	325	344	369	
75th:		322	395	428	458	
Mean:		272.9	352.6	367.3	415.1	

Urology

	Instructor	Assistant Professor	Associate Professor	Professor	Chief	Chair
Count:	8	93	49	56	9	17
25th:	67	225	295	299	305	392
Median:	90	275	336	366	422	487
75th:	131	305	402	427	511	587
Mean:	104.3	263.7	355.2	382.6	470.4	505.2

Vascular Surgery

	Instructor	Assistant Professor	Associate Professor	Professor	Chief	Chair
Count:	2	43	19	23	10	4
25th:		255	280	306	381	
Median:		280	352	361	459	
75th:		319	440	459	535	
Mean:		288.7	361.7	371.6	464.3	

TABLE 15 Summary Statistics on Medical School Faculty Compensation for Southern Region M.D. or Equivalent Degree, Clinical Science Departments/Specialties Total Compensation in Thousands of Dollars (continued)

Other Surgery

	Instructor	Assistant Professor	Associate Professor	Professor	Chief	Chair
Count:	10	41	25	14	6	4
25th:	51	148	232	266	319	
Median:	57	220	300	328	336	
75th:	75	300	446	400	358	
Mean:	64.1	242.6	350.8	343.3	337.3	

Other Clinical Science

Community Health

	Instructor	Assistant Professor	Associate Professor	Professor	Chief	Chair
Count:	2	17	7	0	1	2
25th:		97	117			
Median:		121	171			
75th:		146	181			
Mean:		126.1	153.3			

Emergency Medicine

	Instructor	Assistant Professor	Associate Professor	Professor	Chief	Chair
Count:	21	356	111	36	9	19
25th:	98	206	219	246	301	330
Median:	104	225	243	284	326	389
75th:	212	255	276	334	378	449
Mean:	157.6	234.1	255.7	293.8	338.1	381.6

Family Medicine

	Instructor	Assistant Professor	Associate Professor	Professor	Chief	Chair
Count:	20	498	215	107	9	43
25th:	86	144	154	167	185	244
Median:	129	157	177	192	194	281
75th:	144	176	198	213	212	301
Mean:	143.7	162.5	177.2	198.2	199.8	277.9

Neurology

	Instructor	Assistant Professor	Associate Professor	Professor	Chief	Chair
Count:	21	270	128	135	27	27
25th:	61	140	172	185	176	331
Median:	77	156	189	214	211	368
75th:	120	186	223	256	264	400
Mean:	94.0	168.8	204.8	226.7	225.9	375.0

TABLE 15 Summary Statistics on Medical School Faculty Compensation for Southern Region M.D. or Equivalent Degree, Clinical Science Departments/Specialties Total Compensation in Thousands of Dollars (continued)

Ophthalmology

	Instructor	Assistant Professor	Associate Professor	Professor	Chief	Chair
Count:	40	186	104	89	13	26
25th:	41	162	193	233	294	411
Median:	47	203	245	301	411	510
75th:	71	270	327	424	496	611
Mean:	66.6	229.5	275.2	342.1	413.2	522.1

Otolaryngology

	Instructor	Assistant Professor	Associate Professor	Professor	Chief	Chair
Count:	11	149	74	50	10	24
25th:	50	220	255	312	354	464
Median:	56	245	312	357	425	524
75th:	58	295	371	398	491	644
Mean:	69.6	254.5	306.3	350.7	421.3	544.3

Physical Medicine & Rehabilitation

	Instructor	Assistant Professor	Associate Professor	Professor	Chief	Chair
Count:	0	80	35	18	4	13
25th:		147	178	203		278
Median:		167	197	223		339
75th:		193	237	245		449
Mean:		172.1	219.3	210.2		351.2

Preventive Medicine

	Instructor	Assistant Professor	Associate Professor	Professor	Chief	Chair
Count:	1	9	8	11	0	1
25th:		113	136	206		
Median:		126	185	226		
75th:		143	204	263		
Mean:		132.6	175.3	231.1		

Psychiatry

	Instructor	Assistant Professor	Associate Professor	Professor	Chief	Chair
Count:	7	412	172	142	25	36
25th:	92	140	160	180	185	262
Median:	157	162	185	214	220	349
75th:	166	189	211	257	251	440
Mean:	130.6	167.5	187.9	222.8	233.7	337.3

TABLE 15

Summary Statistics on Medical School Faculty Compensation for Southern Region M.D. or Equivalent Degree, Clinical Science Departments/Specialties Total Compensation in Thousands of Dollars (continued)

Other

	Instructor	Assistant Professor	Associate Professor	Professor	Chief	Chair
Count:	0	26	3	2	0	3
25th:		139				
Median:		169				
75th:		207				
Mean:		166.2				

TABLE 16 Summary Statistics on Medical School Faculty Compensation for Midwestern Region
M.D. or Equivalent Degree, Clinical Science Departments/Specialties
Total Compensation in Thousands of Dollars

CLINICAL SCIENCE - TOTAL ALL DEPARTMENTS/SPECIALTIES

	Instructor	Assistant Professor	Associate Professor	Professor	Chief	Chair
Count:	1,016	7,217	3,507	3,357	501	408
25th:	114	159	185	220	234	346
Median:	165	210	243	285	313	462
75th:	222	297	338	388	449	604
Mean:	182.7	241.4	276.6	316.5	366.9	493.8

Total Anesthesiology

	Instructor	Assistant Professor	Associate Professor	Professor	Chief	Chair
Count:	77	538	175	125	4	21
25th:	235	286	304	326		449
Median:	296	323	358	373		505
75th:	338	382	404	412		547
Mean:	283.3	332.5	356.0	363.2		497.3

Anesthesiology: General

	Instructor	Assistant Professor	Associate Professor	Professor	Chief	Chair
Count:	72	466	154	114	2	21
25th:	247	287	308	327		449
Median:	299	323	360	373		505
75th:	347	370	402	408		547
Mean:	288.3	329.0	356.3	361.1		497.3

Anesthesiology: Pain Management

	Instructor	Assistant Professor	Associate Professor	Professor	Chief	Chair
Count:	0	27	6	2	2	0
25th:		269	235			
Median:		330	303			
75th:		461	404			
Mean:		372.2	335.5			

Anesthesiology: Pediatric

	Instructor	Assistant Professor	Associate Professor	Professor	Chief	Chair
Count:	5	45	15	9	0	0
25th:	138	279	294	320		
Median:	227	348	319	439		
75th:	279	407	459	452		
Mean:	212.0	344.9	361.0	391.6		

TABLE 16 Summary Statistics on Medical School Faculty Compensation for Midwestern Region M.D. or Equivalent Degree, Clinical Science Departments/Specialties Total Compensation in Thousands of Dollars (continued)

Total Dermatology

	Instructor	Assistant Professor	Associate Professor	Professor	Chief	Chair
Count:	9	88	40	32	6	14
25th:	200	201	244	297	270	310
Median:	250	250	313	336	365	465
75th:	310	352	426	534	405	563
Mean:	250.2	293.8	356.9	438.2	360.0	436.2

Dermatology (excluding Mohs Surgery)

	Instructor	Assistant Professor	Associate Professor	Professor	Chief	Chair
Count:	6	73	36	27	5	13
25th:	200	189	244	279	266	255
Median:	256	228	300	329	329	424
75th:	267	299	367	448	450	550
Mean:	255.0	257.6	335.3	417.2	352.0	406.9

Dermatology: Mohs Surgery

	Instructor	Assistant Professor	Associate Professor	Professor	Chief	Chair
Count:	3	15	4	5	1	1
25th:		325		428		
Median:		437		539		
75th:		500		682		
Mean:		470.4		551.6		

Total Medicine

	Instructor	Assistant Professor	Associate Professor	Professor	Chief	Chair
Count:	305	1,908	1,026	1,069	120	34
25th:	128	150	175	212	239	300
Median:	162	185	222	260	303	391
75th:	198	240	287	343	388	500
Mean:	161.7	207.9	242.7	289.2	329.8	393.9

Allergy/Immunology-Med.

	Instructor	Assistant Professor	Associate Professor	Professor	Chief	Chair
Count:	1	23	10	16	2	0
25th:		125	171	178		
Median:		168	195	210		
75th:		201	236	243		
Mean:		173.9	194.5	216.2		

TABLE 16 Summary Statistics on Medical School Faculty Compensation for Midwestern Region M.D. or Equivalent Degree, Clinical Science Departments/Specialties Total Compensation in Thousands of Dollars (continued)

Cardiology: Total

	Instructor	Assistant Professor	Associate Professor	Professor	Chief	Chair
Count:	16	271	179	215	11	5
25th:	118	225	254	280	459	435
Median:	139	277	303	382	520	525
75th:	206	396	405	442	591	733
Mean:	160.6	299.7	323.4	370.2	534.9	571.8

Cardiology: Invasive Interventional-Med.

	Instructor	Assistant Professor	Associate Professor	Professor	Chief	Chair
Count:	5	116	79	77	6	2
25th:	88	239	268	356	500	
Median:	200	309	328	428	529	
75th:	278	435	441	458	566	
Mean:	186.2	327.2	349.9	425.2	540.5	

Cardiology: Invasive Non-interventional-Med.

	Instructor	Assistant Professor	Associate Professor	Professor	Chief	Chair
Count:	2	23	26	12	2	0
25th:		227	225	236		
Median:		293	245	365		
75th:		370	364	443		
Mean:		317.8	297.7	372.3		

Cardiology: Non-invasive-Med.

	Instructor	Assistant Professor	Associate Professor	Professor	Chief	Chair
Count:	9	132	74	126	3	3
25th:	127	208	247	257		
Median:	140	260	278	323		
75th:	197	327	374	433		
Mean:	160.1	272.4	304.2	336.4		

Critical/Intensive Care-Med.

	Instructor	Assistant Professor	Associate Professor	Professor	Chief	Chair
Count:	1	21	11	6	1	0
25th:		147	174	238		
Median:		166	178	249		
75th:		297	192	291		
Mean:		213.2	203.8	272.8		

TABLE 16 Summary Statistics on Medical School Faculty Compensation for Midwestern Region M.D. or Equivalent Degree, Clinical Science Departments/Specialties Total Compensation in Thousands of Dollars (continued)

Endocrinology-Med.

	Instructor	Assistant Professor	Associate Professor	Professor	Chief	Chair
Count:	12	98	56	74	11	0
25th:	98	128	136	185	195	
Median:	117	141	165	218	230	
75th:	144	173	194	240	289	
Mean:	128.3	153.3	168.2	216.9	249.2	

Gastroenterology-Med.

	Instructor	Assistant Professor	Associate Professor	Professor	Chief	Chair
Count:	7	148	114	119	13	3
25th:	61	211	246	273	343	
Median:	116	254	309	362	362	
75th:	150	335	410	410	444	
Mean:	106.1	273.0	315.3	352.6	420.5	

General Internal Medicine

	Instructor	Assistant Professor	Associate Professor	Professor	Chief	Chair
Count:	108	442	194	151	8	12
25th:	155	144	162	195	226	240
Median:	177	170	188	224	253	307
75th:	222	207	230	273	285	378
Mean:	177.1	177.8	200.4	240.6	269.9	308.8

Geriatrics-Med.

	Instructor	Assistant Professor	Associate Professor	Professor	Chief	Chair
Count:	6	44	28	12	3	2
25th:	102	135	163	184		
Median:	157	145	178	205		
75th:	190	172	201	234		
Mean:	153.7	157.2	188.6	227.0		

Hematology/Oncology-Med.

	Instructor	Assistant Professor	Associate Professor	Professor	Chief	Chair
Count:	20	267	137	170	18	1
25th:	94	160	189	240	359	
Median:	128	179	232	284	395	
75th:	143	238	304	331	433	
Mean:	140.5	206.5	246.8	302.5	392.3	

TABLE 16 **Summary Statistics on Medical School Faculty Compensation for Midwestern Region M.D. or Equivalent Degree, Clinical Science Departments/Specialties Total Compensation in Thousands of Dollars (continued)**

Hospital Medicine

	Instructor	Assistant Professor	Associate Professor	Professor	Chief	Chair
Count:	96	126	8	2	5	0
25th:	143	160	166		234	
Median:	166	195	185		250	
75th:	196	213	226		330	
Mean:	170.5	191.3	197.3		275.2	

Infectious Disease-Med.

	Instructor	Assistant Professor	Associate Professor	Professor	Chief	Chair
Count:	9	94	55	73	13	5
25th:	75	123	149	181	216	321
Median:	114	140	168	205	242	475
75th:	141	175	188	232	293	524
Mean:	113.4	152.7	179.5	209.0	254.3	432.8

Nephrology-Med.

	Instructor	Assistant Professor	Associate Professor	Professor	Chief	Chair
Count:	7	122	72	64	10	1
25th:	80	147	179	212	282	
Median:	101	170	210	239	284	
75th:	107	204	255	263	335	
Mean:	98.9	177.7	218.3	241.3	308.1	

Pulmonary-Med.

	Instructor	Assistant Professor	Associate Professor	Professor	Chief	Chair
Count:	4	127	94	97	12	1
25th:		158	182	210	277	
Median:		185	206	248	303	
75th:		248	266	308	337	
Mean:		205.2	225.9	263.0	312.2	

Rheumatology-Med.

	Instructor	Assistant Professor	Associate Professor	Professor	Chief	Chair
Count:	7	61	36	36	10	1
25th:	58	134	137	191	198	
Median:	118	145	172	218	246	
75th:	127	178	236	251	284	
Mean:	96.3	156.7	190.4	221.7	243.9	

TABLE 16 Summary Statistics on Medical School Faculty Compensation for Midwestern Region
M.D. or Equivalent Degree, Clinical Science Departments/Specialties
Total Compensation in Thousands of Dollars (continued)

Other Medicine

	Instructor	Assistant Professor	Associate Professor	Professor	Chief	Chair
Count:	11	64	32	34	3	3
25th:	112	181	187	252		
Median:	178	224	257	313		
75th:	236	286	329	396		
Mean:	169.2	236.9	260.0	333.5		

Total OB/GYN

	Instructor	Assistant Professor	Associate Professor	Professor	Chief	Chair
Count:	19	253	135	90	30	24
25th:	165	192	214	267	267	445
Median:	176	231	261	325	354	495
75th:	247	300	327	438	423	587
Mean:	203.1	252.5	285.7	350.6	358.7	513.1

OB/GYN: General

	Instructor	Assistant Professor	Associate Professor	Professor	Chief	Chair
Count:	18	167	81	40	10	8
25th:	165	191	206	242	250	333
Median:	175	227	246	309	265	452
75th:	235	297	301	367	287	539
Mean:	200.7	250.4	266.6	312.1	286.8	432.6

OB/GYN: Gynecologic Oncology

	Instructor	Assistant Professor	Associate Professor	Professor	Chief	Chair
Count:	0	19	14	13	5	3
25th:		242	283	271	367	
Median:		265	371	343	528	
75th:		331	461	456	541	
Mean:		294.3	386.6	376.0	468.6	

OB/GYN: Maternal & Fetal

	Instructor	Assistant Professor	Associate Professor	Professor	Chief	Chair
Count:	0	33	19	22	5	9
25th:		231	281	314	365	445
Median:		274	313	348	369	484
75th:		326	359	502	574	549
Mean:		283.1	318.8	414.0	449.4	498.1

TABLE 16 Summary Statistics on Medical School Faculty Compensation for Midwestern Region M.D. or Equivalent Degree, Clinical Science Departments/Specialties Total Compensation in Thousands of Dollars (continued)

OB/GYN: Reproductive Endocrinology

	Instructor	Assistant Professor	Associate Professor	Professor	Chief	Chair
Count:	0	13	11	6	4	2
25th:		175	200	278		
Median:		212	245	403		
75th:		270	284	441		
Mean:		230.9	252.6	370.7		

OB/GYN: Other OB/GYN

	Instructor	Assistant Professor	Associate Professor	Professor	Chief	Chair
Count:	1	21	10	9	6	2
25th:		176	250	279	214	
Median:		192	288	322	361	
75th:		222	311	351	423	
Mean:		196.0	272.3	316.4	332.5	

Total Pathology

	Instructor	Assistant Professor	Associate Professor	Professor	Chief	Chair
Count:	24	231	160	214	11	27
25th:	74	165	197	238	249	315
Median:	115	194	248	285	295	392
75th:	207	253	304	341	319	507
Mean:	140.0	213.8	251.5	291.3	284.4	412.5

Pathology: Anatomic

	Instructor	Assistant Professor	Associate Professor	Professor	Chief	Chair
Count:	7	138	83	86	7	12
25th:	216	174	226	249	279	352
Median:	237	210	263	299	304	391
75th:	263	295	361	373	323	455
Mean:	225.3	237.6	283.8	308.5	295.0	399.8

Pathology: Clinical

	Instructor	Assistant Professor	Associate Professor	Professor	Chief	Chair
Count:	8	66	58	85	3	7
25th:	67	164	197	256		385
Median:	95	183	224	296		438
75th:	169	210	275	352		598
Mean:	114.6	188.3	235.5	305.7		491.6

TABLE 16 Summary Statistics on Medical School Faculty Compensation for Midwestern Region M.D. or Equivalent Degree, Clinical Science Departments/Specialties Total Compensation in Thousands of Dollars (continued)

Pathology: Other Pathology

	Instructor	Assistant Professor	Associate Professor	Professor	Chief	Chair
Count:	9	27	19	43	1	8
25th:	69	122	107	180		261
Median:	100	165	146	226		301
75th:	125	180	217	264		496
Mean:	96.2	155.0	159.6	228.3		362.5

Total Pediatrics

	Instructor	Assistant Professor	Associate Professor	Professor	Chief	Chair
Count:	211	1,212	559	459	162	23
25th:	69	138	166	202	204	324
Median:	113	161	196	236	236	353
75th:	130	191	230	284	283	464
Mean:	110.8	170.9	202.6	247.5	254.8	408.0

Adolescent Medicine

	Instructor	Assistant Professor	Associate Professor	Professor	Chief	Chair
Count:	2	13	5	3	6	0
25th:		120	158		168	
Median:		125	173		194	
75th:		142	190		236	
Mean:		129.5	173.6		196.3	

Allergy/Immunology-Peds.

	Instructor	Assistant Professor	Associate Professor	Professor	Chief	Chair
Count:	8	18	8	12	6	0
25th:	58	136	177	200	227	
Median:	78	148	188	221	235	
75th:	90	163	191	277	315	
Mean:	78.8	160.4	191.9	241.4	256.0	

Child & Adolescent Psychiatry

	Instructor	Assistant Professor	Associate Professor	Professor	Chief	Chair
Count:	3	28	10	5	6	0
25th:		158	178	185	187	
Median:		174	220	226	211	
75th:		212	232	230	243	
Mean:		179.9	206.2	211.0	224.8	

TABLE 16

Summary Statistics on Medical School Faculty Compensation for Midwestern Region M.D. or Equivalent Degree, Clinical Science Departments/Specialties Total Compensation in Thousands of Dollars (continued)

Critical/Intensive Care-Peds.

	Instructor	Assistant Professor	Associate Professor	Professor	Chief	Chair
Count:	23	98	39	11	9	1
25th:	70	172	207	229	233	
Median:	116	186	240	272	265	
75th:	161	206	270	304	379	
Mean:	115.1	196.4	250.8	279.6	293.0	

Emergency Medicine-Peds.

	Instructor	Assistant Professor	Associate Professor	Professor	Chief	Chair
Count:	17	85	39	20	5	0
25th:	65	163	195	221	263	
Median:	76	178	215	249	334	
75th:	140	193	231	258	343	
Mean:	106.4	179.4	216.4	244.5	309.2	

Endocrinology-Peds.

	Instructor	Assistant Professor	Associate Professor	Professor	Chief	Chair
Count:	5	46	14	17	9	0
25th:	59	127	139	186	188	
Median:	61	137	156	199	219	
75th:	152	147	170	217	246	
Mean:	96.4	140.9	156.4	206.9	218.7	

Gastroenterology-Peds.

	Instructor	Assistant Professor	Associate Professor	Professor	Chief	Chair
Count:	9	59	29	27	7	0
25th:	57	155	193	202	209	
Median:	61	160	207	245	255	
75th:	117	180	222	303	283	
Mean:	82.2	170.0	203.2	259.1	254.9	

General Pediatrics

	Instructor	Assistant Professor	Associate Professor	Professor	Chief	Chair
Count:	24	289	110	80	12	8
25th:	114	134	146	195	204	293
Median:	128	151	169	233	237	323
75th:	162	191	202	290	271	339
Mean:	136.9	169.6	180.6	245.9	235.8	346.1

TABLE 16 Summary Statistics on Medical School Faculty Compensation for Midwestern Region M.D. or Equivalent Degree, Clinical Science Departments/Specialties Total Compensation in Thousands of Dollars (continued)

Genetics-Peds.

	Instructor	Assistant Professor	Associate Professor	Professor	Chief	Chair
Count:	1	19	12	20	8	0
25th:		122	155	167	176	
Median:		133	162	178	212	
75th:		150	171	228	223	
Mean:		132.7	166.0	196.6	211.3	

Hematology/Oncology-Peds.

	Instructor	Assistant Professor	Associate Professor	Professor	Chief	Chair
Count:	12	87	47	38	13	4
25th:	60	131	166	207	195	
Median:	111	138	176	238	211	
75th:	115	149	208	258	233	
Mean:	93.0	140.9	190.1	251.3	222.7	

Hospital Medicine-Peds.

	Instructor	Assistant Professor	Associate Professor	Professor	Chief	Chair
Count:	50	44	4	1	4	0
25th:	112	132				
Median:	117	138				
75th:	127	152				
Mean:	122.2	146.6				

Infectious Disease-Peds.

	Instructor	Assistant Professor	Associate Professor	Professor	Chief	Chair
Count:	2	26	12	26	11	3
25th:		123	135	181	213	
Median:		128	146	211	228	
75th:		132	180	240	255	
Mean:		130.3	154.3	212.2	231.5	

Neonatology

	Instructor	Assistant Professor	Associate Professor	Professor	Chief	Chair
Count:	18	126	53	60	11	4
25th:	61	171	200	245	300	
Median:	76	197	229	262	339	
75th:	122	222	253	302	371	
Mean:	98.9	206.7	233.3	266.4	348.8	

TABLE 16 Summary Statistics on Medical School Faculty Compensation for Midwestern Region M.D. or Equivalent Degree, Clinical Science Departments/Specialties Total Compensation in Thousands of Dollars (continued)

Nephrology-Peds.

	Instructor	Assistant Professor	Associate Professor	Professor	Chief	Chair
Count:	3	21	12	18	9	0
25th:		136	151	162	190	
Median:		140	169	193	224	
75th:		147	178	210	258	
Mean:		141.5	170.3	197.7	218.1	

Neurology-Peds.

	Instructor	Assistant Professor	Associate Professor	Professor	Chief	Chair
Count:	0	42	25	23	5	0
25th:		151	182	210	220	
Median:		157	195	222	263	
75th:		176	204	234	302	
Mean:		162.6	197.7	220.4	261.4	

Pediatric Cardiology

	Instructor	Assistant Professor	Associate Professor	Professor	Chief	Chair
Count:	13	81	60	39	9	1
25th:	61	175	222	260	288	
Median:	110	195	235	297	389	
75th:	180	219	270	359	454	
Mean:	122.0	199.9	238.4	317.5	382.7	

Pulmonary-Peds.

	Instructor	Assistant Professor	Associate Professor	Professor	Chief	Chair
Count:	7	42	32	29	7	1
25th:	59	143	175	195	221	
Median:	61	153	185	223	254	
75th:	111	170	215	271	304	
Mean:	87.1	159.7	194.9	236.8	253.0	

Rheumatology-Peds.

	Instructor	Assistant Professor	Associate Professor	Professor	Chief	Chair
Count:	5	14	9	3	7	0
25th:	59	135	149		180	
Median:	90	143	166		221	
75th:	123	157	182		301	
Mean:	90.4	146.2	165.7		259.3	

TABLE 16

Summary Statistics on Medical School Faculty Compensation for Midwestern Region M.D. or Equivalent Degree, Clinical Science Departments/Specialties Total Compensation in Thousands of Dollars (continued)

Other Pediatrics

	Instructor	Assistant Professor	Associate Professor	Professor	Chief	Chair
Count:	9	74	39	27	18	1
25th:	80	132	155	202	192	
Median:	112	151	189	261	222	
75th:	115	180	226	300	274	
Mean:	102.3	162.7	197.2	260.5	244.7	

Total Radiology

	Instructor	Assistant Professor	Associate Professor	Professor	Chief	Chair
Count:	75	548	209	249	15	38
25th:	230	306	328	335	361	528
Median:	352	378	400	396	431	614
75th:	487	473	471	468	536	678
Mean:	337.3	388.4	406.2	402.0	463.5	613.3

Diagnostic Radiology: Total

	Instructor	Assistant Professor	Associate Professor	Professor	Chief	Chair
Count:	52	359	120	146	10	17
25th:	240	305	316	328	361	508
Median:	374	390	409	380	479	600
75th:	540	459	490	449	536	676
Mean:	364.3	390.1	405.0	393.5	453.7	598.7

Diagnostic Radiology: Interventional

	Instructor	Assistant Professor	Associate Professor	Professor	Chief	Chair
Count:	19	96	37	27	1	2
25th:	399	355	440	370		
Median:	540	440	500	420		
75th:	540	540	540	540		
Mean:	473.2	440.3	498.3	439.0		

Diagnostic Radiology: Non-interventional

	Instructor	Assistant Professor	Associate Professor	Professor	Chief	Chair
Count:	33	263	83	119	9	15
25th:	140	285	295	328	348	502
Median:	355	371	340	358	464	600
75th:	451	437	431	441	526	682
Mean:	301.6	371.8	363.4	383.1	442.9	604.3

TABLE 16

Summary Statistics on Medical School Faculty Compensation for Midwestern Region
M.D. or Equivalent Degree, Clinical Science Departments/Specialties
Total Compensation in Thousands of Dollars (continued)

Nuclear Medicine

	Instructor	Assistant Professor	Associate Professor	Professor	Chief	Chair
Count:	0	25	10	18	2	0
25th:		311	309	280		
Median:		360	344	340		
75th:		540	399	412		
Mean:		413.3	365.2	348.7		

Radiation Oncology

	Instructor	Assistant Professor	Associate Professor	Professor	Chief	Chair
Count:	15	77	36	40	1	18
25th:	230	274	333	356		538
Median:	285	330	393	429		632
75th:	371	390	449	493		678
Mean:	309.9	340.1	380.2	405.4		625.8

Other Radiology

	Instructor	Assistant Professor	Associate Professor	Professor	Chief	Chair
Count:	8	87	43	45	2	3
25th:	110	335	376	378		
Median:	180	389	407	432		
75th:	318	540	540	542		
Mean:	213.4	417.3	440.9	448.1		

Total Surgery

	Instructor	Assistant Professor	Associate Professor	Professor	Chief	Chair
Count:	41	806	487	490	119	85
25th:	96	250	306	342	425	531
Median:	195	315	402	435	528	637
75th:	297	418	500	536	681	815
Mean:	216.9	346.9	421.0	453.9	571.5	701.1

General Surgery

	Instructor	Assistant Professor	Associate Professor	Professor	Chief	Chair
Count:	4	151	93	109	13	16
25th:		211	266	300	412	468
Median:		254	320	378	508	627
75th:		334	408	445	574	815
Mean:		266.2	330.9	374.9	502.2	615.1

TABLE 16 Summary Statistics on Medical School Faculty Compensation for Midwestern Region
M.D. or Equivalent Degree, Clinical Science Departments/Specialties
Total Compensation in Thousands of Dollars (continued)

Neurosurgery

	Instructor	Assistant Professor	Associate Professor	Professor	Chief	Chair
Count:	5	95	54	46	6	14
25th:	78	337	408	419	522	656
Median:	125	406	493	585	538	815
75th:	250	503	653	678	691	936
Mean:	156.2	435.2	521.3	543.4	529.5	920.9

Orthopaedic Surgery

	Instructor	Assistant Professor	Associate Professor	Professor	Chief	Chair
Count:	14	181	94	98	19	19
25th:	169	300	348	396	445	577
Median:	278	384	505	505	530	650
75th:	302	505	568	563	691	807
Mean:	266.5	419.8	482.6	501.3	542.6	748.3

Pediatric Surgery

	Instructor	Assistant Professor	Associate Professor	Professor	Chief	Chair
Count:	2	19	21	15	9	0
25th:		300	392	507	554	
Median:		337	444	582	633	
75th:		421	561	705	727	
Mean:		336.1	482.7	589.7	626.7	

Plastic Surgery

	Instructor	Assistant Professor	Associate Professor	Professor	Chief	Chair
Count:	3	50	22	24	11	5
25th:		262	330	387	469	556
Median:		326	416	465	655	597
75th:		465	475	534	780	1,123
Mean:		360.5	403.8	476.0	630.9	790.6

Surgical Oncology

	Instructor	Assistant Professor	Associate Professor	Professor	Chief	Chair
Count:	0	17	20	15	6	4
25th:		205	213	261	393	
Median:		234	274	338	455	
75th:		251	358	399	520	
Mean:		234.3	289.5	327.4	451.7	

TABLE 16 Summary Statistics on Medical School Faculty Compensation for Midwestern Region M.D. or Equivalent Degree, Clinical Science Departments/Specialties Total Compensation in Thousands of Dollars (continued)

Thoracic & Cardiovascular Surgery

	Instructor	Assistant Professor	Associate Professor	Professor	Chief	Chair
Count:	6	66	41	38	15	5
25th:	92	275	400	420	541	483
Median:	174	326	478	558	740	542
75th:	186	458	602	651	980	925
Mean:	222.3	374.4	487.5	529.5	890.9	671.6

Transplant Surgery

	Instructor	Assistant Professor	Associate Professor	Professor	Chief	Chair
Count:	0	36	35	34	9	1
25th:		281	350	309	449	
Median:		306	445	402	508	
75th:		392	561	490	677	
Mean:		339.7	464.1	420.2	570.9	

Trauma/Critical Care Surgery

	Instructor	Assistant Professor	Associate Professor	Professor	Chief	Chair
Count:	1	46	22	12	5	2
25th:		250	305	319	398	
Median:		295	357	361	417	
75th:		350	426	387	565	
Mean:		309.1	372.4	354.6	468.6	

Urology

	Instructor	Assistant Professor	Associate Professor	Professor	Chief	Chair
Count:	4	89	65	55	6	15
25th:		244	304	358	388	414
Median:		292	380	434	460	516
75th:		368	433	516	700	624
Mean:		306.2	372.4	471.7	560.3	558.5

Vascular Surgery

	Instructor	Assistant Professor	Associate Professor	Professor	Chief	Chair
Count:	0	28	13	26	13	1
25th:		246	322	340	371	
Median:		277	384	392	438	
75th:		349	434	537	590	
Mean:		297.8	377.5	407.4	461.2	

TABLE 16 Summary Statistics on Medical School Faculty Compensation for Midwestern Region M.D. or Equivalent Degree, Clinical Science Departments/Specialties Total Compensation in Thousands of Dollars (continued)

Other Surgery

	Instructor	Assistant Professor	Associate Professor	Professor	Chief	Chair
Count:	2	28	7	18	7	3
25th:		163	300	345	271	
Median:		243	350	432	363	
75th:		306	437	438	404	
Mean:		247.3	341.1	391.0	356.6	

Other Clinical Science

Community Health

	Instructor	Assistant Professor	Associate Professor	Professor	Chief	Chair
Count:	9	14	5	0	1	0
25th:	200	208	108			
Median:	222	222	125			
75th:	222	230	181			
Mean:	212.2	217.3	140.4			

Emergency Medicine

	Instructor	Assistant Professor	Associate Professor	Professor	Chief	Chair
Count:	83	313	89	34	4	14
25th:	190	211	243	243		380
Median:	210	247	272	270		439
75th:	264	285	294	340		478
Mean:	218.9	247.2	268.6	291.7		437.6

Family Medicine

	Instructor	Assistant Professor	Associate Professor	Professor	Chief	Chair
Count:	49	393	150	79	3	27
25th:	170	147	169	175		272
Median:	220	167	189	202		297
75th:	222	193	210	226		355
Mean:	194.4	173.1	191.0	208.4		300.6

Neurology

	Instructor	Assistant Professor	Associate Professor	Professor	Chief	Chair
Count:	18	301	168	183	8	23
25th:	64	138	161	199	184	318
Median:	74	167	197	249	206	377
75th:	125	208	242	263	219	432
Mean:	113.2	176.3	197.9	238.7	208.3	381.1

TABLE 16 Summary Statistics on Medical School Faculty Compensation for Midwestern Region M.D. or Equivalent Degree, Clinical Science Departments/Specialties Total Compensation in Thousands of Dollars (continued)

Ophthalmology

	Instructor	Assistant Professor	Associate Professor	Professor	Chief	Chair
Count:	31	122	67	90	1	16
25th:	56	154	206	245		438
Median:	98	211	291	308		477
75th:	165	277	373	379		575
Mean:	130.6	225.1	319.0	326.5		502.3

Otolaryngology

	Instructor	Assistant Professor	Associate Professor	Professor	Chief	Chair
Count:	3	107	57	68	11	18
25th:		205	274	276	372	507
Median:		258	329	359	434	576
75th:		328	394	418	488	626
Mean:		290.4	341.1	374.2	422.2	578.1

Physical Medicine & Rehabilitation

	Instructor	Assistant Professor	Associate Professor	Professor	Chief	Chair
Count:	28	125	36	24	1	10
25th:	147	149	178	213		285
Median:	164	191	203	237		339
75th:	212	251	245	303		398
Mean:	188.6	192.4	209.8	243.8		351.6

Preventive Medicine

	Instructor	Assistant Professor	Associate Professor	Professor	Chief	Chair
Count:	10	13	16	4	0	5
25th:	141	129	171			219
Median:	236	188	236			226
75th:	236	236	237			240
Mean:	196.6	179.3	216.4			228.6

Psychiatry

	Instructor	Assistant Professor	Associate Professor	Professor	Chief	Chair
Count:	24	232	118	127	5	29
25th:	132	144	158	171	190	256
Median:	152	164	184	200	234	321
75th:	170	193	215	234	284	409
Mean:	155.3	169.9	188.9	208.6	236.2	333.9

TABLE 16

Summary Statistics on Medical School Faculty Compensation for Midwestern Region M.D. or Equivalent Degree, Clinical Science Departments/Specialties Total Compensation in Thousands of Dollars (continued)

Other

	Instructor	Assistant Professor	Associate Professor	Professor	Chief	Chair
Count:	0	13	10	20	0	0
25th:		128	130	229		
Median:		175	210	263		
75th:		241	239	311		
Mean:		175.8	193.3	270.0		

TABLE 17 Summary Statistics on Medical School Faculty Compensation for Western Region
M.D. or Equivalent Degree, Clinical Science Departments/Specialties
Total Compensation in Thousands of Dollars

CLINICAL SCIENCE - TOTAL ALL DEPARTMENTS/SPECIALTIES

	Instructor	Assistant Professor	Associate Professor	Professor	Chief	Chair
Count:	612	3,802	2,258	2,756	402	246
25th:	80	151	175	211	238	349
Median:	119	193	221	269	293	462
75th:	159	271	306	351	384	612
Mean:	127.6	221.1	256.0	302.3	327.5	505.2

Total Anesthesiology

	Instructor	Assistant Professor	Associate Professor	Professor	Chief	Chair
Count:	22	314	162	164	7	13
25th:	220	266	284	295	285	441
Median:	259	303	315	327	358	464
75th:	283	336	364	375	409	577
Mean:	237.0	301.6	324.3	336.3	352.3	510.3

Anesthesiology: General

	Instructor	Assistant Professor	Associate Professor	Professor	Chief	Chair
Count:	19	233	121	130	5	11
25th:	223	263	281	291	309	449
Median:	263	300	311	322	358	464
75th:	283	337	368	368	399	560
Mean:	248.0	298.7	321.9	333.4	354.4	499.8

Anesthesiology: Pain Management

	Instructor	Assistant Professor	Associate Professor	Professor	Chief	Chair
Count:	1	35	17	12	0	2
25th:		292	293	304		
Median:		312	316	327		
75th:		319	352	350		
Mean:		309.5	319.4	319.8		

Anesthesiology: Pediatric

	Instructor	Assistant Professor	Associate Professor	Professor	Chief	Chair
Count:	2	46	24	22	2	0
25th:		267	311	322		
Median:		307	347	370		
75th:		346	367	405		
Mean:		310.4	339.8	362.6		

TABLE 17 Summary Statistics on Medical School Faculty Compensation for Western Region M.D. or Equivalent Degree, Clinical Science Departments/Specialties Total Compensation in Thousands of Dollars (continued)

Total Dermatology

	Instructor	Assistant Professor	Associate Professor	Professor	Chief	Chair
Count:	5	56	31	32	7	8
25th:	66	214	215	249	282	370
Median:	184	244	267	348	339	430
75th:	252	351	394	420	418	483
Mean:	163.8	301.4	317.1	365.4	361.9	434.1

Dermatology (excluding Mohs Surgery)

	Instructor	Assistant Professor	Associate Professor	Professor	Chief	Chair
Count:	4	43	27	29	6	7
25th:		206	197	241	282	428
Median:		233	265	342	326	430
75th:		293	390	383	400	527
Mean:		257.9	288.4	328.7	337.3	457.3

Dermatology: Mohs Surgery

	Instructor	Assistant Professor	Associate Professor	Professor	Chief	Chair
Count:	1	13	4	3	1	1
25th:		258				
Median:		407				
75th:		645				
Mean:		445.3				

Total Medicine

	Instructor	Assistant Professor	Associate Professor	Professor	Chief	Chair
Count:	188	917	610	762	116	20
25th:	89	142	166	205	227	258
Median:	120	169	195	245	264	383
75th:	145	211	235	304	322	495
Mean:	125.3	184.4	212.4	269.1	281.7	398.9

Allergy/Immunology-Med.

	Instructor	Assistant Professor	Associate Professor	Professor	Chief	Chair
Count:	3	5	3	12	2	0
25th:		115		195		
Median:		138		236		
75th:		207		312		
Mean:		156.0		300.4		

TABLE 17 Summary Statistics on Medical School Faculty Compensation for Western Region M.D. or Equivalent Degree, Clinical Science Departments/Specialties Total Compensation in Thousands of Dollars (continued)

Cardiology: Total

	Instructor	Assistant Professor	Associate Professor	Professor	Chief	Chair
Count:	19	101	75	121	9	2
25th:	100	178	215	240	283	
Median:	134	225	235	275	356	
75th:	219	276	310	329	406	
Mean:	166.5	236.5	270.3	297.3	364.3	

Cardiology: Invasive Interventional-Med.

	Instructor	Assistant Professor	Associate Professor	Professor	Chief	Chair
Count:	4	17	18	17	5	0
25th:		239	278	266	283	
Median:		259	319	355	356	
75th:		310	395	463	480	
Mean:		280.8	340.2	380.7	376.4	

Cardiology: Invasive Non-interventional-Med.

	Instructor	Assistant Professor	Associate Professor	Professor	Chief	Chair
Count:	0	12	12	17	1	0
25th:		195	223	250		
Median:		237	300	295		
75th:		280	395	390		
Mean:		248.3	327.1	320.7		

Cardiology: Non-invasive-Med.

	Instructor	Assistant Professor	Associate Professor	Professor	Chief	Chair
Count:	15	72	45	87	3	2
25th:	90	173	183	223		
Median:	134	216	222	260		
75th:	175	266	247	294		
Mean:	161.9	224.1	227.1	276.5		

Critical/Intensive Care-Med.

	Instructor	Assistant Professor	Associate Professor	Professor	Chief	Chair
Count:	5	18	18	11	0	0
25th:	100	146	178	200		
Median:	175	188	182	208		
75th:	175	210	225	225		
Mean:	144.8	201.6	211.3	217.7		

TABLE 17 Summary Statistics on Medical School Faculty Compensation for Western Region M.D. or Equivalent Degree, Clinical Science Departments/Specialties Total Compensation in Thousands of Dollars (continued)

Endocrinology-Med.

	Instructor	Assistant Professor	Associate Professor	Professor	Chief	Chair
Count:	4	37	28	62	7	3
25th:		106	153	180	222	
Median:		130	168	212	243	
75th:		163	202	290	279	
Mean:		134.1	175.0	242.3	243.0	

Gastroenterology-Med.

	Instructor	Assistant Professor	Associate Professor	Professor	Chief	Chair
Count:	7	68	48	57	11	1
25th:	80	199	215	232	292	
Median:	95	221	251	297	345	
75th:	174	266	329	358	409	
Mean:	116.0	244.2	277.5	324.4	348.5	

General Internal Medicine

	Instructor	Assistant Professor	Associate Professor	Professor	Chief	Chair
Count:	50	176	113	121	13	6
25th:	110	137	149	185	237	172
Median:	129	152	172	215	251	245
75th:	145	171	192	261	294	683
Mean:	125.8	158.1	175.7	235.7	289.5	373.3

Geriatrics-Med.

	Instructor	Assistant Professor	Associate Professor	Professor	Chief	Chair
Count:	5	30	26	19	6	2
25th:	93	121	151	179	206	
Median:	129	151	178	222	250	
75th:	133	172	209	260	272	
Mean:	115.8	151.3	185.8	217.8	252.0	

Hematology/Oncology-Med.

	Instructor	Assistant Professor	Associate Professor	Professor	Chief	Chair
Count:	29	127	93	119	14	0
25th:	81	170	196	228	260	
Median:	85	202	225	281	322	
75th:	101	253	258	345	347	
Mean:	100.0	224.5	235.2	306.1	307.2	

TABLE 17 Summary Statistics on Medical School Faculty Compensation for Western Region M.D. or Equivalent Degree, Clinical Science Departments/Specialties Total Compensation in Thousands of Dollars (continued)

Hospital Medicine

	Instructor	Assistant Professor	Associate Professor	Professor	Chief	Chair
Count:	24	112	34	14	6	0
25th:	141	161	182	210	203	
Median:	143	177	196	239	210	
75th:	158	193	230	288	227	
Mean:	150.6	180.0	207.7	249.9	237.5	

Infectious Disease-Med.

	Instructor	Assistant Professor	Associate Professor	Professor	Chief	Chair
Count:	10	65	57	63	14	1
25th:	83	117	146	190	195	
Median:	85	130	166	217	239	
75th:	89	150	195	243	256	
Mean:	86.2	131.9	177.0	230.2	234.8	

Nephrology-Med.

	Instructor	Assistant Professor	Associate Professor	Professor	Chief	Chair
Count:	3	50	34	56	8	0
25th:		145	173	216	262	
Median:		167	195	259	298	
75th:		191	235	299	317	
Mean:		172.9	213.4	270.8	290.5	

Pulmonary-Med.

	Instructor	Assistant Professor	Associate Professor	Professor	Chief	Chair
Count:	15	72	42	61	8	4
25th:	98	151	176	215	242	
Median:	130	182	196	242	294	
75th:	154	203	252	298	314	
Mean:	137.6	181.8	211.5	259.7	281.9	

Rheumatology-Med.

	Instructor	Assistant Professor	Associate Professor	Professor	Chief	Chair
Count:	8	35	23	28	9	0
25th:	86	118	145	191	211	
Median:	94	136	167	225	220	
75th:	105	158	215	295	283	
Mean:	97.6	141.6	176.0	247.3	237.3	

TABLE 17 Summary Statistics on Medical School Faculty Compensation for Western Region M.D. or Equivalent Degree, Clinical Science Departments/Specialties Total Compensation in Thousands of Dollars (continued)

Other Medicine

	Instructor	Assistant Professor	Associate Professor	Professor	Chief	Chair
Count:	6	21	16	18	9	1
25th:	82	114	144	174	221	
Median:	83	135	164	198	247	
75th:	117	154	181	257	272	
Mean:	102.8	138.4	182.4	252.3	250.4	

Total OB/GYN

	Instructor	Assistant Professor	Associate Professor	Professor	Chief	Chair
Count:	39	162	72	84	22	17
25th:	63	175	203	230	252	374
Median:	77	218	223	290	298	403
75th:	149	263	275	337	358	499
Mean:	111.7	229.9	263.2	310.5	306.8	430.7

OB/GYN: General

	Instructor	Assistant Professor	Associate Professor	Professor	Chief	Chair
Count:	10	87	40	31	5	4
25th:	90	175	195	190	188	
Median:	151	192	212	254	233	
75th:	193	251	255	317	294	
Mean:	166.6	220.6	243.9	255.7	239.0	

OB/GYN: Gynecologic Oncology

	Instructor	Assistant Professor	Associate Professor	Professor	Chief	Chair
Count:	7	16	9	10	7	2
25th:	62	219	232	258	299	
Median:	66	226	285	327	350	
75th:	68	248	392	367	361	
Mean:	76.4	225.9	331.7	311.8	340.0	

OB/GYN: Maternal & Fetal

	Instructor	Assistant Professor	Associate Professor	Professor	Chief	Chair
Count:	15	33	15	25	3	5
25th:	65	169	204	290		417
Median:	76	221	252	331		492
75th:	153	296	440	413		554
Mean:	111.5	246.3	295.1	409.2		486.6

TABLE 17 Summary Statistics on Medical School Faculty Compensation for Western Region M.D. or Equivalent Degree, Clinical Science Departments/Specialties Total Compensation in Thousands of Dollars (continued)

OB/GYN: Reproductive Endocrinology

	Instructor	Assistant Professor	Associate Professor	Professor	Chief	Chair
Count:	0	17	4	11	2	6
25th:		199		226		374
Median:		270		281		398
75th:		307		300		490
Mean:		264.2		280.2		429.2

OB/GYN: Other OB/GYN

	Instructor	Assistant Professor	Associate Professor	Professor	Chief	Chair
Count:	7	9	4	7	5	0
25th:	60	130		200	222	
Median:	69	232		234	283	
75th:	80	255		271	362	
Mean:	69.1	201.6		246.9	290.0	

Total Pathology

	Instructor	Assistant Professor	Associate Professor	Professor	Chief	Chair
Count:	25	159	113	205	14	18
25th:	56	158	191	222	190	322
Median:	69	175	217	254	240	389
75th:	99	195	242	305	258	512
Mean:	83.0	178.6	222.7	274.3	234.9	444.6

Pathology: Anatomic

	Instructor	Assistant Professor	Associate Professor	Professor	Chief	Chair
Count:	17	87	62	97	6	8
25th:	56	161	194	238	210	314
Median:	56	178	223	266	245	373
75th:	98	192	236	318	253	481
Mean:	78.2	184.9	223.9	293.2	233.3	388.9

Pathology: Clinical

	Instructor	Assistant Professor	Associate Professor	Professor	Chief	Chair
Count:	5	49	32	67	8	7
25th:	75	154	186	209	184	313
Median:	84	172	212	243	223	354
75th:	141	202	241	279	278	600
Mean:	103.0	175.4	215.6	260.4	236.1	410.0

TABLE 17 Summary Statistics on Medical School Faculty Compensation for Western Region M.D. or Equivalent Degree, Clinical Science Departments/Specialties Total Compensation in Thousands of Dollars (continued)

Pathology: Other Pathology

	Instructor	Assistant Professor	Associate Professor	Professor	Chief	Chair
Count:	3	23	19	41	0	3
25th:		125	160	193		
Median:		166	202	253		
75th:		187	275	292		
Mean:		162.0	231.0	252.2		

Total Pediatrics

	Instructor	Assistant Professor	Associate Professor	Professor	Chief	Chair
Count:	108	640	397	399	92	16
25th:	107	132	155	185	189	335
Median:	132	149	180	220	223	443
75th:	155	179	221	269	271	605
Mean:	136.2	159.1	197.9	238.5	236.6	452.9

Adolescent Medicine

	Instructor	Assistant Professor	Associate Professor	Professor	Chief	Chair
Count:	1	11	5	2	3	0
25th:		122	152			
Median:		128	164			
75th:		132	185			
Mean:		128.0	167.4			

Allergy/Immunology-Peds.

	Instructor	Assistant Professor	Associate Professor	Professor	Chief	Chair
Count:	1	12	7	12	2	0
25th:		131	142	162		
Median:		143	160	203		
75th:		175	233	226		
Mean:		150.8	177.7	201.3		

Child & Adolescent Psychiatry

	Instructor	Assistant Professor	Associate Professor	Professor	Chief	Chair
Count:	0	12	13	17	3	0
25th:		133	149	193		
Median:		168	194	224		
75th:		179	208	277		
Mean:		159.1	186.9	233.6		

TABLE 17 Summary Statistics on Medical School Faculty Compensation for Western Region M.D. or Equivalent Degree, Clinical Science Departments/Specialties Total Compensation in Thousands of Dollars (continued)

Critical/Intensive Care-Peds.

	Instructor	Assistant Professor	Associate Professor	Professor	Chief	Chair
Count:	9	58	32	18	5	0
25th:	160	180	212	273	274	
Median:	174	216	239	315	327	
75th:	194	235	273	358	354	
Mean:	184.3	210.2	245.0	323.7	316.4	

Emergency Medicine-Peds.

	Instructor	Assistant Professor	Associate Professor	Professor	Chief	Chair
Count:	27	44	23	11	3	0
25th:	122	153	183	200		
Median:	143	165	194	225		
75th:	154	197	275	302		
Mean:	138.4	178.1	234.6	240.3		

Endocrinology-Peds.

	Instructor	Assistant Professor	Associate Professor	Professor	Chief	Chair
Count:	2	26	15	18	7	0
25th:		120	140	176	179	
Median:		132	173	197	186	
75th:		143	186	224	242	
Mean:		126.9	165.3	200.1	203.7	

Gastroenterology-Peds.

	Instructor	Assistant Professor	Associate Professor	Professor	Chief	Chair
Count:	2	20	21	18	4	2
25th:		142	181	208		
Median:		161	193	224		
75th:		180	208	233		
Mean:		167.7	193.3	231.4		

General Pediatrics

	Instructor	Assistant Professor	Associate Professor	Professor	Chief	Chair
Count:	14	150	66	62	10	7
25th:	61	128	146	160	160	223
Median:	122	138	157	184	211	357
75th:	132	160	179	223	231	523
Mean:	103.8	146.8	169.6	203.8	201.1	375.0

TABLE 17 Summary Statistics on Medical School Faculty Compensation for Western Region M.D. or Equivalent Degree, Clinical Science Departments/Specialties Total Compensation in Thousands of Dollars (continued)

Genetics-Peds.

	Instructor	Assistant Professor	Associate Professor	Professor	Chief	Chair
Count:	2	18	15	24	6	0
25th:		106	132	174	172	
Median:		117	143	193	194	
75th:		129	154	259	202	
Mean:		116.0	143.3	216.4	189.2	

Hematology/Oncology-Peds.

	Instructor	Assistant Professor	Associate Professor	Professor	Chief	Chair
Count:	10	51	44	41	5	0
25th:	75	133	160	202	200	
Median:	88	140	168	219	270	
75th:	106	159	192	275	283	
Mean:	91.4	154.1	188.6	246.0	247.0	

Hospital Medicine-Peds.

	Instructor	Assistant Professor	Associate Professor	Professor	Chief	Chair
Count:	10	43	11	4	1	0
25th:	114	131	149			
Median:	117	138	158			
75th:	132	153	173			
Mean:	123.0	144.9	163.5			

Infectious Disease-Peds.

	Instructor	Assistant Professor	Associate Professor	Professor	Chief	Chair
Count:	1	17	17	24	5	0
25th:		111	128	177	185	
Median:		116	145	190	215	
75th:		133	171	241	222	
Mean:		122.1	149.4	212.3	205.8	

Neonatology

	Instructor	Assistant Professor	Associate Professor	Professor	Chief	Chair
Count:	11	49	36	49	6	2
25th:	140	157	198	222	257	
Median:	168	182	227	253	308	
75th:	326	214	303	325	331	
Mean:	201.6	193.2	264.4	291.2	303.3	

Nephrology-Peds.

	Instructor	Assistant Professor	Associate Professor	Professor	Chief	Chair
Count:	0	18	10	17	6	1
25th:		128	149	197	170	
Median:		133	162	202	180	
75th:		143	189	263	222	
Mean:		137.0	170.5	236.6	187.5	

Neurology-Peds.

	Instructor	Assistant Professor	Associate Professor	Professor	Chief	Chair
Count:	6	23	14	16	2	1
25th:	115	139	160	182		
Median:	132	143	166	207		
75th:	145	159	177	238		
Mean:	138.3	147.9	169.9	211.6		

Pediatric Cardiology

	Instructor	Assistant Professor	Associate Professor	Professor	Chief	Chair
Count:	3	41	40	31	6	1
25th:		168	221	235	213	
Median:		180	235	265	307	
75th:		195	309	306	412	
Mean:		183.0	254.5	281.8	317.0	

Pulmonary-Peds.

	Instructor	Assistant Professor	Associate Professor	Professor	Chief	Chair
Count:	4	17	17	14	6	0
25th:		135	147	177	200	
Median:		141	162	196	204	
75th:		157	173	225	233	
Mean:		144.7	161.1	202.7	229.7	

Rheumatology-Peds.

	Instructor	Assistant Professor	Associate Professor	Professor	Chief	Chair
Count:	3	8	1	4	4	0
25th:		132				
Median:		152				
75th:		170				
Mean:		151.1				

TABLE 17 Summary Statistics on Medical School Faculty Compensation for Western Region M.D. or Equivalent Degree, Clinical Science Departments/Specialties Total Compensation in Thousands of Dollars (continued)

Other Pediatrics

	Instructor	Assistant Professor	Associate Professor	Professor	Chief	Chair
Count:	2	22	10	17	8	2
25th:		129	141	169	194	
Median:		140	155	218	220	
75th:		162	186	262	264	
Mean:		148.0	164.8	235.8	227.6	

Total Radiology

	Instructor	Assistant Professor	Associate Professor	Professor	Chief	Chair
Count:	31	235	124	202	22	27
25th:	60	263	293	317	343	486
Median:	68	297	336	362	393	568
75th:	133	328	385	420	434	650
Mean:	103.9	299.4	344.4	375.7	409.6	580.3

Diagnostic Radiology: Total

	Instructor	Assistant Professor	Associate Professor	Professor	Chief	Chair
Count:	27	184	94	165	21	13
25th:	60	270	293	316	331	466
Median:	68	300	336	358	394	561
75th:	82	329	380	418	453	660
Mean:	89.1	299.9	340.5	373.9	411.4	561.6

Diagnostic Radiology: Interventional

	Instructor	Assistant Professor	Associate Professor	Professor	Chief	Chair
Count:	1	35	19	41	2	3
25th:		294	337	328		
Median:		320	370	369		
75th:		372	428	454		
Mean:		322.7	397.4	394.2		

Diagnostic Radiology: Non-interventional

	Instructor	Assistant Professor	Associate Professor	Professor	Chief	Chair
Count:	26	149	75	124	19	10
25th:	60	262	284	315	319	446
Median:	68	293	322	356	392	537
75th:	82	320	377	397	419	650
Mean:	89.9	294.5	326.1	367.1	404.5	542.8

TABLE 17 Summary Statistics on Medical School Faculty Compensation for Western Region M.D. or Equivalent Degree, Clinical Science Departments/Specialties Total Compensation in Thousands of Dollars (continued)

Nuclear Medicine

	Instructor	Assistant Professor	Associate Professor	Professor	Chief	Chair
Count:	0	6	6	12	0	0
25th:		235	273	280		
Median:		280	312	335		
75th:		315	312	397		
Mean:		279.3	294.8	346.9		

Radiation Oncology

	Instructor	Assistant Professor	Associate Professor	Professor	Chief	Chair
Count:	4	39	22	24	1	14
25th:		259	312	366		529
Median:		280	365	405		589
75th:		326	424	439		650
Mean:		304.5	386.2	406.5		597.7

Other Radiology

	Instructor	Assistant Professor	Associate Professor	Professor	Chief	Chair
Count:	0	6	2	1	0	0
25th:		185				
Median:		274				
75th:		381				
Mean:		271.7				

Total Surgery

	Instructor	Assistant Professor	Associate Professor	Professor	Chief	Chair
Count:	43	498	279	331	79	47
25th:	60	249	296	329	378	545
Median:	75	306	377	397	460	680
75th:	100	391	491	543	566	790
Mean:	101.5	327.6	399.5	451.1	494.7	752.5

General Surgery

	Instructor	Assistant Professor	Associate Professor	Professor	Chief	Chair
Count:	3	74	36	62	5	6
25th:		216	270	303	327	501
Median:		250	312	354	486	628
75th:		325	361	455	606	695
Mean:		267.1	312.5	382.3	470.2	564.3

TABLE 17 Summary Statistics on Medical School Faculty Compensation for Western Region M.D. or Equivalent Degree, Clinical Science Departments/Specialties Total Compensation in Thousands of Dollars (continued)

Neurosurgery

	Instructor	Assistant Professor	Associate Professor	Professor	Chief	Chair
Count:	7	55	30	50	3	10
25th:	57	365	406	292		659
Median:	88	400	481	484		735
75th:	100	461	584	627		810
Mean:	137.4	403.4	480.4	510.0		754.6

Orthopaedic Surgery

	Instructor	Assistant Professor	Associate Professor	Professor	Chief	Chair
Count:	4	117	68	68	8	13
25th:		314	359	346	367	511
Median:		365	445	430	432	723
75th:		449	566	570	589	786
Mean:		386.8	468.0	467.5	469.9	683.5

Pediatric Surgery

	Instructor	Assistant Professor	Associate Professor	Professor	Chief	Chair
Count:	0	21	19	9	8	1
25th:		284	369	376	406	
Median:		385	438	519	562	
75th:		428	613	697	672	
Mean:		351.4	464.0	528.1	548.0	

Plastic Surgery

	Instructor	Assistant Professor	Associate Professor	Professor	Chief	Chair
Count:	3	27	12	15	9	2
25th:		243	279	340	339	
Median:		267	355	452	524	
75th:		399	543	485	623	
Mean:		352.4	405.0	416.7	501.8	

Surgical Oncology

	Instructor	Assistant Professor	Associate Professor	Professor	Chief	Chair
Count:	0	16	7	5	5	2
25th:		208	204	255	314	
Median:		243	248	283	431	
75th:		289	298	576	482	
Mean:		261.3	260.1	388.8	404.2	

TABLE 17 Summary Statistics on Medical School Faculty Compensation for Western Region M.D. or Equivalent Degree, Clinical Science Departments/Specialties Total Compensation in Thousands of Dollars (continued)

Thoracic & Cardiovascular Surgery

	Instructor	Assistant Professor	Associate Professor	Professor	Chief	Chair
Count:	4	34	22	29	11	3
25th:		284	337	442	410	
Median:		307	406	545	475	
75th:		456	500	739	597	
Mean:		370.6	421.3	632.6	572.6	

Transplant Surgery

	Instructor	Assistant Professor	Associate Professor	Professor	Chief	Chair
Count:	8	18	13	9	5	3
25th:	70	258	323	380	489	
Median:	80	281	408	548	770	
75th:	91	344	525	702	925	
Mean:	81.8	287.3	432.7	545.1	719.6	

Trauma/Critical Care Surgery

	Instructor	Assistant Professor	Associate Professor	Professor	Chief	Chair
Count:	2	45	14	22	8	0
25th:		236	280	320	428	
Median:		275	354	363	456	
75th:		320	396	417	496	
Mean:		285.1	344.1	387.2	442.0	

Urology

	Instructor	Assistant Professor	Associate Professor	Professor	Chief	Chair
Count:	11	57	39	39	7	7
25th:	64	235	247	343	350	400
Median:	71	263	323	382	460	546
75th:	115	322	399	450	566	641
Mean:	89.8	269.0	330.1	403.6	491.7	645.7

Vascular Surgery

	Instructor	Assistant Professor	Associate Professor	Professor	Chief	Chair
Count:	0	18	11	18	9	0
25th:		241	229	288	311	
Median:		273	291	347	342	
75th:		320	349	463	424	
Mean:		282.4	298.6	362.7	395.2	

TABLE 17 Summary Statistics on Medical School Faculty Compensation for Western Region M.D. or Equivalent Degree, Clinical Science Departments/Specialties Total Compensation in Thousands of Dollars (continued)

Other Surgery

	Instructor	Assistant Professor	Associate Professor	Professor	Chief	Chair
Count:	1	16	8	5	1	0
25th:		195	171	192		
Median:		255	269	292		
75th:		287	408	325		
Mean:		240.7	324.3	265.2		

Other Clinical Science

Community Health

	Instructor	Assistant Professor	Associate Professor	Professor	Chief	Chair
Count:	0	0	1	4	0	0
25th:						
Median:						
75th:						
Mean:						

Emergency Medicine

	Instructor	Assistant Professor	Associate Professor	Professor	Chief	Chair
Count:	21	121	83	67	7	9
25th:	90	195	225	243	320	339
Median:	158	212	241	268	340	394
75th:	205	237	262	297	353	512
Mean:	146.5	222.1	247.1	279.2	333.4	421.9

Family Medicine

	Instructor	Assistant Professor	Associate Professor	Professor	Chief	Chair
Count:	22	142	84	79	0	12
25th:	110	142	155	173		226
Median:	137	155	167	192		272
75th:	157	181	185	219		291
Mean:	130.5	162.0	172.3	206.5		265.6

Neurology

	Instructor	Assistant Professor	Associate Professor	Professor	Chief	Chair
Count:	18	155	83	127	11	12
25th:	57	130	160	186	250	317
Median:	59	150	180	215	273	376
75th:	85	174	220	266	333	459
Mean:	75.7	157.6	189.8	239.8	278.3	419.5

TABLE 17 Summary Statistics on Medical School Faculty Compensation for Western Region M.D. or Equivalent Degree, Clinical Science Departments/Specialties Total Compensation in Thousands of Dollars (continued)

Ophthalmology

	Instructor	Assistant Professor	Associate Professor	Professor	Chief	Chair
Count:	19	88	55	70	4	13
25th:	53	177	225	238		446
Median:	53	203	311	301		534
75th:	78	301	417	415		635
Mean:	72.1	241.3	334.6	368.9		537.8

Otolaryngology

	Instructor	Assistant Professor	Associate Professor	Professor	Chief	Chair
Count:	5	65	44	44	12	9
25th:	54	222	292	345	332	448
Median:	65	260	330	423	370	494
75th:	65	318	381	534	417	605
Mean:	60.6	282.0	351.4	432.4	413.1	501.3

Physical Medicine & Rehabilitation

	Instructor	Assistant Professor	Associate Professor	Professor	Chief	Chair
Count:	2	35	18	8	4	6
25th:		156	188	214		202
Median:		181	192	243		304
75th:		212	266	253		375
Mean:		190.7	216.0	243.5		294.5

Preventive Medicine

	Instructor	Assistant Professor	Associate Professor	Professor	Chief	Chair
Count:	1	13	4	9	1	2
25th:		102		204		
Median:		125		229		
75th:		136		287		
Mean:		121.9		239.4		

Psychiatry

	Instructor	Assistant Professor	Associate Professor	Professor	Chief	Chair
Count:	62	196	96	167	4	16
25th:	152	151	172	192		292
Median:	163	168	190	236		367
75th:	185	196	217	302		532
Mean:	166.9	182.6	203.6	257.3		403.9

TABLE 17 Summary Statistics on Medical School Faculty Compensation for Western Region M.D. or Equivalent Degree, Clinical Science Departments/Specialties Total Compensation in Thousands of Dollars (continued)

Other

	Instructor	Assistant Professor	Associate Professor	Professor	Chief	Chair
Count:	1	6	2	2	0	1
25th:		124				
Median:		152				
75th:		178				
Mean:		154.8				

TABLE 18 Summary Statistics on Medical School Faculty Compensation for All Schools
Ph.D. or Other Doctoral Degree, Basic Science Departments/Specialties
Total Compensation in Thousands of Dollars

BASIC SCIENCE - TOTAL ALL DEPARTMENTS/SPECIALTIES

	Instructor	Assistant Professor	Associate Professor	Professor	Chief	Chair
Count:	601	4,002	3,170	4,289	31	539
25th:	48	71	96	132	180	211
Median:	54	86	110	159	207	258
75th:	64	99	127	192	231	310
Mean:	58.3	86.3	112.9	168.0	209.5	264.7

Anatomy

	Instructor	Assistant Professor	Associate Professor	Professor	Chief	Chair
Count:	37	248	248	293	2	44
25th:	50	69	90	121		191
Median:	53	80	103	141		247
75th:	66	94	117	169		302
Mean:	57.9	81.8	104.9	150.2		237.6

Biochemistry

	Instructor	Assistant Professor	Associate Professor	Professor	Chief	Chair
Count:	74	524	486	753	2	82
25th:	50	68	92	129		200
Median:	56	83	106	155		252
75th:	64	95	121	193		294
Mean:	59.6	83.3	108.3	166.4		251.4

Bioethics/Medical Humanities

	Instructor	Assistant Professor	Associate Professor	Professor	Chief	Chair
Count:	0	39	39	28	1	5
25th:		80	91	113		159
Median:		85	103	138		177
75th:		95	131	183		262
Mean:		88.6	112.1	149.9		203.6

Biomedical Informatics

	Instructor	Assistant Professor	Associate Professor	Professor	Chief	Chair
Count:	5	71	27	14	3	2
25th:	65	93	114	153		
Median:	79	108	137	185		
75th:	86	120	160	220		
Mean:	76.0	112.1	143.0	201.6		

TABLE 18 Summary Statistics on Medical School Faculty Compensation for All Schools Ph.D. or Other Doctoral Degree, Basic Science Departments/Specialties Total Compensation in Thousands of Dollars (continued)

Biostatistics

	Instructor	Assistant Professor	Associate Professor	Professor	Chief	Chair
Count:	9	209	131	133	8	12
25th:	77	90	113	159	220	237
Median:	86	96	125	179	232	265
75th:	90	105	143	204	252	309
Mean:	82.4	96.9	130.0	186.7	231.9	267.7

Genetics

	Instructor	Assistant Professor	Associate Professor	Professor	Chief	Chair
Count:	45	255	165	171	1	15
25th:	58	78	104	144		270
Median:	66	94	123	173		322
75th:	75	108	142	223		380
Mean:	70.4	94.6	126.6	186.1		344.5

Microbiology

	Instructor	Assistant Professor	Associate Professor	Professor	Chief	Chair
Count:	50	533	446	638	2	82
25th:	48	70	95	132		219
Median:	55	85	109	158		259
75th:	66	96	127	191		312
Mean:	57.7	83.7	111.8	166.5		266.3

Molecular & Cellular Biology

	Instructor	Assistant Professor	Associate Professor	Professor	Chief	Chair
Count:	117	439	322	402	1	45
25th:	48	69	97	140		214
Median:	53	84	112	168		268
75th:	59	99	130	197		352
Mean:	56.0	85.5	114.5	173.9		282.1

Neurosciences

	Instructor	Assistant Professor	Associate Professor	Professor	Chief	Chair
Count:	32	271	213	293	0	32
25th:	49	70	98	137		210
Median:	52	86	109	161		250
75th:	60	96	125	193		318
Mean:	56.3	84.3	113.5	172.4		274.6

TABLE 18

Summary Statistics on Medical School Faculty Compensation for All Schools Ph.D. or Other Doctoral Degree, Basic Science Departments/Specialties Total Compensation in Thousands of Dollars (continued)

Pharmacology

	Instructor	Assistant Professor	Associate Professor	Professor	Chief	Chair
Count:	76	485	394	580	3	88
25th:	46	67	95	129		216
Median:	53	84	106	158		265
75th:	61	95	122	192		306
Mean:	55.8	82.9	108.8	167.7		266.2

Physiology

	Instructor	Assistant Professor	Associate Professor	Professor	Chief	Chair
Count:	89	425	361	593	2	70
25th:	43	68	96	130		235
Median:	50	84	108	155		265
75th:	56	93	122	182		307
Mean:	51.5	82.8	109.3	160.5		270.7

Other Basic Sciences

	Instructor	Assistant Professor	Associate Professor	Professor	Chief	Chair
Count:	67	503	338	391	6	62
25th:	50	75	97	135	203	203
Median:	60	88	114	166	210	256
75th:	69	102	132	204	217	311
Mean:	61.7	89.5	117.6	175.4	215.5	257.3

TABLE 19 Summary Statistics on Medical School Faculty Compensation for Public Schools Ph.D. or Other Doctoral Degree, Basic Science Departments/Specialties Total Compensation in Thousands of Dollars

BASIC SCIENCE - TOTAL ALL DEPARTMENTS/SPECIALTIES

	Instructor	Assistant Professor	Associate Professor	Professor	Chief	Chair
Count:	277	2,166	1,859	2,531	18	318
25th:	47	70	94	127	180	201
Median:	52	84	106	152	212	249
75th:	59	95	121	184	231	289
Mean:	54.6	83.1	108.9	161.8	210.5	248.9

Anatomy

	Instructor	Assistant Professor	Associate Professor	Professor	Chief	Chair
Count:	21	189	172	211	1	30
25th:	50	69	89	121		191
Median:	57	80	100	142		250
75th:	65	94	116	168		305
Mean:	57.8	81.5	102.8	150.3		242.3

Biochemistry

	Instructor	Assistant Professor	Associate Professor	Professor	Chief	Chair
Count:	30	303	308	441	1	51
25th:	45	63	93	126		200
Median:	53	80	107	150		230
75th:	58	93	120	185		273
Mean:	53.9	79.4	108.0	161.0		242.6

Bioethics/Medical Humanities

	Instructor	Assistant Professor	Associate Professor	Professor	Chief	Chair
Count:	0	28	27	20	0	3
25th:		80	94	110		
Median:		84	104	141		
75th:		95	134	183		
Mean:		87.6	114.3	146.3		

Biomedical Informatics

	Instructor	Assistant Professor	Associate Professor	Professor	Chief	Chair
Count:	2	37	15	10	2	2
25th:		92	99	150		
Median:		104	135	160		
75th:		111	146	200		
Mean:		103.3	128.3	169.8		

TABLE 19

Summary Statistics on Medical School Faculty Compensation for Public Schools Ph.D. or Other Doctoral Degree, Basic Science Departments/Specialties Total Compensation in Thousands of Dollars (continued)

Biostatistics

	Instructor	Assistant Professor	Associate Professor	Professor	Chief	Chair
Count:	2	76	57	55	5	4
25th:		90	109	161	199	
Median:		95	124	179	230	
75th:		103	141	214	250	
Mean:		97.1	129.2	194.6	225.6	

Genetics

	Instructor	Assistant Professor	Associate Professor	Professor	Chief	Chair
Count:	5	100	72	93	0	10
25th:	56	76	101	136		240
Median:	60	90	110	156		292
75th:	65	98	136	190		323
Mean:	60.2	87.0	117.4	170.6		289.7

Microbiology

	Instructor	Assistant Professor	Associate Professor	Professor	Chief	Chair
Count:	20	316	260	400	2	50
25th:	50	70	93	128		213
Median:	54	83	104	152		253
75th:	61	94	120	184		297
Mean:	54.7	82.3	107.3	160.6		258.5

Molecular & Cellular Biology

	Instructor	Assistant Professor	Associate Professor	Professor	Chief	Chair
Count:	60	224	191	197	0	25
25th:	47	67	90	130		208
Median:	52	81	107	156		262
75th:	55	94	126	186		305
Mean:	51.2	81.9	110.2	163.5		261.0

Neurosciences

	Instructor	Assistant Professor	Associate Professor	Professor	Chief	Chair
Count:	16	125	108	159	0	15
25th:	46	67	97	132		200
Median:	50	85	105	154		237
75th:	55	94	118	187		304
Mean:	54.1	82.5	108.5	167.5		253.1

TABLE 19 Summary Statistics on Medical School Faculty Compensation for Public Schools Ph.D. or Other Doctoral Degree, Basic Science Departments/Specialties Total Compensation in Thousands of Dollars (continued)

Pharmacology

	Instructor	Assistant Professor	Associate Professor	Professor	Chief	Chair
Count:	45	299	264	357	2	53
25th:	46	68	94	126		203
Median:	50	83	105	147		264
75th:	61	94	119	184		296
Mean:	55.5	80.8	107.2	163.6		255.0

Physiology

	Instructor	Assistant Professor	Associate Professor	Professor	Chief	Chair
Count:	48	257	229	401	2	45
25th:	45	68	95	130		209
Median:	50	82	107	153		255
75th:	54	92	120	179		283
Mean:	52.8	81.6	107.5	159.7		247.5

Other Basic Sciences

	Instructor	Assistant Professor	Associate Professor	Professor	Chief	Chair
Count:	28	212	156	187	3	30
25th:	51	74	93	120		177
Median:	58	86	107	151		214
75th:	65	96	125	190		261
Mean:	59.1	86.5	109.2	160.9		218.9

TABLE 20 Summary Statistics on Medical School Faculty Compensation for Private Schools
Ph.D. or Other Doctoral Degree, Basic Science Departments/Specialties
Total Compensation in Thousands of Dollars

BASIC SCIENCE - TOTAL ALL DEPARTMENTS/SPECIALTIES

	Instructor	Assistant Professor	Associate Professor	Professor	Chief	Chair
Count:	324	1,836	1,311	1,758	13	221
25th:	50	73	100	141	173	232
Median:	57	90	115	170	193	283
75th:	70	103	134	202	229	335
Mean:	61.4	90.0	118.5	177.0	208.1	287.4

Anatomy

	Instructor	Assistant Professor	Associate Professor	Professor	Chief	Chair
Count:	16	59	76	82	1	14
25th:	49	68	95	120		190
Median:	50	79	108	141		233
75th:	70	95	124	171		287
Mean:	58.0	82.7	109.8	150.0		227.5

Biochemistry

	Instructor	Assistant Professor	Associate Professor	Professor	Chief	Chair
Count:	44	221	178	312	1	31
25th:	53	72	92	136		192
Median:	60	87	105	164		273
75th:	66	102	122	203		335
Mean:	63.6	88.7	108.8	174.0		265.8

Bioethics/Medical Humanities

	Instructor	Assistant Professor	Associate Professor	Professor	Chief	Chair
Count:	0	11	12	8	1	2
25th:		74	87	123		
Median:		87	98	138		
75th:		103	130	190		
Mean:		91.4	107.3	159.0		

Biomedical Informatics

	Instructor	Assistant Professor	Associate Professor	Professor	Chief	Chair
Count:	3	34	12	4	1	0
25th:		108	126			
Median:		118	150			
75th:		124	201			
Mean:		121.8	161.3			

TABLE 20 Summary Statistics on Medical School Faculty Compensation for Private Schools Ph.D. or Other Doctoral Degree, Basic Science Departments/Specialties Total Compensation in Thousands of Dollars (continued)

Biostatistics

	Instructor	Assistant Professor	Associate Professor	Professor	Chief	Chair
Count:	7	133	74	78	3	8
25th:	82	90	116	159		237
Median:	86	96	125	178		259
75th:	93	105	147	203		292
Mean:	86.3	96.7	130.6	181.0		264.0

Genetics

	Instructor	Assistant Professor	Associate Professor	Professor	Chief	Chair
Count:	40	155	93	78	1	5
25th:	59	79	110	155		317
Median:	67	101	130	201		380
75th:	75	115	147	244		629
Mean:	71.7	99.5	133.7	204.5		454.2

Microbiology

	Instructor	Assistant Professor	Associate Professor	Professor	Chief	Chair
Count:	30	217	186	238	0	32
25th:	46	68	101	141		227
Median:	56	87	115	171		267
75th:	71	100	133	203		325
Mean:	59.7	85.9	117.9	176.3		278.5

Molecular & Cellular Biology

	Instructor	Assistant Professor	Associate Professor	Professor	Chief	Chair
Count:	57	215	131	205	1	20
25th:	52	74	105	147		214
Median:	55	90	117	178		320
75th:	67	105	134	207		389
Mean:	60.9	89.3	120.9	183.9		308.5

Neurosciences

	Instructor	Assistant Professor	Associate Professor	Professor	Chief	Chair
Count:	16	146	105	134	0	17
25th:	50	73	98	145		241
Median:	56	87	115	167		286
75th:	62	99	138	199		355
Mean:	58.5	85.8	118.7	178.2		293.5

TABLE 20 Summary Statistics on Medical School Faculty Compensation for Private Schools Ph.D. or Other Doctoral Degree, Basic Science Departments/Specialties Total Compensation in Thousands of Dollars (continued)

Pharmacology

	Instructor	Assistant Professor	Associate Professor	Professor	Chief	Chair
Count:	31	186	130	223	1	35
25th:	50	66	98	137		234
Median:	54	87	112	171		296
75th:	62	99	125	200		330
Mean:	56.2	86.2	112.2	174.3		283.2

Physiology

	Instructor	Assistant Professor	Associate Professor	Professor	Chief	Chair
Count:	41	168	132	192	0	25
25th:	40	69	98	128		245
Median:	45	85	110	160		307
75th:	59	96	125	187		378
Mean:	49.9	84.8	112.3	162.2		312.5

Other Basic Sciences

	Instructor	Assistant Professor	Associate Professor	Professor	Chief	Chair
Count:	39	291	182	204	3	32
25th:	50	77	107	156		252
Median:	61	90	120	182		298
75th:	75	103	139	215		339
Mean:	63.5	91.7	124.8	188.6		293.3

TABLE 21 Summary Statistics on Medical School Faculty Compensation for Northeastern Region Ph.D. or Other Doctoral Degree, Basic Science Departments/Specialties Total Compensation in Thousands of Dollars

BASIC SCIENCE - TOTAL ALL DEPARTMENTS/SPECIALTIES

	Instructor	Assistant Professor	Associate Professor	Professor	Chief	Chair
Count:	210	1,225	945	1,225	7	166
25th:	52	74	102	144	151	228
Median:	60	90	115	170	186	285
75th:	70	103	130	200	207	331
Mean:	63.6	89.7	117.4	175.8	181.7	281.3

Anatomy

	Instructor	Assistant Professor	Associate Professor	Professor	Chief	Chair
Count:	4	49	61	64	2	11
25th:		71	95	126		230
Median:		84	108	147		250
75th:		97	125	171		301
Mean:		83.9	111.9	150.7		253.0

Biochemistry

	Instructor	Assistant Professor	Associate Professor	Professor	Chief	Chair
Count:	29	144	130	206	2	26
25th:	60	74	97	143		202
Median:	63	90	109	164		257
75th:	81	102	119	200		322
Mean:	69.6	87.9	109.9	172.7		262.3

Bioethics/Medical Humanities

	Instructor	Assistant Professor	Associate Professor	Professor	Chief	Chair
Count:	0	3	16	8	0	2
25th:			99	125		
Median:			119	169		
75th:			139	206		
Mean:			117.8	171.4		

Biomedical Informatics

	Instructor	Assistant Professor	Associate Professor	Professor	Chief	Chair
Count:	1	25	5	3	1	0
25th:		92	104			
Median:		113	130			
75th:		123	190			
Mean:		114.2	143.2			

Biostatistics

	Instructor	Assistant Professor	Associate Professor	Professor	Chief	Chair
Count:	0	66	33	42	0	3
25th:		82	114	159		
Median:		93	124	179		
75th:		104	130	205		
Mean:		91.3	124.1	185.4		

Genetics

	Instructor	Assistant Professor	Associate Professor	Professor	Chief	Chair
Count:	14	58	32	37	0	3
25th:	60	80	123	152		
Median:	73	105	133	180		
75th:	100	114	147	217		
Mean:	81.1	101.9	136.3	191.4		

Microbiology

	Instructor	Assistant Professor	Associate Professor	Professor	Chief	Chair
Count:	21	191	154	206	1	27
25th:	55	72	103	145		234
Median:	62	90	114	172		291
75th:	72	102	130	201		347
Mean:	64.8	87.5	116.8	176.1		290.9

Molecular & Cellular Biology

	Instructor	Assistant Professor	Associate Professor	Professor	Chief	Chair
Count:	62	161	99	133	0	18
25th:	52	71	103	155		201
Median:	55	90	120	180		271
75th:	66	107	135	206		381
Mean:	59.5	91.4	124.1	187.4		287.2

Neurosciences

	Instructor	Assistant Professor	Associate Professor	Professor	Chief	Chair
Count:	15	130	87	122	0	13
25th:	50	74	99	145		211
Median:	57	88	112	167		287
75th:	70	98	129	196		355
Mean:	61.8	86.0	116.1	175.8		289.7

TABLE 21 Summary Statistics on Medical School Faculty Compensation for Northeastern Region Ph.D. or Other Doctoral Degree, Basic Science Departments/Specialties Total Compensation in Thousands of Dollars (continued)

Pharmacology

	Instructor	Assistant Professor	Associate Professor	Professor	Chief	Chair
Count:	24	117	120	165	0	24
25th:	52	66	101	142		237
Median:	58	86	114	170		274
75th:	64	97	126	200		322
Mean:	59.2	83.9	113.8	174.1		285.2

Physiology

	Instructor	Assistant Professor	Associate Professor	Professor	Chief	Chair
Count:	15	99	94	132	1	17
25th:	46	68	103	141		232
Median:	59	91	114	167		296
75th:	66	101	126	189		328
Mean:	58.1	89.6	113.1	166.3		291.3

Other Basic Sciences

	Instructor	Assistant Professor	Associate Professor	Professor	Chief	Chair
Count:	25	182	114	107	0	22
25th:	51	75	105	156		220
Median:	57	90	123	180		289
75th:	68	106	137	206		338
Mean:	62.2	91.9	124.1	184.1		284.0

TABLE 22 Summary Statistics on Medical School Faculty Compensation for Southern Region
Ph.D. or Other Doctoral Degree, Basic Science Departments/Specialties
Total Compensation in Thousands of Dollars

BASIC SCIENCE - TOTAL ALL DEPARTMENTS/SPECIALTIES

	Instructor	Assistant Professor	Associate Professor	Professor	Chief	Chair
Count:	244	1,514	1,136	1,445	10	182
25th:	47	67	92	124	171	205
Median:	52	82	107	151	216	255
75th:	59	95	123	185	252	300
Mean:	54.7	82.6	110.3	160.1	221.3	259.9

Anatomy

	Instructor	Assistant Professor	Associate Professor	Professor	Chief	Chair
Count:	10	93	90	107	0	16
25th:	50	65	90	115		177
Median:	56	76	100	130		206
75th:	59	85	112	161		278
Mean:	57.4	76.0	101.8	139.3		217.4

Biochemistry

	Instructor	Assistant Professor	Associate Professor	Professor	Chief	Chair
Count:	35	213	182	267	0	32
25th:	49	64	89	119		200
Median:	55	75	100	147		257
75th:	58	90	119	189		301
Mean:	54.2	77.0	104.7	160.2		259.4

Bioethics/Medical Humanities

	Instructor	Assistant Professor	Associate Professor	Professor	Chief	Chair
Count:	0	21	12	9	0	2
25th:		80	101	100		
Median:		82	111	126		
75th:		96	140	206		
Mean:		87.9	124.4	147.4		

Biomedical Informatics

	Instructor	Assistant Professor	Associate Professor	Professor	Chief	Chair
Count:	3	21	9	1	0	0
25th:		102	104			
Median:		108	140			
75th:		123	167			
Mean:		111.8	143.3			

TABLE 22 Summary Statistics on Medical School Faculty Compensation for Southern Region Ph.D. or Other Doctoral Degree, Basic Science Departments/Specialties Total Compensation in Thousands of Dollars (continued)

Biostatistics

	Instructor	Assistant Professor	Associate Professor	Professor	Chief	Chair
Count:	4	91	46	41	3	5
25th:		93	113	155		241
Median:		98	125	180		269
75th:		104	138	197		331
Mean:		99.0	128.0	180.2		282.4

Genetics

	Instructor	Assistant Professor	Associate Professor	Professor	Chief	Chair
Count:	24	131	63	48	1	6
25th:	53	73	105	156		322
Median:	60	92	123	207		361
75th:	70	111	142	247		600
Mean:	62.5	93.2	129.0	204.0		428.7

Microbiology

	Instructor	Assistant Professor	Associate Professor	Professor	Chief	Chair
Count:	11	195	165	219	1	29
25th:	48	65	92	120		215
Median:	52	80	104	143		250
75th:	56	89	120	180		277
Mean:	52.9	77.7	108.5	154.1		251.0

Molecular & Cellular Biology

	Instructor	Assistant Professor	Associate Professor	Professor	Chief	Chair
Count:	51	175	149	154	0	12
25th:	46	65	88	134		236
Median:	50	79	109	163		291
75th:	56	93	123	185		325
Mean:	52.0	79.6	108.9	165.3		286.4

Neurosciences

	Instructor	Assistant Professor	Associate Professor	Professor	Chief	Chair
Count:	17	88	72	84	0	11
25th:	46	62	97	135		237
Median:	50	83	111	157		249
75th:	52	92	123	183		343
Mean:	51.5	80.3	113.9	169.7		284.0

TABLE 22 Summary Statistics on Medical School Faculty Compensation for Southern Region Ph.D. or Other Doctoral Degree, Basic Science Departments/Specialties Total Compensation in Thousands of Dollars (continued)

Pharmacology

	Instructor	Assistant Professor	Associate Professor	Professor	Chief	Chair
Count:	32	201	135	223	2	32
25th:	46	66	91	123		194
Median:	50	84	102	145		255
75th:	57	94	115	183		293
Mean:	52.3	82.6	104.2	155.9		248.5

Physiology

	Instructor	Assistant Professor	Associate Professor	Professor	Chief	Chair
Count:	45	149	133	197	1	23
25th:	45	66	92	120		192
Median:	50	80	105	144		250
75th:	54	90	119	171		293
Mean:	51.4	78.1	106.5	149.5		246.0

Other Basic Sciences

	Instructor	Assistant Professor	Associate Professor	Professor	Chief	Chair
Count:	12	136	80	95	2	14
25th:	51	73	98	129		230
Median:	59	85	114	175		256
75th:	73	100	130	227		311
Mean:	61.9	86.8	121.2	182.1		268.8

TABLE 23

Summary Statistics on Medical School Faculty Compensation for Midwestern Region Ph.D. or Other Doctoral Degree, Basic Science Departments/Specialties Total Compensation in Thousands of Dollars

BASIC SCIENCE - TOTAL ALL DEPARTMENTS/SPECIALTIES

	Instructor	Assistant Professor	Associate Professor	Professor	Chief	Chair
Count:	100	930	787	1,050	5	125
25th:	43	74	93	127	173	201
Median:	50	85	104	151	187	254
75th:	63	95	121	181	230	308
Mean:	54.3	84.9	108.4	159.1	198.4	258.2

Anatomy

	Instructor	Assistant Professor	Associate Professor	Professor	Chief	Chair
Count:	12	78	78	85	0	11
25th:	48	72	87	121		190
Median:	50	84	102	141		254
75th:	58	95	117	165		314
Mean:	53.4	83.4	104.1	151.9		245.6

Biochemistry

	Instructor	Assistant Professor	Associate Professor	Professor	Chief	Chair
Count:	10	126	123	195	0	14
25th:	45	70	89	127		200
Median:	48	84	104	149		233
75th:	50	93	124	175		270
Mean:	49.7	84.6	107.0	153.9		236.9

Bioethics/Medical Humanities

	Instructor	Assistant Professor	Associate Professor	Professor	Chief	Chair
Count:	0	12	8	8	1	1
25th:		74	83	128		
Median:		85	89	141		
75th:		99	93	165		
Mean:		88.4	88.4	144.8		

Biomedical Informatics

	Instructor	Assistant Professor	Associate Professor	Professor	Chief	Chair
Count:	0	12	7	4	1	1
25th:		90	122			
Median:		111	137			
75th:		122	156			
Mean:		119.5	135.6			

TABLE 23 Summary Statistics on Medical School Faculty Compensation for Midwestern Region Ph.D. or Other Doctoral Degree, Basic Science Departments/Specialties Total Compensation in Thousands of Dollars (continued)

Biostatistics

	Instructor	Assistant Professor	Associate Professor	Professor	Chief	Chair
Count:	5	42	35	32	1	3
25th:	80	87	105	159		
Median:	86	93	115	174		
75th:	90	105	160	197		
Mean:	85.0	94.4	127.8	176.2		

Genetics

	Instructor	Assistant Professor	Associate Professor	Professor	Chief	Chair
Count:	7	45	45	42	0	4
25th:	67	80	96	122		
Median:	68	89	104	142		
75th:	70	99	131	164		
Mean:	76.0	89.4	115.3	159.5		

Microbiology

	Instructor	Assistant Professor	Associate Professor	Professor	Chief	Chair
Count:	11	107	94	139	0	18
25th:	37	71	93	129		213
Median:	43	87	104	150		252
75th:	52	95	123	176		322
Mean:	47.5	84.0	109.0	159.2		262.6

Molecular & Cellular Biology

	Instructor	Assistant Professor	Associate Professor	Professor	Chief	Chair
Count:	3	54	39	63	1	6
25th:		80	96	127		235
Median:		85	103	150		263
75th:		95	117	191		368
Mean:		84.7	104.6	165.1		301.2

Neurosciences

	Instructor	Assistant Professor	Associate Professor	Professor	Chief	Chair
Count:	0	42	39	50	0	6
25th:		71	95	129		198
Median:		85	101	145		232
75th:		92	112	169		263
Mean:		81.6	104.7	153.2		248.2

TABLE 23 Summary Statistics on Medical School Faculty Compensation for Midwestern Region Ph.D. or Other Doctoral Degree, Basic Science Departments/Specialties Total Compensation in Thousands of Dollars (continued)

Pharmacology

	Instructor	Assistant Professor	Associate Professor	Professor	Chief	Chair
Count:	12	128	109	125	1	25
25th:	45	63	93	127		199
Median:	46	81	104	153		256
75th:	53	90	116	185		323
Mean:	49.8	79.7	105.6	159.5		263.7

Physiology

	Instructor	Assistant Professor	Associate Professor	Professor	Chief	Chair
Count:	22	135	102	173	0	19
25th:	38	70	95	131		242
Median:	40	83	104	153		265
75th:	45	90	120	182		326
Mean:	44.6	80.8	107.3	160.8		282.8

Other Basic Sciences

	Instructor	Assistant Professor	Associate Professor	Professor	Chief	Chair
Count:	18	149	108	134	0	17
25th:	48	77	91	128		173
Median:	57	87	108	158		220
75th:	62	98	125	193		292
Mean:	59.7	88.8	109.6	164.4		234.0

TABLE 24 Summary Statistics on Medical School Faculty Compensation for Western Region Ph.D. or Other Doctoral Degree, Basic Science Departments/Specialties Total Compensation in Thousands of Dollars

BASIC SCIENCE - TOTAL ALL DEPARTMENTS/SPECIALTIES

	Instructor	Assistant Professor	Associate Professor	Professor	Chief	Chair
Count:	47	333	302	569	9	66
25th:	48	81	100	140	205	208
Median:	55	92	116	172	230	252
75th:	70	108	140	222	235	275
Mean:	61.9	93.7	120.0	187.8	224.1	248.3

Anatomy

	Instructor	Assistant Professor	Associate Professor	Professor	Chief	Chair
Count:	11	28	19	37	0	6
25th:	48	80	85	131		207
Median:	59	87	95	164		248
75th:	66	105	121	206		275
Mean:	57.1	93.1	100.5	177.1		248.7

Biochemistry

	Instructor	Assistant Professor	Associate Professor	Professor	Chief	Chair
Count:	0	41	51	85	0	10
25th:		80	107	145		190
Median:		93	116	181		224
75th:		114	130	237		258
Mean:		96.2	119.8	199.2		217.5

Bioethics/Medical Humanities

	Instructor	Assistant Professor	Associate Professor	Professor	Chief	Chair
Count:	0	3	3	3	0	0
25th:						
Median:						
75th:						
Mean:						

Biomedical Informatics

	Instructor	Assistant Professor	Associate Professor	Professor	Chief	Chair
Count:	1	13	6	6	1	1
25th:		92	126	153		
Median:		101	140	175		
75th:		108	160	200		
Mean:		101.9	151.0	189.8		

TABLE 24 Summary Statistics on Medical School Faculty Compensation for Western Region Ph.D. or Other Doctoral Degree, Basic Science Departments/Specialties Total Compensation in Thousands of Dollars (continued)

Biostatistics

	Instructor	Assistant Professor	Associate Professor	Professor	Chief	Chair
Count:	0	10	17	18	4	1
25th:		116	140	177		
Median:		128	148	193		
75th:		129	162	232		
Mean:		124.2	151.5	223.1		

Genetics

	Instructor	Assistant Professor	Associate Professor	Professor	Chief	Chair
Count:	0	21	25	44	0	2
25th:		85	106	152		
Median:		93	136	172		
75th:		106	150	214		
Mean:		94.8	128.4	187.3		

Microbiology

	Instructor	Assistant Professor	Associate Professor	Professor	Chief	Chair
Count:	7	40	33	74	0	8
25th:	50	81	93	144		207
Median:	55	96	107	180		242
75th:	64	112	133	230		286
Mean:	59.9	94.2	112.6	189.5		247.4

Molecular & Cellular Biology

	Instructor	Assistant Professor	Associate Professor	Professor	Chief	Chair
Count:	1	49	35	52	0	9
25th:		72	100	128		193
Median:		89	116	168		262
75th:		104	145	209		281
Mean:		88.2	122.5	175.7		253.3

Neurosciences

	Instructor	Assistant Professor	Associate Professor	Professor	Chief	Chair
Count:	0	11	15	37	0	2
25th:		95	100	140		
Median:		100	110	192		
75th:		120	145	233		
Mean:		105.2	119.7	193.4		

TABLE 24 Summary Statistics on Medical School Faculty Compensation for Western Region Ph.D. or Other Doctoral Degree, Basic Science Departments/Specialties Total Compensation in Thousands of Dollars (continued)

Pharmacology

	Instructor	Assistant Professor	Associate Professor	Professor	Chief	Chair
Count:	8	39	30	67	0	7
25th:	52	82	103	133		246
Median:	58	90	115	176		285
75th:	86	104	136	259		323
Mean:	68.3	91.6	121.5	206.4		291.4

Physiology

	Instructor	Assistant Professor	Associate Professor	Professor	Chief	Chair
Count:	7	42	32	91	0	11
25th:	43	79	103	140		247
Median:	50	91	114	161		269
75th:	52	100	129	196		291
Mean:	59.1	90.1	116.1	175.3		269.8

Other Basic Sciences

	Instructor	Assistant Professor	Associate Professor	Professor	Chief	Chair
Count:	12	36	36	55	4	9
25th:	47	75	92	128		193
Median:	62	87	111	159		213
75th:	74	106	139	205		262
Mean:	63.4	90.6	113.3	173.5		218.4

TABLE 25

Summary Statistics on Medical School Faculty Compensation for All Schools
Ph.D. or Other Doctoral Degree, Clinical Science Departments/Specialties
Total Compensation in Thousands of Dollars

CLINICAL SCIENCE - TOTAL ALL DEPARTMENTS/SPECIALTIES

	Instructor	Assistant Professor	Associate Professor	Professor	Chief	Chair
Count:	1,040	6,105	3,399	3,424	139	50
25th:	55	74	98	137	165	182
Median:	66	86	116	168	209	234
75th:	82	102	140	206	258	282
Mean:	72.7	92.6	124.0	177.7	214.9	253.5

Total Anesthesiology

	Instructor	Assistant Professor	Associate Professor	Professor	Chief	Chair
Count:	23	120	64	74	0	0
25th:	64	75	101	148		
Median:	77	89	124	178		
75th:	134	107	155	217		
Mean:	99.7	111.2	143.7	191.3		

Anesthesiology: General

	Instructor	Assistant Professor	Associate Professor	Professor	Chief	Chair
Count:	21	111	60	67	0	0
25th:	62	75	100	148		
Median:	77	90	124	178		
75th:	134	109	155	217		
Mean:	94.5	112.9	144.1	191.2		

Anesthesiology: Pain Management

	Instructor	Assistant Professor	Associate Professor	Professor	Chief	Chair
Count:	1	7	3	6	0	0
25th:		80		158		
Median:		88		168		
75th:		100		190		
Mean:		90.7		180.5		

Anesthesiology: Pediatric

	Instructor	Assistant Professor	Associate Professor	Professor	Chief	Chair
Count:	1	2	1	1	0	0
25th:						
Median:						
75th:						
Mean:						

TABLE 25

Summary Statistics on Medical School Faculty Compensation for All Schools Ph.D. or Other Doctoral Degree, Clinical Science Departments/Specialties Total Compensation in Thousands of Dollars (continued)

Total Dermatology

	Instructor	Assistant Professor	Associate Professor	Professor	Chief	Chair
Count:	11	57	24	32	1	0
25th:	52	74	100	125		
Median:	55	87	130	160		
75th:	72	101	162	216		
Mean:	60.6	95.3	136.9	169.2		

Dermatology (excluding Mohs Surgery)

	Instructor	Assistant Professor	Associate Professor	Professor	Chief	Chair
Count:	11	56	24	30	1	0
25th:	52	74	100	122		
Median:	55	87	130	163		
75th:	72	100	162	220		
Mean:	60.6	94.2	136.9	170.3		

Dermatology: Mohs Surgery

	Instructor	Assistant Professor	Associate Professor	Professor	Chief	Chair
Count:	0	1	0	2	0	0
25th:						
Median:						
75th:						
Mean:						

Total Medicine

	Instructor	Assistant Professor	Associate Professor	Professor	Chief	Chair
Count:	271	1,407	691	562	19	5
25th:	52	69	94	134	180	186
Median:	60	82	113	166	205	252
75th:	70	95	135	200	225	389
Mean:	64.3	85.3	117.4	173.0	207.3	280.0

Allergy/Immunology-Med.

	Instructor	Assistant Professor	Associate Professor	Professor	Chief	Chair
Count:	10	27	25	23	1	1
25th:	50	78	100	144		
Median:	57	88	122	171		
75th:	62	97	137	200		
Mean:	56.8	90.3	119.4	170.5		

TABLE 25 Summary Statistics on Medical School Faculty Compensation for All Schools Ph.D. or Other Doctoral Degree, Clinical Science Departments/Specialties Total Compensation in Thousands of Dollars (continued)

Cardiology: Total

	Instructor	Assistant Professor	Associate Professor	Professor	Chief	Chair
Count:	20	149	67	62	0	0
25th:	54	66	92	133		
Median:	59	78	118	163		
75th:	74	95	141	200		
Mean:	62.3	84.5	122.6	173.9		

Cardiology: Invasive Interventional-Med.

	Instructor	Assistant Professor	Associate Professor	Professor	Chief	Chair
Count:	0	17	10	7	0	0
25th:		63	91	136		
Median:		84	127	151		
75th:		116	135	230		
Mean:		87.1	120.0	172.1		

Cardiology: Invasive Non-interventional-Med.

	Instructor	Assistant Professor	Associate Professor	Professor	Chief	Chair
Count:	2	0	0	2	0	0
25th:						
Median:						
75th:						
Mean:						

Cardiology: Non-invasive-Med.

	Instructor	Assistant Professor	Associate Professor	Professor	Chief	Chair
Count:	18	132	57	53	0	0
25th:	53	67	94	131		
Median:	59	78	113	163		
75th:	74	93	143	196		
Mean:	62.3	84.2	123.0	171.2		

Critical/Intensive Care-Med.

	Instructor	Assistant Professor	Associate Professor	Professor	Chief	Chair
Count:	1	0	2	0	0	0
25th:						
Median:						
75th:						
Mean:						

Summary Statistics on Medical School Faculty Compensation for All Schools Ph.D. or Other Doctoral Degree, Clinical Science Departments/Specialties Total Compensation in Thousands of Dollars (continued)

Endocrinology-Med.

	Instructor	Assistant Professor	Associate Professor	Professor	Chief	Chair
Count:	28	117	66	42	2	0
25th:	50	62	95	133		
Median:	55	75	109	158		
75th:	67	89	125	185		
Mean:	62.8	78.4	114.5	161.0		

Gastroenterology-Med.

	Instructor	Assistant Professor	Associate Professor	Professor	Chief	Chair
Count:	17	88	43	31	0	0
25th:	50	70	100	133		
Median:	60	82	109	162		
75th:	68	92	136	214		
Mean:	60.1	85.2	116.8	180.0		

General Internal Medicine

	Instructor	Assistant Professor	Associate Professor	Professor	Chief	Chair
Count:	24	127	83	71	0	0
25th:	64	75	102	130		
Median:	82	90	124	174		
75th:	104	108	150	206		
Mean:	90.1	95.7	128.5	177.3		

Geriatrics-Med.

	Instructor	Assistant Professor	Associate Professor	Professor	Chief	Chair
Count:	8	65	32	29	1	0
25th:	54	74	95	123		
Median:	60	84	105	170		
75th:	64	98	121	188		
Mean:	59.6	87.2	111.8	167.8		

Hematology/Oncology-Med.

	Instructor	Assistant Professor	Associate Professor	Professor	Chief	Chair
Count:	58	232	104	111	4	0
25th:	52	72	97	132		
Median:	59	82	124	168		
75th:	69	94	141	225		
Mean:	63.7	84.6	121.4	178.8		

TABLE 25 Summary Statistics on Medical School Faculty Compensation for All Schools Ph.D. or Other Doctoral Degree, Clinical Science Departments/Specialties Total Compensation in Thousands of Dollars (continued)

Hospital Medicine

	Instructor	Assistant Professor	Associate Professor	Professor	Chief	Chair
Count:	0	1	0	0	0	0
25th:						
Median:						
75th:						
Mean:						

Infectious Disease-Med.

	Instructor	Assistant Professor	Associate Professor	Professor	Chief	Chair
Count:	27	122	42	38	2	0
25th:	53	72	95	136		
Median:	60	85	107	154		
75th:	65	97	139	189		
Mean:	60.1	87.4	113.9	164.3		

Nephrology-Med.

	Instructor	Assistant Professor	Associate Professor	Professor	Chief	Chair
Count:	12	90	46	25	0	0
25th:	52	62	84	125		
Median:	64	77	90	148		
75th:	75	92	110	182		
Mean:	63.6	79.6	101.4	158.7		

Pulmonary-Med.

	Instructor	Assistant Professor	Associate Professor	Professor	Chief	Chair
Count:	16	123	44	37	0	0
25th:	50	63	90	147		
Median:	54	75	107	170		
75th:	66	84	124	194		
Mean:	58.5	77.9	109.1	170.4		

Rheumatology-Med.

	Instructor	Assistant Professor	Associate Professor	Professor	Chief	Chair
Count:	10	52	21	28	0	0
25th:	55	62	89	140		
Median:	65	80	103	160		
75th:	70	92	124	172		
Mean:	64.6	81.4	110.1	157.0		

Other Medicine

	Instructor	Assistant Professor	Associate Professor	Professor	Chief	Chair
Count:	40	214	116	65	9	4
25th:	54	75	97	148	144	
Median:	61	87	116	183	197	
75th:	66	99	133	218	241	
Mean:	60.8	89.1	118.4	184.2	197.2	

Total OB/GYN

	Instructor	Assistant Professor	Associate Professor	Professor	Chief	Chair
Count:	22	129	94	98	3	1
25th:	53	78	96	138		
Median:	61	89	109	165		
75th:	75	109	128	217		
Mean:	65.5	97.3	121.2	179.5		

OB/GYN: General

	Instructor	Assistant Professor	Associate Professor	Professor	Chief	Chair
Count:	7	40	35	35	0	0
25th:	58	81	100	140		
Median:	62	89	115	167		
75th:	76	107	128	217		
Mean:	74.0	98.7	123.2	176.8		

OB/GYN: Gynecologic Oncology

	Instructor	Assistant Professor	Associate Professor	Professor	Chief	Chair
Count:	1	2	2	6	0	0
25th:				135		
Median:				166		
75th:				215		
Mean:				175.0		

OB/GYN: Maternal & Fetal

	Instructor	Assistant Professor	Associate Professor	Professor	Chief	Chair
Count:	1	8	5	5	0	0
25th:		75	101	142		
Median:		84	120	149		
75th:		95	257	194		
Mean:		82.6	167.0	163.8		

TABLE 25 Summary Statistics on Medical School Faculty Compensation for All Schools Ph.D. or Other Doctoral Degree, Clinical Science Departments/Specialties Total Compensation in Thousands of Dollars (continued)

OB/GYN: Reproductive Endocrinology

	Instructor	Assistant Professor	Associate Professor	Professor	Chief	Chair
Count:	1	31	13	19	1	1
25th:		81	89	156		
Median:		112	120	205		
75th:		136	173	288		
Mean:		117.6	133.9	223.1		

OB/GYN: Other OB/GYN

	Instructor	Assistant Professor	Associate Professor	Professor	Chief	Chair
Count:	12	48	39	33	2	0
25th:	45	75	95	122		
Median:	58	85	107	157		
75th:	71	93	124	189		
Mean:	61.3	85.8	110.8	160.6		

Total Pathology

	Instructor	Assistant Professor	Associate Professor	Professor	Chief	Chair
Count:	81	508	333	486	12	2
25th:	50	72	106	142	202	
Median:	62	92	124	172	246	
75th:	80	112	155	205	279	
Mean:	65.2	98.4	131.1	180.3	245.1	

Pathology: Anatomic

	Instructor	Assistant Professor	Associate Professor	Professor	Chief	Chair
Count:	15	80	63	70	0	0
25th:	62	85	108	142		
Median:	72	111	127	169		
75th:	98	163	181	203		
Mean:	75.8	123.9	136.3	180.6		

Pathology: Clinical

	Instructor	Assistant Professor	Associate Professor	Professor	Chief	Chair
Count:	20	108	91	136	4	2
25th:	50	82	117	150		
Median:	66	102	140	181		
75th:	80	122	170	221		
Mean:	65.2	108.1	144.3	190.9		

TABLE 25 Summary Statistics on Medical School Faculty Compensation for All Schools Ph.D. or Other Doctoral Degree, Clinical Science Departments/Specialties Total Compensation in Thousands of Dollars (continued)

Pathology: Other Pathology

	Instructor	Assistant Professor	Associate Professor	Professor	Chief	Chair
Count:	46	320	179	280	8	0
25th:	50	67	98	139	192	
Median:	58	87	115	168	223	
75th:	74	102	139	201	274	
Mean:	61.7	88.7	122.5	175.0	233.9	

Total Pediatrics

	Instructor	Assistant Professor	Associate Professor	Professor	Chief	Chair
Count:	105	776	379	337	23	2
25th:	59	75	96	132	170	
Median:	70	86	111	165	209	
75th:	86	98	132	203	296	
Mean:	72.8	89.1	116.8	171.1	230.0	

Adolescent Medicine

	Instructor	Assistant Professor	Associate Professor	Professor	Chief	Chair
Count:	0	10	4	4	0	0
25th:		76				
Median:		82				
75th:		88				
Mean:		81.5				

Allergy/Immunology-Peds.

	Instructor	Assistant Professor	Associate Professor	Professor	Chief	Chair
Count:	1	16	7	2	0	0
25th:		76	91			
Median:		88	109			
75th:		95	114			
Mean:		85.5	106.0			

Child & Adolescent Psychiatry

	Instructor	Assistant Professor	Associate Professor	Professor	Chief	Chair
Count:	8	80	43	40	4	0
25th:	70	77	99	132		
Median:	75	85	112	172		
75th:	84	91	130	211		
Mean:	79.6	89.9	117.9	174.1		

Critical/Intensive Care-Peds.

	Instructor	Assistant Professor	Associate Professor	Professor	Chief	Chair
Count:	6	7	3	4	0	0
25th:	78	66				
Median:	89	98				
75th:	93	103				
Mean:	84.7	88.3				

Emergency Medicine-Peds.

	Instructor	Assistant Professor	Associate Professor	Professor	Chief	Chair
Count:	1	4	1	0	0	0
25th:						
Median:						
75th:						
Mean:						

Endocrinology-Peds.

	Instructor	Assistant Professor	Associate Professor	Professor	Chief	Chair
Count:	5	20	5	7	0	0
25th:	47	69	82	123		
Median:	50	79	100	177		
75th:	64	89	105	206		
Mean:	54.4	81.5	94.8	168.6		

Gastroenterology-Peds.

	Instructor	Assistant Professor	Associate Professor	Professor	Chief	Chair
Count:	4	14	12	5	0	0
25th:		75	96	136		
Median:		86	126	169		
75th:		100	144	210		
Mean:		89.9	130.7	172.0		

General Pediatrics

	Instructor	Assistant Professor	Associate Professor	Professor	Chief	Chair
Count:	22	89	40	42	1	1
25th:	52	77	96	135		
Median:	65	86	108	157		
75th:	72	99	122	187		
Mean:	65.7	90.7	111.9	163.4		

Genetics-Peds.

	Instructor	Assistant Professor	Associate Professor	Professor	Chief	Chair
Count:	2	32	24	22	3	0
25th:		75	91	112		
Median:		85	103	141		
75th:		96	121	187		
Mean:		89.3	107.8	156.6		

Hematology/Oncology-Peds.

	Instructor	Assistant Professor	Associate Professor	Professor	Chief	Chair
Count:	9	71	31	16	0	0
25th:	55	75	88	147		
Median:	65	82	118	199		
75th:	94	96	140	237		
Mean:	73.1	84.8	117.1	195.5		

Hospital Medicine-Peds.

	Instructor	Assistant Professor	Associate Professor	Professor	Chief	Chair
Count:	0	0	0	0	0	0
25th:						
Median:						
75th:						
Mean:						

Infectious Disease-Peds.

	Instructor	Assistant Professor	Associate Professor	Professor	Chief	Chair
Count:	8	28	13	10	0	0
25th:	56	70	106	123		
Median:	71	84	106	152		
75th:	108	100	133	176		
Mean:	80.1	88.5	116.1	150.1		

Neonatology

	Instructor	Assistant Professor	Associate Professor	Professor	Chief	Chair
Count:	5	41	24	23	0	0
25th:	67	68	89	145		
Median:	70	78	106	172		
75th:	98	98	142	200		
Mean:	80.0	87.8	113.8	170.6		

TABLE 25 Summary Statistics on Medical School Faculty Compensation for All Schools Ph.D. or Other Doctoral Degree, Clinical Science Departments/Specialties Total Compensation in Thousands of Dollars (continued)

Nephrology-Peds.

	Instructor	Assistant Professor	Associate Professor	Professor	Chief	Chair
Count:	0	8	1	1	0	0
25th:		68				
Median:		75				
75th:		83				
Mean:		75.3				

Neurology-Peds.

	Instructor	Assistant Professor	Associate Professor	Professor	Chief	Chair
Count:	6	26	8	10	0	0
25th:	60	73	114	135		
Median:	74	86	125	177		
75th:	75	98	136	230		
Mean:	79.7	85.7	129.3	182.7		

Pediatric Cardiology

	Instructor	Assistant Professor	Associate Professor	Professor	Chief	Chair
Count:	3	13	7	6	0	0
25th:		71	94	128		
Median:		93	100	168		
75th:		102	120	253		
Mean:		96.5	104.7	185.8		

Pulmonary-Peds.

	Instructor	Assistant Professor	Associate Professor	Professor	Chief	Chair
Count:	2	21	11	9	0	0
25th:		70	80	115		
Median:		82	90	127		
75th:		89	129	164		
Mean:		79.8	103.9	135.0		

Rheumatology-Peds.

	Instructor	Assistant Professor	Associate Professor	Professor	Chief	Chair
Count:	0	2	2	1	0	0
25th:						
Median:						
75th:						
Mean:						

TABLE 25

Summary Statistics on Medical School Faculty Compensation for All Schools
Ph.D. or Other Doctoral Degree, Clinical Science Departments/Specialties
Total Compensation in Thousands of Dollars (continued)

Other Pediatrics

	Instructor	Assistant Professor	Associate Professor	Professor	Chief	Chair
Count:	23	294	143	135	15	1
25th:	61	76	100	138	183	
Median:	69	89	116	166	221	
75th:	90	101	133	208	303	
Mean:	73.7	91.2	119.8	176.6	248.9	

Total Radiology

	Instructor	Assistant Professor	Associate Professor	Professor	Chief	Chair
Count:	136	595	380	330	28	3
25th:	61	85	115	161	199	
Median:	75	102	142	194	227	
75th:	108	139	180	227	278	
Mean:	85.9	116.5	151.1	201.3	235.7	

Diagnostic Radiology: Total

	Instructor	Assistant Professor	Associate Professor	Professor	Chief	Chair
Count:	68	175	130	111	7	0
25th:	59	85	111	165	175	
Median:	74	95	132	191	212	
75th:	90	110	163	225	240	
Mean:	76.6	109.8	141.6	201.4	203.4	

Diagnostic Radiology: Interventional

	Instructor	Assistant Professor	Associate Professor	Professor	Chief	Chair
Count:	3	7	1	4	0	0
25th:		72				
Median:		115				
75th:		257				
Mean:		171.1				

Diagnostic Radiology: Non-interventional

	Instructor	Assistant Professor	Associate Professor	Professor	Chief	Chair
Count:	65	168	129	107	7	0
25th:	61	85	110	165	175	
Median:	75	95	131	190	212	
75th:	90	107	163	225	240	
Mean:	77.2	107.2	141.0	201.4	203.4	

Summary Statistics on Medical School Faculty Compensation for All Schools Ph.D. or Other Doctoral Degree, Clinical Science Departments/Specialties Total Compensation in Thousands of Dollars (continued)

Nuclear Medicine

	Instructor	Assistant Professor	Associate Professor	Professor	Chief	Chair
Count:	2	10	8	11	1	0
25th:		60	88	148		
Median:		81	117	202		
75th:		102	140	241		
Mean:		82.0	116.9	207.6		

Radiation Oncology

	Instructor	Assistant Professor	Associate Professor	Professor	Chief	Chair
Count:	46	241	121	112	16	0
25th:	65	99	143	180	208	
Median:	107	134	180	206	253	
75th:	135	160	216	250	304	
Mean:	107.3	133.2	178.3	213.5	256.3	

Other Radiology

	Instructor	Assistant Professor	Associate Professor	Professor	Chief	Chair
Count:	20	169	121	96	4	3
25th:	61	80	112	146		
Median:	66	95	134	178		
75th:	73	110	155	208		
Mean:	68.0	101.5	136.3	186.2		

Total Surgery

	Instructor	Assistant Professor	Associate Professor	Professor	Chief	Chair
Count:	100	465	251	295	13	2
25th:	54	68	98	133	226	
Median:	65	82	117	172	285	
75th:	88	99	136	216	314	
Mean:	72.5	88.8	128.6	184.5	253.2	

General Surgery

	Instructor	Assistant Professor	Associate Professor	Professor	Chief	Chair
Count:	25	77	38	44	2	0
25th:	55	71	101	133		
Median:	79	85	115	160		
75th:	103	106	145	206		
Mean:	81.6	95.3	131.2	172.7		

TABLE 25 Summary Statistics on Medical School Faculty Compensation for All Schools Ph.D. or Other Doctoral Degree, Clinical Science Departments/Specialties Total Compensation in Thousands of Dollars (continued)

Neurosurgery

	Instructor	Assistant Professor	Associate Professor	Professor	Chief	Chair
Count:	18	94	42	61	1	1
25th:	55	65	101	142		
Median:	62	82	125	183		
75th:	71	91	136	214		
Mean:	66.8	91.4	145.5	189.3		

Orthopaedic Surgery

	Instructor	Assistant Professor	Associate Professor	Professor	Chief	Chair
Count:	22	86	58	63	3	0
25th:	52	72	93	129		
Median:	56	84	110	180		
75th:	96	104	136	235		
Mean:	75.3	93.3	133.4	184.1		

Pediatric Surgery

	Instructor	Assistant Professor	Associate Professor	Professor	Chief	Chair
Count:	4	17	5	0	0	0
25th:		58	80			
Median:		74	103			
75th:		92	119			
Mean:		76.1	100.0			

Plastic Surgery

	Instructor	Assistant Professor	Associate Professor	Professor	Chief	Chair
Count:	0	8	4	6	0	0
25th:		63		101		
Median:		78		132		
75th:		92		203		
Mean:		80.9		154.0		

Surgical Oncology

	Instructor	Assistant Professor	Associate Professor	Professor	Chief	Chair
Count:	2	18	4	3	0	0
25th:		58				
Median:		75				
75th:		96				
Mean:		81.1				

TABLE 25 Summary Statistics on Medical School Faculty Compensation for All Schools Ph.D. or Other Doctoral Degree, Clinical Science Departments/Specialties Total Compensation in Thousands of Dollars (continued)

Thoracic & Cardiovascular Surgery

	Instructor	Assistant Professor	Associate Professor	Professor	Chief	Chair
Count:	2	21	14	16	1	0
25th:		68	85	121		
Median:		80	117	153		
75th:		102	133	185		
Mean:		86.1	116.4	153.9		

Transplant Surgery

	Instructor	Assistant Professor	Associate Professor	Professor	Chief	Chair
Count:	10	22	16	17	0	1
25th:	57	69	108	179		
Median:	62	93	127	203		
75th:	80	103	153	313		
Mean:	68.8	90.7	128.6	232.1		

Trauma/Critical Care Surgery

	Instructor	Assistant Professor	Associate Professor	Professor	Chief	Chair
Count:	1	10	3	7	0	0
25th:		65		150		
Median:		68		208		
75th:		73		210		
Mean:		69.1		179.1		

Urology

	Instructor	Assistant Professor	Associate Professor	Professor	Chief	Chair
Count:	7	49	28	36	1	0
25th:	55	66	108	142		
Median:	59	80	121	171		
75th:	88	98	139	202		
Mean:	66.4	82.2	122.1	178.1		

Vascular Surgery

	Instructor	Assistant Professor	Associate Professor	Professor	Chief	Chair
Count:	2	7	3	3	0	0
25th:		73				
Median:		85				
75th:		121				
Mean:		95.4				

TABLE 25 Summary Statistics on Medical School Faculty Compensation for All Schools Ph.D. or Other Doctoral Degree, Clinical Science Departments/Specialties Total Compensation in Thousands of Dollars (continued)

Other Surgery

	Instructor	Assistant Professor	Associate Professor	Professor	Chief	Chair
Count:	7	56	36	39	5	0
25th:	53	71	96	130	260	
Median:	60	86	114	167	299	
75th:	69	98	126	248	325	
Mean:	61.4	84.8	112.6	196.5	293.4	

Other Clinical Science

Community Health

	Instructor	Assistant Professor	Associate Professor	Professor	Chief	Chair
Count:	9	112	70	77	6	7
25th:	53	80	95	140	134	182
Median:	75	90	109	163	152	206
75th:	97	102	139	210	170	235
Mean:	74.0	92.9	117.3	172.7	148.2	204.3

Emergency Medicine

	Instructor	Assistant Professor	Associate Professor	Professor	Chief	Chair
Count:	3	26	13	11	1	0
25th:		68	93	125		
Median:		92	135	149		
75th:		150	170	165		
Mean:		123.8	135.9	165.7		

Family Medicine

	Instructor	Assistant Professor	Associate Professor	Professor	Chief	Chair
Count:	15	163	95	90	4	4
25th:	60	75	91	109		
Median:	71	85	105	131		
75th:	75	98	123	159		
Mean:	68.7	88.5	109.6	138.1		

Neurology

	Instructor	Assistant Professor	Associate Professor	Professor	Chief	Chair
Count:	72	295	126	128	4	1
25th:	53	72	94	138		
Median:	63	88	113	170		
75th:	75	104	138	203		
Mean:	68.2	91.4	120.0	188.1		

TABLE 25 Summary Statistics on Medical School Faculty Compensation for All Schools Ph.D. or Other Doctoral Degree, Clinical Science Departments/Specialties Total Compensation in Thousands of Dollars (continued)

Ophthalmology

	Instructor	Assistant Professor	Associate Professor	Professor	Chief	Chair
Count:	19	139	96	126	0	0
25th:	47	70	98	137		
Median:	65	81	112	164		
75th:	98	97	130	200		
Mean:	71.4	87.0	115.4	172.2		

Otolaryngology

	Instructor	Assistant Professor	Associate Professor	Professor	Chief	Chair
Count:	10	80	62	77	3	0
25th:	59	74	89	133		
Median:	71	83	103	169		
75th:	107	94	121	195		
Mean:	81.5	88.7	109.7	164.8		

Physical Medicine & Rehabilitation

	Instructor	Assistant Professor	Associate Professor	Professor	Chief	Chair
Count:	24	136	98	47	3	6
25th:	66	76	92	114		176
Median:	70	83	99	127		184
75th:	83	91	118	153		193
Mean:	79.3	86.0	107.3	136.8		184.3

Preventive Medicine

	Instructor	Assistant Professor	Associate Professor	Professor	Chief	Chair
Count:	5	126	86	76	1	6
25th:	55	83	110	151		219
Median:	70	92	125	176		293
75th:	79	100	143	196		398
Mean:	67.4	92.4	127.1	184.2		329.2

Psychiatry

	Instructor	Assistant Professor	Associate Professor	Professor	Chief	Chair
Count:	124	881	468	509	16	3
25th:	64	75	98	139	133	
Median:	75	85	112	164	176	
75th:	90	100	136	208	229	
Mean:	79.7	89.7	119.5	175.8	177.1	

TABLE 25

Summary Statistics on Medical School Faculty Compensation for All Schools Ph.D. or Other Doctoral Degree, Clinical Science Departments/Specialties Total Compensation in Thousands of Dollars (continued)

Other

	Instructor	Assistant Professor	Associate Professor	Professor	Chief	Chair
Count:	10	90	69	69	2	8
25th:	70	71	95	138		149
Median:	75	85	114	161		238
75th:	85	100	131	199		276
Mean:	77.5	86.7	114.7	174.1		231.5

TABLE 26

Summary Statistics on Medical School Faculty Compensation for Public Schools Ph.D. or Other Doctoral Degree, Clinical Science Departments/Specialties Total Compensation in Thousands of Dollars

CLINICAL SCIENCE - TOTAL ALL DEPARTMENTS/SPECIALTIES

	Instructor	Assistant Professor	Associate Professor	Professor	Chief	Chair
Count:	345	3,006	1,835	2,028	76	30
25th:	53	73	95	133	167	188
Median:	65	85	111	164	202	223
75th:	77	99	135	200	251	270
Mean:	68.3	89.5	118.8	174.0	213.1	236.0

Total Anesthesiology

	Instructor	Assistant Professor	Associate Professor	Professor	Chief	Chair
Count:	12	57	34	42	0	0
25th:	60	74	88	158		
Median:	79	80	115	178		
75th:	98	98	138	217		
Mean:	89.9	92.6	140.2	189.7		

Anesthesiology: General

	Instructor	Assistant Professor	Associate Professor	Professor	Chief	Chair
Count:	10	50	32	37	0	0
25th:	50	73	88	151		
Median:	77	80	122	178		
75th:	86	96	147	217		
Mean:	77.1	92.8	142.5	189.9		

Anesthesiology: Pain Management

	Instructor	Assistant Professor	Associate Professor	Professor	Chief	Chair
Count:	1	5	2	4	0	0
25th:		84				
Median:		88				
75th:		104				
Mean:		92.4				

Anesthesiology: Pediatric

	Instructor	Assistant Professor	Associate Professor	Professor	Chief	Chair
Count:	1	2	0	1	0	0
25th:						
Median:						
75th:						
Mean:						

TABLE 26

Summary Statistics on Medical School Faculty Compensation for Public Schools
Ph.D. or Other Doctoral Degree, Clinical Science Departments/Specialties
Total Compensation in Thousands of Dollars (continued)

Total Dermatology

	Instructor	Assistant Professor	Associate Professor	Professor	Chief	Chair
Count:	6	21	10	14	1	0
25th:	49	71	96	108		
Median:	53	91	103	134		
75th:	55	100	140	185		
Mean:	52.7	88.7	124.3	154.8		

Dermatology (excluding Mohs Surgery)

	Instructor	Assistant Professor	Associate Professor	Professor	Chief	Chair
Count:	6	21	10	14	1	0
25th:	49	71	96	108		
Median:	53	91	103	134		
75th:	55	100	140	185		
Mean:	52.7	88.7	124.3	154.8		

Dermatology: Mohs Surgery

	Instructor	Assistant Professor	Associate Professor	Professor	Chief	Chair
Count:	0	0	0	0	0	0
25th:						
Median:						
75th:						
Mean:						

Total Medicine

	Instructor	Assistant Professor	Associate Professor	Professor	Chief	Chair
Count:	97	686	367	321	7	4
25th:	50	67	90	126	198	
Median:	56	81	107	159	206	
75th:	65	93	129	195	270	
Mean:	59.2	82.6	112.8	169.7	222.0	

Allergy/Immunology-Med.

	Instructor	Assistant Professor	Associate Professor	Professor	Chief	Chair
Count:	3	11	11	9	0	1
25th:		78	86	124		
Median:		84	94	170		
75th:		95	136	217		
Mean:		84.9	105.6	168.2		

Summary Statistics on Medical School Faculty Compensation for Public Schools Ph.D. or Other Doctoral Degree, Clinical Science Departments/Specialties Total Compensation in Thousands of Dollars (continued)

Cardiology: Total

	Instructor	Assistant Professor	Associate Professor	Professor	Chief	Chair
Count:	9	69	38	42	0	0
25th:	49	65	89	125		
Median:	54	78	111	158		
75th:	70	95	134	200		
Mean:	60.1	82.5	117.4	170.3		

Cardiology: Invasive Interventional-Med.

	Instructor	Assistant Professor	Associate Professor	Professor	Chief	Chair
Count:	0	5	0	3	0	0
25th:		64				
Median:		114				
75th:		129				
Mean:		99.6				

Cardiology: Invasive Non-interventional-Med.

	Instructor	Assistant Professor	Associate Professor	Professor	Chief	Chair
Count:	0	0	0	2	0	0
25th:						
Median:						
75th:						
Mean:						

Cardiology: Non-invasive-Med.

	Instructor	Assistant Professor	Associate Professor	Professor	Chief	Chair
Count:	9	64	38	37	0	0
25th:	49	65	89	126		
Median:	54	78	111	158		
75th:	70	93	134	197		
Mean:	60.1	81.2	117.4	167.7		

Critical/Intensive Care-Med.

	Instructor	Assistant Professor	Associate Professor	Professor	Chief	Chair
Count:	1	0	1	0	0	0
25th:						
Median:						
75th:						
Mean:						

TABLE 26

Summary Statistics on Medical School Faculty Compensation for Public Schools Ph.D. or Other Doctoral Degree, Clinical Science Departments/Specialties Total Compensation in Thousands of Dollars (continued)

Endocrinology-Med.

	Instructor	Assistant Professor	Associate Professor	Professor	Chief	Chair
Count:	14	80	32	26	2	0
25th:	46	60	91	146		
Median:	53	73	102	161		
75th:	56	86	117	185		
Mean:	50.9	74.7	106.7	164.1		

Gastroenterology-Med.

	Instructor	Assistant Professor	Associate Professor	Professor	Chief	Chair
Count:	8	50	25	20	0	0
25th:	51	65	101	124		
Median:	54	83	114	180		
75th:	66	91	130	230		
Mean:	59.8	79.9	114.5	193.9		

General Internal Medicine

	Instructor	Assistant Professor	Associate Professor	Professor	Chief	Chair
Count:	2	55	46	36	0	0
25th:		67	101	124		
Median:		85	112	172		
75th:		100	137	200		
Mean:		87.6	119.9	173.8		

Geriatrics-Med.

	Instructor	Assistant Professor	Associate Professor	Professor	Chief	Chair
Count:	4	36	19	24	1	0
25th:		74	95	126		
Median:		90	106	171		
75th:		99	122	197		
Mean:		90.4	118.2	177.6		

Hematology/Oncology-Med.

	Instructor	Assistant Professor	Associate Professor	Professor	Chief	Chair
Count:	10	85	41	47	1	0
25th:	47	70	86	110		
Median:	49	82	115	157		
75th:	59	91	136	209		
Mean:	52.7	81.0	114.8	171.1		

TABLE 26 Summary Statistics on Medical School Faculty Compensation for Public Schools Ph.D. or Other Doctoral Degree, Clinical Science Departments/Specialties Total Compensation in Thousands of Dollars (continued)

Hospital Medicine

	Instructor	Assistant Professor	Associate Professor	Professor	Chief	Chair
Count:	0	1	0	0	0	0
25th:						
Median:						
75th:						
Mean:						

Infectious Disease-Med.

	Instructor	Assistant Professor	Associate Professor	Professor	Chief	Chair
Count:	14	63	27	30	1	0
25th:	52	66	95	136		
Median:	54	82	107	156		
75th:	62	93	139	190		
Mean:	56.4	83.8	113.2	167.7		

Nephrology-Med.

	Instructor	Assistant Professor	Associate Professor	Professor	Chief	Chair
Count:	5	38	26	11	0	0
25th:	48	66	80	116		
Median:	65	75	89	128		
75th:	70	89	99	157		
Mean:	60.2	80.2	96.7	133.4		

Pulmonary-Med.

	Instructor	Assistant Professor	Associate Professor	Professor	Chief	Chair
Count:	8	68	26	24	0	0
25th:	50	63	87	139		
Median:	58	74	101	163		
75th:	64	84	120	190		
Mean:	57.9	78.6	101.4	166.3		

Rheumatology-Med.

	Instructor	Assistant Professor	Associate Professor	Professor	Chief	Chair
Count:	3	28	14	17	0	0
25th:		62	82	146		
Median:		78	97	168		
75th:		88	106	177		
Mean:		75.8	106.6	163.8		

TABLE 26 **Summary Statistics on Medical School Faculty Compensation for Public Schools Ph.D. or Other Doctoral Degree, Clinical Science Departments/Specialties Total Compensation in Thousands of Dollars (continued)**

Other Medicine

	Instructor	Assistant Professor	Associate Professor	Professor	Chief	Chair
Count:	16	102	61	35	2	3
25th:	57	75	101	126		
Median:	65	87	115	168		
75th:	67	102	136	200		
Mean:	64.6	89.8	118.5	166.9		

Total OB/GYN

	Instructor	Assistant Professor	Associate Professor	Professor	Chief	Chair
Count:	6	74	57	60	2	1
25th:	59	76	95	136		
Median:	62	88	109	161		
75th:	66	100	128	216		
Mean:	61.5	89.9	120.6	173.7		

OB/GYN: General

	Instructor	Assistant Professor	Associate Professor	Professor	Chief	Chair
Count:	2	22	24	19	0	0
25th:		80	100	126		
Median:		84	115	162		
75th:		90	125	217		
Mean:		88.0	124.5	173.4		

OB/GYN: Gynecologic Oncology

	Instructor	Assistant Professor	Associate Professor	Professor	Chief	Chair
Count:	1	0	1	6	0	0
25th:				135		
Median:				166		
75th:				215		
Mean:				175.0		

OB/GYN: Maternal & Fetal

	Instructor	Assistant Professor	Associate Professor	Professor	Chief	Chair
Count:	1	6	3	5	0	0
25th:		70		142		
Median:		84		149		
75th:		87		194		
Mean:		79.8		163.8		

TABLE 26 Summary Statistics on Medical School Faculty Compensation for Public Schools Ph.D. or Other Doctoral Degree, Clinical Science Departments/Specialties Total Compensation in Thousands of Dollars (continued)

OB/GYN: Reproductive Endocrinology

	Instructor	Assistant Professor	Associate Professor	Professor	Chief	Chair
Count:	1	20	9	13	0	1
25th:		82	87	153		
Median:		106	105	172		
75th:		126	127	249		
Mean:		103.0	109.6	199.2		

OB/GYN: Other OB/GYN

	Instructor	Assistant Professor	Associate Professor	Professor	Chief	Chair
Count:	1	26	20	17	2	0
25th:		74	94	122		
Median:		82	109	142		
75th:		93	126	199		
Mean:		83.7	110.2	156.9		

Total Pathology

	Instructor	Assistant Professor	Associate Professor	Professor	Chief	Chair
Count:	26	231	187	288	7	1
25th:	46	72	100	137	189	
Median:	54	90	116	163	225	
75th:	70	102	144	198	255	
Mean:	59.4	91.2	123.8	175.2	225.4	

Pathology: Anatomic

	Instructor	Assistant Professor	Associate Professor	Professor	Chief	Chair
Count:	4	25	31	37	0	0
25th:		81	108	134		
Median:		94	118	155		
75th:		102	133	188		
Mean:		95.1	125.5	174.2		

Pathology: Clinical

	Instructor	Assistant Professor	Associate Professor	Professor	Chief	Chair
Count:	8	51	57	78	3	1
25th:	47	97	117	138		
Median:	51	104	140	171		
75th:	83	122	162	212		
Mean:	61.9	111.8	140.0	185.6		

Summary Statistics on Medical School Faculty Compensation for Public Schools Ph.D. or Other Doctoral Degree, Clinical Science Departments/Specialties Total Compensation in Thousands of Dollars (continued)

Pathology: Other Pathology

	Instructor	Assistant Professor	Associate Professor	Professor	Chief	Chair
Count:	14	155	99	173	4	0
25th:	46	65	95	138		
Median:	54	84	109	163		
75th:	60	96	128	199		
Mean:	55.9	83.7	113.9	170.8		

Total Pediatrics

	Instructor	Assistant Professor	Associate Professor	Professor	Chief	Chair
Count:	50	436	235	217	16	2
25th:	62	75	96	128	173	
Median:	69	86	111	163	197	
75th:	89	96	132	199	309	
Mean:	74.8	87.2	115.5	165.8	233.0	

Adolescent Medicine

	Instructor	Assistant Professor	Associate Professor	Professor	Chief	Chair
Count:	0	5	2	2	0	0
25th:		71				
Median:		78				
75th:		87				
Mean:		78.6				

Allergy/Immunology-Peds.

	Instructor	Assistant Professor	Associate Professor	Professor	Chief	Chair
Count:	0	9	7	2	0	0
25th:		75	91			
Median:		86	109			
75th:		96	114			
Mean:		85.7	106.0			

Child & Adolescent Psychiatry

	Instructor	Assistant Professor	Associate Professor	Professor	Chief	Chair
Count:	3	57	31	31	3	0
25th:		75	98	119		
Median:		82	108	168		
75th:		89	130	205		
Mean:		83.2	111.6	170.0		

Summary Statistics on Medical School Faculty Compensation for Public Schools Ph.D. or Other Doctoral Degree, Clinical Science Departments/Specialties Total Compensation in Thousands of Dollars (continued)

Critical/Intensive Care-Peds.

	Instructor	Assistant Professor	Associate Professor	Professor	Chief	Chair
Count:	4	5	2	4	0	0
25th:		73				
Median:		98				
75th:		103				
Mean:		89.8				

Emergency Medicine-Peds.

	Instructor	Assistant Professor	Associate Professor	Professor	Chief	Chair
Count:	1	3	1	0	0	0
25th:						
Median:						
75th:						
Mean:						

Endocrinology-Peds.

	Instructor	Assistant Professor	Associate Professor	Professor	Chief	Chair
Count:	3	13	4	7	0	0
25th:		65		123		
Median:		79		177		
75th:		89		206		
Mean:		80.5		168.6		

Gastroenterology-Peds.

	Instructor	Assistant Professor	Associate Professor	Professor	Chief	Chair
Count:	4	10	6	2	0	0
25th:		72	95			
Median:		83	129			
75th:		100	147			
Mean:		84.3	143.8			

General Pediatrics

	Instructor	Assistant Professor	Associate Professor	Professor	Chief	Chair
Count:	11	54	25	26	1	1
25th:	52	77	96	130		
Median:	67	85	108	150		
75th:	76	91	119	185		
Mean:	68.0	87.3	111.9	155.8		

Summary Statistics on Medical School Faculty Compensation for Public Schools Ph.D. or Other Doctoral Degree, Clinical Science Departments/Specialties Total Compensation in Thousands of Dollars (continued)

Genetics-Peds.

	Instructor	Assistant Professor	Associate Professor	Professor	Chief	Chair
Count:	2	26	19	17	1	0
25th:		75	96	102		
Median:		85	106	140		
75th:		97	125	198		
Mean:		87.4	111.7	157.2		

Hematology/Oncology-Peds.

	Instructor	Assistant Professor	Associate Professor	Professor	Chief	Chair
Count:	1	35	12	6	0	0
25th:		79	90	195		
Median:		87	118	203		
75th:		96	141	205		
Mean:		86.4	114.6	199.0		

Hospital Medicine-Peds.

	Instructor	Assistant Professor	Associate Professor	Professor	Chief	Chair
Count:	0	0	0	0	0	0
25th:						
Median:						
75th:						
Mean:						

Infectious Disease-Peds.

	Instructor	Assistant Professor	Associate Professor	Professor	Chief	Chair
Count:	6	13	8	8	0	0
25th:	59	69	106	118		
Median:	78	80	109	139		
75th:	119	99	133	179		
Mean:	84.5	83.1	118.5	147.1		

Neonatology

	Instructor	Assistant Professor	Associate Professor	Professor	Chief	Chair
Count:	4	18	13	15	0	0
25th:		75	85	114		
Median:		82	106	185		
75th:		96	142	200		
Mean:		85.5	112.1	172.9		

TABLE 26 Summary Statistics on Medical School Faculty Compensation for Public Schools
Ph.D. or Other Doctoral Degree, Clinical Science Departments/Specialties
Total Compensation in Thousands of Dollars (continued)

Nephrology-Peds.

	Instructor	Assistant Professor	Associate Professor	Professor	Chief	Chair
Count:	0	5	0	1	0	0
25th:		69				
Median:		75				
75th:		92				
Mean:		79.4				

Neurology-Peds.

	Instructor	Assistant Professor	Associate Professor	Professor	Chief	Chair
Count:	2	14	6	5	0	0
25th:		71	113	114		
Median:		78	119	166		
75th:		91	125	227		
Mean:		79.9	127.2	169.6		

Pediatric Cardiology

	Instructor	Assistant Professor	Associate Professor	Professor	Chief	Chair
Count:	2	6	5	6	0	0
25th:		80	85	128		
Median:		89	96	168		
75th:		96	106	253		
Mean:		97.3	95.4	185.8		

Pulmonary-Peds.

	Instructor	Assistant Professor	Associate Professor	Professor	Chief	Chair
Count:	0	11	6	5	0	0
25th:		70	79	140		
Median:		82	95	160		
75th:		96	129	172		
Mean:		82.1	107.0	156.6		

Rheumatology-Peds.

	Instructor	Assistant Professor	Associate Professor	Professor	Chief	Chair
Count:	0	1	1	1	0	0
25th:						
Median:						
75th:						
Mean:						

TABLE 26 **Summary Statistics on Medical School Faculty Compensation for Public Schools Ph.D. or Other Doctoral Degree, Clinical Science Departments/Specialties Total Compensation in Thousands of Dollars (continued)**

Other Pediatrics

	Instructor	Assistant Professor	Associate Professor	Professor	Chief	Chair
Count:	7	151	87	79	11	1
25th:	67	78	101	130	181	
Median:	68	90	117	163	209	
75th:	90	101	133	198	322	
Mean:	77.0	90.5	119.0	167.3	248.8	

Total Radiology

	Instructor	Assistant Professor	Associate Professor	Professor	Chief	Chair
Count:	29	278	171	180	17	2
25th:	54	84	111	160	191	
Median:	66	103	138	186	214	
75th:	110	135	173	227	257	
Mean:	77.9	112.4	147.1	197.8	230.7	

Diagnostic Radiology: Total

	Instructor	Assistant Professor	Associate Professor	Professor	Chief	Chair
Count:	5	60	38	57	5	0
25th:	53	85	116	163	180	
Median:	62	93	130	176	212	
75th:	101	105	151	202	230	
Mean:	74.0	105.2	140.8	185.0	206.4	

Diagnostic Radiology: Interventional

	Instructor	Assistant Professor	Associate Professor	Professor	Chief	Chair
Count:	1	6	0	2	0	0
25th:		72				
Median:		110				
75th:		178				
Mean:		133.0				

Diagnostic Radiology: Non-interventional

	Instructor	Assistant Professor	Associate Professor	Professor	Chief	Chair
Count:	4	54	38	55	5	0
25th:		85	116	162	180	
Median:		93	130	176	212	
75th:		103	151	198	230	
Mean:		102.1	140.8	183.3	206.4	

TABLE 26 Summary Statistics on Medical School Faculty Compensation for Public Schools Ph.D. or Other Doctoral Degree, Clinical Science Departments/Specialties Total Compensation in Thousands of Dollars (continued)

Nuclear Medicine

	Instructor	Assistant Professor	Associate Professor	Professor	Chief	Chair
Count:	0	3	3	7	0	0
25th:				143		
Median:				232		
75th:				290		
Mean:				213.4		

Radiation Oncology

	Instructor	Assistant Professor	Associate Professor	Professor	Chief	Chair
Count:	17	136	63	62	9	0
25th:	56	100	130	187	199	
Median:	80	132	173	208	250	
75th:	112	151	205	255	291	
Mean:	86.1	127.6	172.1	222.3	250.1	

Other Radiology

	Instructor	Assistant Professor	Associate Professor	Professor	Chief	Chair
Count:	7	79	67	54	3	2
25th:	52	76	105	140		
Median:	59	90	129	166		
75th:	66	105	143	203		
Mean:	60.7	93.6	129.9	181.3		

Total Surgery

	Instructor	Assistant Professor	Associate Professor	Professor	Chief	Chair
Count:	27	214	119	177	3	0
25th:	55	68	97	133		
Median:	70	83	114	168		
75th:	90	95	130	209		
Mean:	78.4	88.0	116.7	181.7		

General Surgery

	Instructor	Assistant Professor	Associate Professor	Professor	Chief	Chair
Count:	7	43	20	35	1	0
25th:	51	67	104	133		
Median:	55	80	115	160		
75th:	101	92	128	201		
Mean:	74.7	86.1	118.2	171.5		

TABLE 26 Summary Statistics on Medical School Faculty Compensation for Public Schools Ph.D. or Other Doctoral Degree, Clinical Science Departments/Specialties Total Compensation in Thousands of Dollars (continued)

Neurosurgery

	Instructor	Assistant Professor	Associate Professor	Professor	Chief	Chair
Count:	4	45	19	39	0	0
25th:		68	103	134		
Median:		85	125	183		
75th:		92	138	210		
Mean:		94.6	126.6	191.0		

Orthopaedic Surgery

	Instructor	Assistant Professor	Associate Professor	Professor	Chief	Chair
Count:	2	42	30	38	1	0
25th:		72	88	125		
Median:		84	101	152		
75th:		104	123	196		
Mean:		92.0	109.0	168.1		

Pediatric Surgery

	Instructor	Assistant Professor	Associate Professor	Professor	Chief	Chair
Count:	1	5	0	0	0	0
25th:		70				
Median:		85				
75th:		105				
Mean:		86.6				

Plastic Surgery

	Instructor	Assistant Professor	Associate Professor	Professor	Chief	Chair
Count:	0	3	2	1	0	0
25th:						
Median:						
75th:						
Mean:						

Surgical Oncology

	Instructor	Assistant Professor	Associate Professor	Professor	Chief	Chair
Count:	0	7	2	1	0	0
25th:		55				
Median:		72				
75th:		76				
Mean:		67.1				

TABLE 26 Summary Statistics on Medical School Faculty Compensation for Public Schools
Ph.D. or Other Doctoral Degree, Clinical Science Departments/Specialties
Total Compensation in Thousands of Dollars (continued)

Thoracic & Cardiovascular Surgery

	Instructor	Assistant Professor	Associate Professor	Professor	Chief	Chair
Count:	2	7	8	11	1	0
25th:		75	82	117		
Median:		85	117	155		
75th:		97	129	190		
Mean:		86.6	111.3	156.9		

Transplant Surgery

	Instructor	Assistant Professor	Associate Professor	Professor	Chief	Chair
Count:	4	10	5	12	0	0
25th:		75	99	179		
Median:		95	124	186		
75th:		103	150	305		
Mean:		93.6	124.2	218.8		

Trauma/Critical Care Surgery

	Instructor	Assistant Professor	Associate Professor	Professor	Chief	Chair
Count:	1	9	3	6	0	0
25th:		60		150		
Median:		69		181		
75th:		79		210		
Mean:		69.3		172.8		

Urology

	Instructor	Assistant Professor	Associate Professor	Professor	Chief	Chair
Count:	3	21	13	15	0	0
25th:		63	105	112		
Median:		85	117	154		
75th:		102	127	190		
Mean:		83.9	117.4	162.3		

Vascular Surgery

	Instructor	Assistant Professor	Associate Professor	Professor	Chief	Chair
Count:	1	5	2	2	0	0
25th:		73				
Median:		85				
75th:		130				
Mean:		98.0				

TABLE 26 Summary Statistics on Medical School Faculty Compensation for Public Schools Ph.D. or Other Doctoral Degree, Clinical Science Departments/Specialties Total Compensation in Thousands of Dollars (continued)

Other Surgery

	Instructor	Assistant Professor	Associate Professor	Professor	Chief	Chair
Count:	2	17	15	17	0	0
25th:		75	97	138		
Median:		90	112	168		
75th:		98	126	279		
Mean:		88.0	114.0	224.7		

Other Clinical Science

Community Health

	Instructor	Assistant Professor	Associate Professor	Professor	Chief	Chair
Count:	0	55	41	41	3	3
25th:		80	95	119		
Median:		88	109	152		
75th:		100	138	174		
Mean:		91.6	116.9	152.7		

Emergency Medicine

	Instructor	Assistant Professor	Associate Professor	Professor	Chief	Chair
Count:	1	11	9	8	1	0
25th:		80	97	134		
Median:		93	135	147		
75th:		199	177	151		
Mean:		124.5	143.8	142.8		

Family Medicine

	Instructor	Assistant Professor	Associate Professor	Professor	Chief	Chair
Count:	5	106	60	69	1	2
25th:	62	74	90	110		
Median:	74	83	105	130		
75th:	81	99	124	159		
Mean:	71.8	89.6	111.1	138.7		

Neurology

	Instructor	Assistant Professor	Associate Professor	Professor	Chief	Chair
Count:	17	120	53	72	2	1
25th:	47	75	90	139		
Median:	57	90	102	176		
75th:	65	107	133	207		
Mean:	58.2	93.8	109.1	198.6		

TABLE 26 Summary Statistics on Medical School Faculty Compensation for Public Schools
Ph.D. or Other Doctoral Degree, Clinical Science Departments/Specialties
Total Compensation in Thousands of Dollars (continued)

Ophthalmology

	Instructor	Assistant Professor	Associate Professor	Professor	Chief	Chair
Count:	11	74	53	81	0	0
25th:	46	70	95	136		
Median:	70	81	109	163		
75th:	100	99	123	203		
Mean:	74.8	88.3	113.3	174.7		

Otolaryngology

	Instructor	Assistant Professor	Associate Professor	Professor	Chief	Chair
Count:	2	33	40	47	1	0
25th:		76	89	133		
Median:		80	101	171		
75th:		91	118	197		
Mean:		82.5	105.4	169.1		

Physical Medicine & Rehabilitation

	Instructor	Assistant Professor	Associate Professor	Professor	Chief	Chair
Count:	11	74	64	32	2	3
25th:	64	75	91	112		
Median:	66	82	97	125		
75th:	78	89	107	152		
Mean:	69.5	84.0	102.9	134.1		

Preventive Medicine

	Instructor	Assistant Professor	Associate Professor	Professor	Chief	Chair
Count:	2	66	53	42	1	5
25th:		82	105	131		209
Median:		90	119	157		270
75th:		95	137	179		445
Mean:		89.6	121.5	171.0		315.4

Psychiatry

	Instructor	Assistant Professor	Associate Professor	Professor	Chief	Chair
Count:	37	426	247	298	11	1
25th:	59	74	95	136	101	
Median:	67	83	109	160	149	
75th:	75	97	132	209	178	
Mean:	70.3	87.5	116.6	173.5	153.2	

TABLE 26 Summary Statistics on Medical School Faculty Compensation for Public Schools Ph.D. or Other Doctoral Degree, Clinical Science Departments/Specialties Total Compensation in Thousands of Dollars (continued)

Other

	Instructor	Assistant Professor	Associate Professor	Professor	Chief	Chair
Count:	6	44	35	39	1	5
25th:	70	71	90	151		124
Median:	74	82	103	170		169
75th:	79	92	120	213		238
Mean:	76.5	83.5	109.3	181.9		178.2

TABLE 27 Summary Statistics on Medical School Faculty Compensation for Private Schools
Ph.D. or Other Doctoral Degree, Clinical Science Departments/Specialties
Total Compensation in Thousands of Dollars

CLINICAL SCIENCE - TOTAL ALL DEPARTMENTS/SPECIALTIES

	Instructor	Assistant Professor	Associate Professor	Professor	Chief	Chair
Count:	695	3,099	1,564	1,396	63	20
25th:	56	74	101	144	152	181
Median:	68	88	122	174	221	249
75th:	85	105	148	213	275	404
Mean:	74.9	95.6	130.0	183.1	217.0	279.7

Total Anesthesiology

	Instructor	Assistant Professor	Associate Professor	Professor	Chief	Chair
Count:	11	63	30	32	0	0
25th:	64	80	115	141		
Median:	76	97	129	178		
75th:	150	128	158	219		
Mean:	110.4	128.1	147.6	193.3		

Anesthesiology: General

	Instructor	Assistant Professor	Associate Professor	Professor	Chief	Chair
Count:	11	61	28	30	0	0
25th:	64	80	115	143		
Median:	76	98	126	178		
75th:	150	133	157	218		
Mean:	110.4	129.4	145.9	192.8		

Anesthesiology: Pain Management

	Instructor	Assistant Professor	Associate Professor	Professor	Chief	Chair
Count:	0	2	1	2	0	0
25th:						
Median:						
75th:						
Mean:						

Anesthesiology: Pediatric

	Instructor	Assistant Professor	Associate Professor	Professor	Chief	Chair
Count:	0	0	1	0	0	0
25th:						
Median:						
75th:						
Mean:						

Total Dermatology

	Instructor	Assistant Professor	Associate Professor	Professor	Chief	Chair
Count:	5	36	14	18	0	0
25th:	56	80	110	143		
Median:	72	87	148	171		
75th:	84	108	175	220		
Mean:	70.2	99.2	145.9	180.3		

Dermatology (excluding Mohs Surgery)

	Instructor	Assistant Professor	Associate Professor	Professor	Chief	Chair
Count:	5	35	14	16	0	0
25th:	56	77	110	138		
Median:	72	87	148	175		
75th:	84	105	175	235		
Mean:	70.2	97.5	145.9	183.9		

Dermatology: Mohs Surgery

	Instructor	Assistant Professor	Associate Professor	Professor	Chief	Chair
Count:	0	1	0	2	0	0
25th:						
Median:						
75th:						
Mean:						

Total Medicine

	Instructor	Assistant Professor	Associate Professor	Professor	Chief	Chair
Count:	174	721	324	241	12	1
25th:	54	71	100	144	165	
Median:	62	84	121	169	194	
75th:	74	97	140	207	219	
Mean:	67.1	87.9	122.7	177.4	198.8	

Allergy/Immunology-Med.

	Instructor	Assistant Professor	Associate Professor	Professor	Chief	Chair
Count:	7	16	14	14	1	0
25th:	50	77	120	156		
Median:	51	90	131	179		
75th:	62	114	143	200		
Mean:	54.3	94.1	130.3	171.9		

TABLE 27 Summary Statistics on Medical School Faculty Compensation for Private Schools Ph.D. or Other Doctoral Degree, Clinical Science Departments/Specialties Total Compensation in Thousands of Dollars (continued)

Cardiology: Total

	Instructor	Assistant Professor	Associate Professor	Professor	Chief	Chair
Count:	11	80	29	20	0	0
25th:	55	69	104	150		
Median:	65	78	130	170		
75th:	75	95	149	214		
Mean:	64.1	86.3	129.4	181.5		

Cardiology: Invasive Interventional-Med.

	Instructor	Assistant Professor	Associate Professor	Professor	Chief	Chair
Count:	0	12	10	4	0	0
25th:		63	91			
Median:		77	127			
75th:		102	135			
Mean:		81.9	120.0			

Cardiology: Invasive Non-interventional-Med.

	Instructor	Assistant Professor	Associate Professor	Professor	Chief	Chair
Count:	2	0	0	0	0	0
25th:						
Median:						
75th:						
Mean:						

Cardiology: Non-invasive-Med.

	Instructor	Assistant Professor	Associate Professor	Professor	Chief	Chair
Count:	9	68	19	16	0	0
25th:	55	70	107	154		
Median:	65	78	130	170		
75th:	75	94	170	196		
Mean:	64.6	87.0	134.4	179.3		

Critical/Intensive Care-Med.

	Instructor	Assistant Professor	Associate Professor	Professor	Chief	Chair
Count:	0	0	1	0	0	0
25th:						
Median:						
75th:						
Mean:						

TABLE 27 Summary Statistics on Medical School Faculty Compensation for Private Schools Ph.D. or Other Doctoral Degree, Clinical Science Departments/Specialties Total Compensation in Thousands of Dollars (continued)

Endocrinology-Med.

	Instructor	Assistant Professor	Associate Professor	Professor	Chief	Chair
Count:	14	37	34	16	0	0
25th:	54	68	103	123		
Median:	67	82	120	143		
75th:	80	103	134	187		
Mean:	74.6	86.6	121.9	155.8		

Gastroenterology-Med.

	Instructor	Assistant Professor	Associate Professor	Professor	Chief	Chair
Count:	9	38	18	11	0	0
25th:	49	75	100	147		
Median:	62	82	109	155		
75th:	70	92	144	164		
Mean:	60.4	92.1	120.1	154.9		

General Internal Medicine

	Instructor	Assistant Professor	Associate Professor	Professor	Chief	Chair
Count:	22	72	37	35	0	0
25th:	64	82	116	141		
Median:	82	93	130	180		
75th:	106	111	156	211		
Mean:	91.7	101.9	139.2	180.9		

Geriatrics-Med.

	Instructor	Assistant Professor	Associate Professor	Professor	Chief	Chair
Count:	4	29	13	5	0	0
25th:		68	96	83		
Median:		82	102	125		
75th:		94	121	156		
Mean:		83.2	102.5	120.4		

Hematology/Oncology-Med.

	Instructor	Assistant Professor	Associate Professor	Professor	Chief	Chair
Count:	48	147	63	64	3	0
25th:	55	72	102	145		
Median:	60	82	125	170		
75th:	71	97	142	226		
Mean:	65.9	86.6	125.8	184.5		

TABLE 27 Summary Statistics on Medical School Faculty Compensation for Private Schools Ph.D. or Other Doctoral Degree, Clinical Science Departments/Specialties Total Compensation in Thousands of Dollars (continued)

Hospital Medicine

	Instructor	Assistant Professor	Associate Professor	Professor	Chief	Chair
Count:	0	0	0	0	0	0
25th:						
Median:						
75th:						
Mean:						

Infectious Disease-Med.

	Instructor	Assistant Professor	Associate Professor	Professor	Chief	Chair
Count:	13	59	15	8	1	0
25th:	54	76	92	138		
Median:	60	87	106	153		
75th:	77	100	143	179		
Mean:	64.0	91.2	115.1	151.6		

Nephrology-Med.

	Instructor	Assistant Professor	Associate Professor	Professor	Chief	Chair
Count:	7	52	20	14	0	0
25th:	52	62	85	143		
Median:	63	77	99	161		
75th:	76	92	123	208		
Mean:	66.0	79.1	107.5	178.6		

Pulmonary-Med.

	Instructor	Assistant Professor	Associate Professor	Professor	Chief	Chair
Count:	8	55	18	13	0	0
25th:	44	63	106	159		
Median:	51	75	117	176		
75th:	70	87	127	200		
Mean:	59.1	77.0	120.2	178.1		

Rheumatology-Med.

	Instructor	Assistant Professor	Associate Professor	Professor	Chief	Chair
Count:	7	24	7	11	0	0
25th:	52	61	93	135		
Median:	57	83	106	154		
75th:	70	99	134	165		
Mean:	59.9	88.0	117.0	146.6		

Summary Statistics on Medical School Faculty Compensation for Private Schools Ph.D. or Other Doctoral Degree, Clinical Science Departments/Specialties Total Compensation in Thousands of Dollars (continued)

Other Medicine

	Instructor	Assistant Professor	Associate Professor	Professor	Chief	Chair
Count:	24	112	55	30	7	1
25th:	53	75	92	172	136	
Median:	59	87	116	196	190	
75th:	65	96	130	239	207	
Mean:	58.3	88.5	118.2	204.4	175.0	

Total OB/GYN

	Instructor	Assistant Professor	Associate Professor	Professor	Chief	Chair
Count:	16	55	37	38	1	0
25th:	52	81	96	140		
Median:	59	90	109	172		
75th:	76	112	140	222		
Mean:	67.0	107.2	122.1	188.8		

OB/GYN: General

	Instructor	Assistant Professor	Associate Professor	Professor	Chief	Chair
Count:	5	18	11	16	0	0
25th:	60	85	100	142		
Median:	76	93	119	169		
75th:	108	118	157	220		
Mean:	82.2	111.7	120.5	180.8		

OB/GYN: Gynecologic Oncology

	Instructor	Assistant Professor	Associate Professor	Professor	Chief	Chair
Count:	0	2	1	0	0	0
25th:						
Median:						
75th:						
Mean:						

OB/GYN: Maternal & Fetal

	Instructor	Assistant Professor	Associate Professor	Professor	Chief	Chair
Count:	0	2	2	0	0	0
25th:						
Median:						
75th:						
Mean:						

TABLE 27 Summary Statistics on Medical School Faculty Compensation for Private Schools Ph.D. or Other Doctoral Degree, Clinical Science Departments/Specialties Total Compensation in Thousands of Dollars (continued)

OB/GYN: Reproductive Endocrinology

	Instructor	Assistant Professor	Associate Professor	Professor	Chief	Chair
Count:	0	11	4	6	1	0
25th:		81		189		
Median:		125		287		
75th:		143		334		
Mean:		144.1		274.8		

OB/GYN: Other OB/GYN

	Instructor	Assistant Professor	Associate Professor	Professor	Chief	Chair
Count:	11	22	19	16	0	0
25th:	40	81	95	122		
Median:	57	87	106	162		
75th:	66	92	121	177		
Mean:	60.1	88.4	111.5	164.4		

Total Pathology

	Instructor	Assistant Professor	Associate Professor	Professor	Chief	Chair
Count:	55	277	146	198	5	1
25th:	52	72	113	154	241	
Median:	63	94	133	185	275	
75th:	80	123	170	216	304	
Mean:	67.9	104.4	140.5	187.6	272.6	

Pathology: Anatomic

	Instructor	Assistant Professor	Associate Professor	Professor	Chief	Chair
Count:	11	55	32	33	0	0
25th:	62	91	107	165		
Median:	72	139	158	190		
75th:	106	180	190	219		
Mean:	79.3	137.0	146.8	187.9		

Pathology: Clinical

	Instructor	Assistant Professor	Associate Professor	Professor	Chief	Chair
Count:	12	57	34	58	1	1
25th:	55	73	118	164		
Median:	70	99	146	198		
75th:	77	123	178	232		
Mean:	67.4	104.8	151.6	198.2		

TABLE 27 Summary Statistics on Medical School Faculty Compensation for Private Schools Ph.D. or Other Doctoral Degree, Clinical Science Departments/Specialties Total Compensation in Thousands of Dollars (continued)

Pathology: Other Pathology

	Instructor	Assistant Professor	Associate Professor	Professor	Chief	Chair
Count:	32	165	80	107	4	0
25th:	50	70	111	141		
Median:	61	90	128	177		
75th:	80	110	157	211		
Mean:	64.2	93.3	133.2	181.8		

Total Pediatrics

	Instructor	Assistant Professor	Associate Professor	Professor	Chief	Chair
Count:	55	340	144	120	7	0
25th:	55	74	96	142	170	
Median:	70	85	117	167	228	
75th:	85	101	133	209	261	
Mean:	71.1	91.7	118.8	180.8	223.3	

Adolescent Medicine

	Instructor	Assistant Professor	Associate Professor	Professor	Chief	Chair
Count:	0	5	2	2	0	0
25th:		78				
Median:		86				
75th:		91				
Mean:		84.4				

Allergy/Immunology-Peds.

	Instructor	Assistant Professor	Associate Professor	Professor	Chief	Chair
Count:	1	7	0	0	0	0
25th:		80				
Median:		89				
75th:		95				
Mean:		85.3				

Child & Adolescent Psychiatry

	Instructor	Assistant Professor	Associate Professor	Professor	Chief	Chair
Count:	5	23	12	9	1	0
25th:	70	85	118	150		
Median:	75	91	129	181		
75th:	100	140	135	222		
Mean:	82.8	106.6	134.3	188.2		

Critical/Intensive Care-Peds.

	Instructor	Assistant Professor	Associate Professor	Professor	Chief	Chair
Count:	2	2	1	0	0	0
25th:						
Median:						
75th:						
Mean:						

Emergency Medicine-Peds.

	Instructor	Assistant Professor	Associate Professor	Professor	Chief	Chair
Count:	0	1	0	0	0	0
25th:						
Median:						
75th:						
Mean:						

Endocrinology-Peds.

	Instructor	Assistant Professor	Associate Professor	Professor	Chief	Chair
Count:	2	7	1	0	0	0
25th:		67				
Median:		72				
75th:		101				
Mean:		83.3				

Gastroenterology-Peds.

	Instructor	Assistant Professor	Associate Professor	Professor	Chief	Chair
Count:	0	4	6	3	0	0
25th:			96			
Median:			119			
75th:			140			
Mean:			117.5			

General Pediatrics

	Instructor	Assistant Professor	Associate Professor	Professor	Chief	Chair
Count:	11	35	15	16	0	0
25th:	50	77	93	139		
Median:	61	92	108	163		
75th:	72	105	130	198		
Mean:	63.5	95.9	112.0	175.6		

TABLE 27 Summary Statistics on Medical School Faculty Compensation for Private Schools Ph.D. or Other Doctoral Degree, Clinical Science Departments/Specialties Total Compensation in Thousands of Dollars (continued)

Genetics-Peds.

	Instructor	Assistant Professor	Associate Professor	Professor	Chief	Chair
Count:	0	6	5	5	2	0
25th:		64	74	130		
Median:		81	82	155		
75th:		94	117	180		
Mean:		97.7	92.6	154.6		

Hematology/Oncology-Peds.

	Instructor	Assistant Professor	Associate Professor	Professor	Chief	Chair
Count:	8	36	19	10	0	0
25th:	55	70	88	146		
Median:	72	78	118	160		
75th:	94	92	140	240		
Mean:	74.1	83.3	118.7	193.4		

Hospital Medicine-Peds.

	Instructor	Assistant Professor	Associate Professor	Professor	Chief	Chair
Count:	0	0	0	0	0	0
25th:						
Median:						
75th:						
Mean:						

Infectious Disease-Peds.

	Instructor	Assistant Professor	Associate Professor	Professor	Chief	Chair
Count:	2	15	5	2	0	0
25th:		70	93			
Median:		86	106			
75th:		103	135			
Mean:		93.2	112.2			

Neonatology

	Instructor	Assistant Professor	Associate Professor	Professor	Chief	Chair
Count:	1	23	11	8	0	0
25th:		65	88	146		
Median:		75	105	159		
75th:		102	143	173		
Mean:		89.6	115.9	166.1		

TABLE 27 Summary Statistics on Medical School Faculty Compensation for Private Schools Ph.D. or Other Doctoral Degree, Clinical Science Departments/Specialties Total Compensation in Thousands of Dollars (continued)

Nephrology-Peds.

	Instructor	Assistant Professor	Associate Professor	Professor	Chief	Chair
Count:	0	3	1	0	0	0
25th:						
Median:						
75th:						
Mean:						

Neurology-Peds.

	Instructor	Assistant Professor	Associate Professor	Professor	Chief	Chair
Count:	4	12	2	5	0	0
25th:		78		156		
Median:		90		195		
75th:		104		237		
Mean:		92.5		195.8		

Pediatric Cardiology

	Instructor	Assistant Professor	Associate Professor	Professor	Chief	Chair
Count:	1	7	2	0	0	0
25th:		60				
Median:		95				
75th:		106				
Mean:		95.9				

Pulmonary-Peds.

	Instructor	Assistant Professor	Associate Professor	Professor	Chief	Chair
Count:	2	10	5	4	0	0
25th:		70	85			
Median:		81	90			
75th:		86	121			
Mean:		77.2	100.2			

Rheumatology-Peds.

	Instructor	Assistant Professor	Associate Professor	Professor	Chief	Chair
Count:	0	1	1	0	0	0
25th:						
Median:						
75th:						
Mean:						

TABLE 27 Summary Statistics on Medical School Faculty Compensation for Private Schools Ph.D. or Other Doctoral Degree, Clinical Science Departments/Specialties Total Compensation in Thousands of Dollars (continued)

Other Pediatrics

	Instructor	Assistant Professor	Associate Professor	Professor	Chief	Chair
Count:	16	143	56	56	4	0
25th:	57	76	100	150		
Median:	71	85	115	176		
75th:	85	103	131	221		
Mean:	72.2	92.0	121.0	189.6		

Total Radiology

	Instructor	Assistant Professor	Associate Professor	Professor	Chief	Chair
Count:	107	317	209	150	11	1
25th:	62	87	115	165	212	
Median:	75	102	145	200	244	
75th:	107	142	192	227	300	
Mean:	88.1	120.0	154.3	205.4	243.5	

Diagnostic Radiology: Total

	Instructor	Assistant Professor	Associate Professor	Professor	Chief	Chair
Count:	63	115	92	54	2	0
25th:	60	84	108	180		
Median:	75	96	133	215		
75th:	90	112	169	248		
Mean:	76.8	112.2	141.9	218.8		

Diagnostic Radiology: Interventional

	Instructor	Assistant Professor	Associate Professor	Professor	Chief	Chair
Count:	2	1	1	2	0	0
25th:						
Median:						
75th:						
Mean:						

Diagnostic Radiology: Non-interventional

	Instructor	Assistant Professor	Associate Professor	Professor	Chief	Chair
Count:	61	114	91	52	2	0
25th:	61	84	107	181		
Median:	75	96	133	218		
75th:	90	112	167	254		
Mean:	77.7	109.7	141.2	220.6		

Summary Statistics on Medical School Faculty Compensation for Private Schools Ph.D. or Other Doctoral Degree, Clinical Science Departments/Specialties Total Compensation in Thousands of Dollars (continued)

Nuclear Medicine

	Instructor	Assistant Professor	Associate Professor	Professor	Chief	Chair
Count:	2	7	5	4	1	0
25th:		72	111			
Median:		98	135			
75th:		113	160			
Mean:		91.7	135.4			

Radiation Oncology

	Instructor	Assistant Professor	Associate Professor	Professor	Chief	Chair
Count:	29	105	58	50	7	0
25th:	67	98	153	160	229	
Median:	115	143	195	196	298	
75th:	153	177	222	238	308	
Mean:	119.7	140.5	185.0	202.5	264.1	

Other Radiology

	Instructor	Assistant Professor	Associate Professor	Professor	Chief	Chair
Count:	13	90	54	42	1	1
25th:	64	88	117	158		
Median:	69	100	143	186		
75th:	76	115	168	212		
Mean:	71.9	108.4	144.2	192.4		

Total Surgery

	Instructor	Assistant Professor	Associate Professor	Professor	Chief	Chair
Count:	73	251	132	118	10	2
25th:	52	66	101	141	224	
Median:	60	82	124	178	260	
75th:	85	100	145	232	299	
Mean:	70.3	89.5	139.4	188.7	241.0	

General Surgery

	Instructor	Assistant Professor	Associate Professor	Professor	Chief	Chair
Count:	18	34	18	9	1	0
25th:	71	79	92	118		
Median:	81	101	116	163		
75th:	104	124	157	254		
Mean:	84.3	106.9	145.7	177.0		

TABLE 27 Summary Statistics on Medical School Faculty Compensation for Private Schools Ph.D. or Other Doctoral Degree, Clinical Science Departments/Specialties Total Compensation in Thousands of Dollars (continued)

Neurosurgery

	Instructor	Assistant Professor	Associate Professor	Professor	Chief	Chair
Count:	14	49	23	22	1	1
25th:	54	63	100	142		
Median:	61	80	125	181		
75th:	67	91	136	229		
Mean:	60.5	88.5	161.2	186.4		

Orthopaedic Surgery

	Instructor	Assistant Professor	Associate Professor	Professor	Chief	Chair
Count:	20	44	28	25	2	0
25th:	51	72	104	144		
Median:	56	82	131	197		
75th:	103	106	151	255		
Mean:	76.5	94.5	159.5	208.4		

Pediatric Surgery

	Instructor	Assistant Professor	Associate Professor	Professor	Chief	Chair
Count:	3	12	5	0	0	0
25th:		56	80			
Median:		67	103			
75th:		80	119			
Mean:		71.7	100.0			

Plastic Surgery

	Instructor	Assistant Professor	Associate Professor	Professor	Chief	Chair
Count:	0	5	2	5	0	0
25th:		74		99		
Median:		90		116		
75th:		110		232		
Mean:		91.2		155.2		

Surgical Oncology

	Instructor	Assistant Professor	Associate Professor	Professor	Chief	Chair
Count:	2	11	2	2	0	0
25th:		70				
Median:		96				
75th:		100				
Mean:		89.9				

TABLE 27 Summary Statistics on Medical School Faculty Compensation for Private Schools Ph.D. or Other Doctoral Degree, Clinical Science Departments/Specialties Total Compensation in Thousands of Dollars (continued)

Thoracic & Cardiovascular Surgery

	Instructor	Assistant Professor	Associate Professor	Professor	Chief	Chair
Count:	0	14	6	5	0	0
25th:		60	93	114		
Median:		75	113	150		
75th:		105	159	180		
Mean:		85.9	123.3	147.4		

Transplant Surgery

	Instructor	Assistant Professor	Associate Professor	Professor	Chief	Chair
Count:	6	12	11	5	0	1
25th:	57	67	109	181		
Median:	58	89	139	232		
75th:	58	106	153	363		
Mean:	64.5	88.3	130.6	264.0		

Trauma/Critical Care Surgery

	Instructor	Assistant Professor	Associate Professor	Professor	Chief	Chair
Count:	0	1	0	1	0	0
25th:						
Median:						
75th:						
Mean:						

Urology

	Instructor	Assistant Professor	Associate Professor	Professor	Chief	Chair
Count:	4	28	15	21	1	0
25th:		66	110	152		
Median:		79	132	179		
75th:		90	143	212		
Mean:		80.9	126.1	189.3		

Vascular Surgery

	Instructor	Assistant Professor	Associate Professor	Professor	Chief	Chair
Count:	1	2	1	1	0	0
25th:						
Median:						
75th:						
Mean:						

TABLE 27 Summary Statistics on Medical School Faculty Compensation for Private Schools
Ph.D. or Other Doctoral Degree, Clinical Science Departments/Specialties
Total Compensation in Thousands of Dollars (continued)

Other Surgery

	Instructor	Assistant Professor	Associate Professor	Professor	Chief	Chair
Count:	5	39	21	22	5	0
25th:	48	68	88	126	260	
Median:	56	84	118	162	299	
75th:	65	98	126	220	325	
Mean:	56.2	83.4	111.5	174.7	293.4	

Other Clinical Science

Community Health

	Instructor	Assistant Professor	Associate Professor	Professor	Chief	Chair
Count:	9	57	29	36	3	4
25th:	53	81	93	146		
Median:	75	93	105	194		
75th:	97	102	144	234		
Mean:	74.0	94.1	117.9	195.5		

Emergency Medicine

	Instructor	Assistant Professor	Associate Professor	Professor	Chief	Chair
Count:	2	15	4	3	0	0
25th:		59				
Median:		78				
75th:		150				
Mean:		123.3				

Family Medicine

	Instructor	Assistant Professor	Associate Professor	Professor	Chief	Chair
Count:	10	57	35	21	3	2
25th:	60	75	93	107		
Median:	70	86	104	139		
75th:	74	95	123	160		
Mean:	67.1	86.5	106.9	136.1		

Neurology

	Instructor	Assistant Professor	Associate Professor	Professor	Chief	Chair
Count:	55	175	73	56	2	0
25th:	54	70	99	137		
Median:	65	85	120	166		
75th:	80	100	144	199		
Mean:	71.2	89.7	127.9	174.6		

TABLE 27 Summary Statistics on Medical School Faculty Compensation for Private Schools Ph.D. or Other Doctoral Degree, Clinical Science Departments/Specialties Total Compensation in Thousands of Dollars (continued)

Ophthalmology

	Instructor	Assistant Professor	Associate Professor	Professor	Chief	Chair
Count:	8	65	43	45	0	0
25th:	48	70	100	138		
Median:	64	82	115	167		
75th:	87	95	135	201		
Mean:	66.8	85.4	118.0	167.8		

Otolaryngology

	Instructor	Assistant Professor	Associate Professor	Professor	Chief	Chair
Count:	8	47	22	30	2	0
25th:	63	74	96	128		
Median:	71	85	113	159		
75th:	98	95	129	190		
Mean:	82.6	93.1	117.5	158.0		

Physical Medicine & Rehabilitation

	Instructor	Assistant Professor	Associate Professor	Professor	Chief	Chair
Count:	13	62	34	15	1	3
25th:	70	78	94	120		
Median:	74	85	105	129		
75th:	96	95	134	158		
Mean:	87.5	88.4	115.5	142.7		

Preventive Medicine

	Instructor	Assistant Professor	Associate Professor	Professor	Chief	Chair
Count:	3	60	33	34	0	1
25th:		90	121	175		
Median:		99	136	191		
75th:		103	154	224		
Mean:		95.6	136.1	200.5		

Psychiatry

	Instructor	Assistant Professor	Associate Professor	Professor	Chief	Chair
Count:	87	455	221	211	5	2
25th:	67	75	101	144	193	
Median:	80	87	116	170	246	
75th:	94	102	142	207	259	
Mean:	83.8	91.8	122.8	179.0	229.8	

TABLE 27

Summary Statistics on Medical School Faculty Compensation for Private Schools Ph.D. or Other Doctoral Degree, Clinical Science Departments/Specialties Total Compensation in Thousands of Dollars (continued)

Other

	Instructor	Assistant Professor	Associate Professor	Professor	Chief	Chair
Count:	4	46	34	30	1	3
25th:		74	109	121		
Median:		89	119	151		
75th:		102	142	162		
Mean:		89.8	120.3	163.9		

TABLE 28 Summary Statistics on Medical School Faculty Compensation for Northeastern Region
Ph.D. or Other Doctoral Degree, Clinical Science Departments/Specialties
Total Compensation in Thousands of Dollars

CLINICAL SCIENCE - TOTAL ALL DEPARTMENTS/SPECIALTIES

	Instructor	Assistant Professor	Associate Professor	Professor	Chief	Chair
Count:	460	1,869	1,039	930	39	14
25th:	60	76	104	148	177	248
Median:	70	89	124	174	215	270
75th:	90	107	151	214	259	356
Mean:	78.4	97.8	132.9	184.3	219.4	307.7

Total Anesthesiology

	Instructor	Assistant Professor	Associate Professor	Professor	Chief	Chair
Count:	9	42	19	19	0	0
25th:	66	82	120	159		
Median:	133	100	158	197		
75th:	165	183	209	271		
Mean:	119.8	147.2	171.3	209.2		

Anesthesiology: General

	Instructor	Assistant Professor	Associate Professor	Professor	Chief	Chair
Count:	9	41	17	17	0	0
25th:	66	82	119	162		
Median:	133	100	158	197		
75th:	165	207	211	270		
Mean:	119.8	148.5	171.2	210.2		

Anesthesiology: Pain Management

	Instructor	Assistant Professor	Associate Professor	Professor	Chief	Chair
Count:	0	1	1	2	0	0
25th:						
Median:						
75th:						
Mean:						

Anesthesiology: Pediatric

	Instructor	Assistant Professor	Associate Professor	Professor	Chief	Chair
Count:	0	0	1	0	0	0
25th:						
Median:						
75th:						
Mean:						

TABLE 28 Summary Statistics on Medical School Faculty Compensation for Northeastern Region Ph.D. or Other Doctoral Degree, Clinical Science Departments/Specialties Total Compensation in Thousands of Dollars (continued)

Total Dermatology

	Instructor	Assistant Professor	Associate Professor	Professor	Chief	Chair
Count:	4	24	12	10	0	0
25th:		68	107	143		
Median:		89	148	177		
75th:		116	185	220		
Mean:		104.9	146.2	183.4		

Dermatology (excluding Mohs Surgery)

	Instructor	Assistant Professor	Associate Professor	Professor	Chief	Chair
Count:	4	23	12	10	0	0
25th:		66	107	143		
Median:		87	148	177		
75th:		115	185	220		
Mean:		102.5	146.2	183.4		

Dermatology: Mohs Surgery

	Instructor	Assistant Professor	Associate Professor	Professor	Chief	Chair
Count:	0	1	0	0	0	0
25th:						
Median:						
75th:						
Mean:						

Total Medicine

	Instructor	Assistant Professor	Associate Professor	Professor	Chief	Chair
Count:	111	426	222	173	7	2
25th:	56	75	101	153	182	
Median:	64	85	121	171	212	
75th:	78	100	139	208	225	
Mean:	71.8	90.8	123.6	179.5	213.7	

Allergy/Immunology-Med.

	Instructor	Assistant Professor	Associate Professor	Professor	Chief	Chair
Count:	6	9	15	8	0	1
25th:	50	73	106	135		
Median:	53	85	120	157		
75th:	60	90	135	187		
Mean:	55.0	82.8	118.9	150.6		

TABLE 28 Summary Statistics on Medical School Faculty Compensation for Northeastern Region Ph.D. or Other Doctoral Degree, Clinical Science Departments/Specialties Total Compensation in Thousands of Dollars (continued)

Cardiology: Total

	Instructor	Assistant Professor	Associate Professor	Professor	Chief	Chair
Count:	5	46	16	14	0	0
25th:	54	68	106	166		
Median:	56	79	128	191		
75th:	74	100	162	230		
Mean:	62.2	90.2	130.1	191.8		

Cardiology: Invasive Interventional-Med.

	Instructor	Assistant Professor	Associate Professor	Professor	Chief	Chair
Count:	0	1	1	2	0	0
25th:						
Median:						
75th:						
Mean:						

Cardiology: Invasive Non-interventional-Med.

	Instructor	Assistant Professor	Associate Professor	Professor	Chief	Chair
Count:	1	0	0	0	0	0
25th:						
Median:						
75th:						
Mean:						

Cardiology: Non-invasive-Med.

	Instructor	Assistant Professor	Associate Professor	Professor	Chief	Chair
Count:	4	45	15	12	0	0
25th:		68	97	166		
Median:		79	130	191		
75th:		100	170	224		
Mean:		89.4	130.6	192.0		

Critical/Intensive Care-Med.

	Instructor	Assistant Professor	Associate Professor	Professor	Chief	Chair
Count:	0	0	1	0	0	0
25th:						
Median:						
75th:						
Mean:						

TABLE 28

Summary Statistics on Medical School Faculty Compensation for Northeastern Region Ph.D. or Other Doctoral Degree, Clinical Science Departments/Specialties Total Compensation in Thousands of Dollars (continued)

Endocrinology-Med.

	Instructor	Assistant Professor	Associate Professor	Professor	Chief	Chair
Count:	11	27	25	8	0	0
25th:	56	71	102	133		
Median:	70	86	120	162		
75th:	80	103	139	183		
Mean:	77.7	89.5	126.2	167.4		

Gastroenterology-Med.

	Instructor	Assistant Professor	Associate Professor	Professor	Chief	Chair
Count:	6	22	11	7	0	0
25th:	54	75	100	148		
Median:	66	86	109	154		
75th:	68	125	147	163		
Mean:	63.2	104.0	124.4	156.1		

General Internal Medicine

	Instructor	Assistant Professor	Associate Professor	Professor	Chief	Chair
Count:	18	49	26	27	0	0
25th:	76	85	102	149		
Median:	87	101	131	187		
75th:	109	115	160	211		
Mean:	96.8	109.7	141.6	187.8		

Geriatrics-Med.

	Instructor	Assistant Professor	Associate Professor	Professor	Chief	Chair
Count:	0	9	6	4	0	0
25th:		88	100			
Median:		98	113			
75th:		115	122			
Mean:		99.7	101.2			

Hematology/Oncology-Med.

	Instructor	Assistant Professor	Associate Professor	Professor	Chief	Chair
Count:	23	107	44	45	4	0
25th:	56	75	121	138		
Median:	70	85	127	169		
75th:	80	99	143	227		
Mean:	73.5	89.4	130.6	179.9		

TABLE 28

Summary Statistics on Medical School Faculty Compensation for Northeastern Region Ph.D. or Other Doctoral Degree, Clinical Science Departments/Specialties Total Compensation in Thousands of Dollars (continued)

Hospital Medicine

	Instructor	Assistant Professor	Associate Professor	Professor	Chief	Chair
Count:	0	0	0	0	0	0
25th:						
Median:						
75th:						
Mean:						

Infectious Disease-Med.

	Instructor	Assistant Professor	Associate Professor	Professor	Chief	Chair
Count:	9	47	15	13	1	0
25th:	60	75	110	153		
Median:	63	83	139	179		
75th:	79	92	170	200		
Mean:	67.4	87.6	133.4	177.8		

Nephrology-Med.

	Instructor	Assistant Professor	Associate Professor	Professor	Chief	Chair
Count:	5	23	11	8	0	0
25th:	58	64	95	150		
Median:	75	77	110	164		
75th:	83	91	138	194		
Mean:	71.2	77.3	117.5	172.5		

Pulmonary-Med.

	Instructor	Assistant Professor	Associate Professor	Professor	Chief	Chair
Count:	5	33	11	12	0	0
25th:	53	64	90	159		
Median:	69	75	110	185		
75th:	89	84	122	204		
Mean:	70.6	78.3	103.9	185.9		

Rheumatology-Med.

	Instructor	Assistant Professor	Associate Professor	Professor	Chief	Chair
Count:	8	12	5	8	0	0
25th:	54	78	93	157		
Median:	59	86	103	163		
75th:	73	97	120	190		
Mean:	63.5	94.8	105.6	169.9		

TABLE 28 Summary Statistics on Medical School Faculty Compensation for Northeastern Region Ph.D. or Other Doctoral Degree, Clinical Science Departments/Specialties Total Compensation in Thousands of Dollars (continued)

Other Medicine

	Instructor	Assistant Professor	Associate Professor	Professor	Chief	Chair
Count:	15	42	36	19	2	1
25th:	48	77	91	171		
Median:	58	87	107	194		
75th:	62	98	123	221		
Mean:	56.2	86.0	110.0	198.4		

Total OB/GYN

	Instructor	Assistant Professor	Associate Professor	Professor	Chief	Chair
Count:	13	44	30	23	1	0
25th:	58	82	93	157		
Median:	62	90	109	170		
75th:	76	110	137	240		
Mean:	71.5	107.8	120.8	207.3		

OB/GYN: General

	Instructor	Assistant Professor	Associate Professor	Professor	Chief	Chair
Count:	5	15	7	7	0	0
25th:	60	85	69	165		
Median:	76	98	120	170		
75th:	108	163	157	240		
Mean:	82.2	116.0	120.0	205.9		

OB/GYN: Gynecologic Oncology

	Instructor	Assistant Professor	Associate Professor	Professor	Chief	Chair
Count:	0	1	1	0	0	0
25th:						
Median:						
75th:						
Mean:						

OB/GYN: Maternal & Fetal

	Instructor	Assistant Professor	Associate Professor	Professor	Chief	Chair
Count:	0	2	2	1	0	0
25th:						
Median:						
75th:						
Mean:						

Summary Statistics on Medical School Faculty Compensation for Northeastern Region Ph.D. or Other Doctoral Degree, Clinical Science Departments/Specialties Total Compensation in Thousands of Dollars (continued)

OB/GYN: Reproductive Endocrinology

	Instructor	Assistant Professor	Associate Professor	Professor	Chief	Chair
Count:	0	7	4	3	1	0
25th:		81				
Median:		112				
75th:		139				
Mean:		156.6				

OB/GYN: Other OB/GYN

	Instructor	Assistant Professor	Associate Professor	Professor	Chief	Chair
Count:	8	19	16	12	0	0
25th:	55	79	98	149		
Median:	59	88	108	171		
75th:	71	90	129	217		
Mean:	64.9	86.8	114.0	191.7		

Total Pathology

	Instructor	Assistant Professor	Associate Professor	Professor	Chief	Chair
Count:	25	183	108	148	5	2
25th:	54	76	112	156	241	
Median:	62	95	130	180	275	
75th:	79	118	175	215	304	
Mean:	68.4	101.0	140.5	188.3	272.6	

Pathology: Anatomic

	Instructor	Assistant Professor	Associate Professor	Professor	Chief	Chair
Count:	10	31	28	27	0	0
25th:	63	74	100	148		
Median:	75	108	118	178		
75th:	106	139	174	217		
Mean:	81.5	116.7	132.0	183.3		

Pathology: Clinical

	Instructor	Assistant Professor	Associate Professor	Professor	Chief	Chair
Count:	4	33	22	36	1	2
25th:		85	124	168		
Median:		106	160	194		
75th:		131	182	237		
Mean:		112.5	158.8	200.5		

TABLE 28 Summary Statistics on Medical School Faculty Compensation for Northeastern Region Ph.D. or Other Doctoral Degree, Clinical Science Departments/Specialties Total Compensation in Thousands of Dollars (continued)

Pathology: Other Pathology

	Instructor	Assistant Professor	Associate Professor	Professor	Chief	Chair
Count:	11	119	58	85	4	0
25th:	49	73	112	151		
Median:	58	91	130	176		
75th:	62	110	165	206		
Mean:	57.2	93.7	137.6	184.7		

Total Pediatrics

	Instructor	Assistant Professor	Associate Professor	Professor	Chief	Chair
Count:	27	173	85	74	6	0
25th:	55	75	98	140	165	
Median:	68	87	111	168	168	
75th:	72	103	139	205	221	
Mean:	66.9	94.1	123.8	176.4	183.7	

Adolescent Medicine

	Instructor	Assistant Professor	Associate Professor	Professor	Chief	Chair
Count:	0	4	1	2	0	0
25th:						
Median:						
75th:						
Mean:						

Allergy/Immunology-Peds.

	Instructor	Assistant Professor	Associate Professor	Professor	Chief	Chair
Count:	1	7	0	0	0	0
25th:		80				
Median:		89				
75th:		100				
Mean:		86.7				

Child & Adolescent Psychiatry

	Instructor	Assistant Professor	Associate Professor	Professor	Chief	Chair
Count:	3	22	13	8	3	0
25th:		83	112	150		
Median:		88	118	194		
75th:		103	130	222		
Mean:		98.6	127.5	191.3		

TABLE 28 Summary Statistics on Medical School Faculty Compensation for Northeastern Region Ph.D. or Other Doctoral Degree, Clinical Science Departments/Specialties Total Compensation in Thousands of Dollars (continued)

Critical/Intensive Care-Peds.

	Instructor	Assistant Professor	Associate Professor	Professor	Chief	Chair
Count:	0	1	0	0	0	0
25th:						
Median:						
75th:						
Mean:						

Emergency Medicine-Peds.

	Instructor	Assistant Professor	Associate Professor	Professor	Chief	Chair
Count:	0	1	0	0	0	0
25th:						
Median:						
75th:						
Mean:						

Endocrinology-Peds.

	Instructor	Assistant Professor	Associate Professor	Professor	Chief	Chair
Count:	1	5	1	0	0	0
25th:		69				
Median:		80				
75th:		118				
Mean:		90.4				

Gastroenterology-Peds.

	Instructor	Assistant Professor	Associate Professor	Professor	Chief	Chair
Count:	0	3	5	3	0	0
25th:			103			
Median:			133			
75th:			226			
Mean:			158.2			

General Pediatrics

	Instructor	Assistant Professor	Associate Professor	Professor	Chief	Chair
Count:	9	22	10	12	0	0
25th:	50	77	93	137		
Median:	55	89	106	152		
75th:	68	98	130	189		
Mean:	58.2	90.8	112.6	171.5		

TABLE 28 Summary Statistics on Medical School Faculty Compensation for Northeastern Region
Ph.D. or Other Doctoral Degree, Clinical Science Departments/Specialties
Total Compensation in Thousands of Dollars (continued)

Genetics-Peds.

	Instructor	Assistant Professor	Associate Professor	Professor	Chief	Chair
Count:	0	3	1	3	2	0
25th:						
Median:						
75th:						
Mean:						

Hematology/Oncology-Peds.

	Instructor	Assistant Professor	Associate Professor	Professor	Chief	Chair
Count:	2	16	5	2	0	0
25th:		67	102			
Median:		78	128			
75th:		97	156			
Mean:		82.6	128.8			

Hospital Medicine-Peds.

	Instructor	Assistant Professor	Associate Professor	Professor	Chief	Chair
Count:	0	0	0	0	0	0
25th:						
Median:						
75th:						
Mean:						

Infectious Disease-Peds.

	Instructor	Assistant Professor	Associate Professor	Professor	Chief	Chair
Count:	1	6	4	0	0	0
25th:		70				
Median:		102				
75th:		155				
Mean:		108.8				

Neonatology

	Instructor	Assistant Professor	Associate Professor	Professor	Chief	Chair
Count:	0	15	7	5	0	0
25th:		55	79	138		
Median:		81	103	152		
75th:		106	122	166		
Mean:		98.9	100.3	152.0		

TABLE 28 Summary Statistics on Medical School Faculty Compensation for Northeastern Region Ph.D. or Other Doctoral Degree, Clinical Science Departments/Specialties Total Compensation in Thousands of Dollars (continued)

Nephrology-Peds.

	Instructor	Assistant Professor	Associate Professor	Professor	Chief	Chair
Count:	0	2	1	0	0	0
25th:						
Median:						
75th:						
Mean:						

Neurology-Peds.

	Instructor	Assistant Professor	Associate Professor	Professor	Chief	Chair
Count:	2	6	2	2	0	0
25th:		74				
Median:		86				
75th:		109				
Mean:		95.2				

Pediatric Cardiology

	Instructor	Assistant Professor	Associate Professor	Professor	Chief	Chair
Count:	1	3	1	0	0	0
25th:						
Median:						
75th:						
Mean:						

Pulmonary-Peds.

	Instructor	Assistant Professor	Associate Professor	Professor	Chief	Chair
Count:	1	3	2	3	0	0
25th:						
Median:						
75th:						
Mean:						

Rheumatology-Peds.

	Instructor	Assistant Professor	Associate Professor	Professor	Chief	Chair
Count:	0	0	1	0	0	0
25th:						
Median:						
75th:						
Mean:						

TABLE 28 Summary Statistics on Medical School Faculty Compensation for Northeastern Region Ph.D. or Other Doctoral Degree, Clinical Science Departments/Specialties Total Compensation in Thousands of Dollars (continued)

Other Pediatrics

	Instructor	Assistant Professor	Associate Professor	Professor	Chief	Chair
Count:	6	54	31	34	1	0
25th:	68	76	97	155		
Median:	80	89	107	197		
75th:	98	112	142	223		
Mean:	79.8	94.7	126.5	191.6		

Total Radiology

	Instructor	Assistant Professor	Associate Professor	Professor	Chief	Chair
Count:	69	195	119	93	6	0
25th:	64	84	115	157	175	
Median:	77	100	145	198	228	
75th:	103	130	188	226	255	
Mean:	87.2	114.4	153.9	203.7	229.0	

Diagnostic Radiology: Total

	Instructor	Assistant Professor	Associate Professor	Professor	Chief	Chair
Count:	48	92	66	36	3	0
25th:	63	85	113	181		
Median:	75	99	135	213		
75th:	92	113	175	225		
Mean:	79.9	114.2	144.8	206.5		

Diagnostic Radiology: Interventional

	Instructor	Assistant Professor	Associate Professor	Professor	Chief	Chair
Count:	1	3	0	1	0	0
25th:						
Median:						
75th:						
Mean:						

Diagnostic Radiology: Non-interventional

	Instructor	Assistant Professor	Associate Professor	Professor	Chief	Chair
Count:	47	89	66	35	3	0
25th:	63	85	113	180		
Median:	75	98	135	213		
75th:	93	112	175	225		
Mean:	80.5	111.1	144.8	206.8		

TABLE 28 Summary Statistics on Medical School Faculty Compensation for Northeastern Region Ph.D. or Other Doctoral Degree, Clinical Science Departments/Specialties Total Compensation in Thousands of Dollars (continued)

Nuclear Medicine

	Instructor	Assistant Professor	Associate Professor	Professor	Chief	Chair
Count:	1	7	4	2	0	0
25th:		53				
Median:		72				
75th:		98				
Mean:		76.3				

Radiation Oncology

	Instructor	Assistant Professor	Associate Professor	Professor	Chief	Chair
Count:	13	57	30	31	2	0
25th:	93	96	147	149		
Median:	107	134	197	208		
75th:	168	161	229	283		
Mean:	126.7	132.5	187.6	211.4		

Other Radiology

	Instructor	Assistant Professor	Associate Professor	Professor	Chief	Chair
Count:	7	39	19	24	1	0
25th:	65	76	126	148		
Median:	69	89	145	166		
75th:	70	106	166	193		
Mean:	69.1	95.0	142.7	190.8		

Total Surgery

	Instructor	Assistant Professor	Associate Professor	Professor	Chief	Chair
Count:	50	145	80	70	4	0
25th:	57	68	103	146		
Median:	67	81	125	182		
75th:	92	105	149	235		
Mean:	76.8	90.6	150.1	190.8		

General Surgery

	Instructor	Assistant Professor	Associate Professor	Professor	Chief	Chair
Count:	13	25	12	6	0	0
25th:	73	75	99	148		
Median:	81	86	119	173		
75th:	107	121	157	193		
Mean:	90.0	104.6	148.9	180.2		

TABLE 28 Summary Statistics on Medical School Faculty Compensation for Northeastern Region Ph.D. or Other Doctoral Degree, Clinical Science Departments/Specialties Total Compensation in Thousands of Dollars (continued)

Neurosurgery

	Instructor	Assistant Professor	Associate Professor	Professor	Chief	Chair
Count:	12	27	11	14	0	0
25th:	61	65	101	158		
Median:	65	74	125	188		
75th:	72	85	290	210		
Mean:	67.3	82.7	203.9	185.9		

Orthopaedic Surgery

	Instructor	Assistant Professor	Associate Professor	Professor	Chief	Chair
Count:	12	31	19	17	2	0
25th:	52	75	109	144		
Median:	76	84	134	235		
75th:	113	107	170	283		
Mean:	88.1	96.0	179.4	220.5		

Pediatric Surgery

	Instructor	Assistant Professor	Associate Professor	Professor	Chief	Chair
Count:	0	7	1	0	0	0
25th:		55				
Median:		57				
75th:		80				
Mean:		68.4				

Plastic Surgery

	Instructor	Assistant Professor	Associate Professor	Professor	Chief	Chair
Count:	0	1	1	1	0	0
25th:						
Median:						
75th:						
Mean:						

Surgical Oncology

	Instructor	Assistant Professor	Associate Professor	Professor	Chief	Chair
Count:	2	3	0	2	0	0
25th:						
Median:						
75th:						
Mean:						

TABLE 28 Summary Statistics on Medical School Faculty Compensation for Northeastern Region Ph.D. or Other Doctoral Degree, Clinical Science Departments/Specialties Total Compensation in Thousands of Dollars (continued)

Thoracic & Cardiovascular Surgery

	Instructor	Assistant Professor	Associate Professor	Professor	Chief	Chair
Count:	0	9	4	2	1	0
25th:		53				
Median:		97				
75th:		108				
Mean:		92.2				

Transplant Surgery

	Instructor	Assistant Professor	Associate Professor	Professor	Chief	Chair
Count:	3	5	6	2	0	0
25th:		62	92			
Median:		111	146			
75th:		134	154			
Mean:		100.4	131.5			

Trauma/Critical Care Surgery

	Instructor	Assistant Professor	Associate Professor	Professor	Chief	Chair
Count:	0	0	0	0	0	0
25th:						
Median:						
75th:						
Mean:						

Urology

	Instructor	Assistant Professor	Associate Professor	Professor	Chief	Chair
Count:	5	18	10	8	1	0
25th:	54	66	105	163		
Median:	59	80	122	198		
75th:	77	85	145	262		
Mean:	64.0	82.6	121.4	207.4		

Vascular Surgery

	Instructor	Assistant Professor	Associate Professor	Professor	Chief	Chair
Count:	0	2	0	1	0	0
25th:						
Median:						
75th:						
Mean:						

TABLE 28 Summary Statistics on Medical School Faculty Compensation for Northeastern Region
Ph.D. or Other Doctoral Degree, Clinical Science Departments/Specialties
Total Compensation in Thousands of Dollars (continued)

Other Surgery

	Instructor	Assistant Professor	Associate Professor	Professor	Chief	Chair
Count:	3	17	16	17	0	0
25th:		64	111	131		
Median:		78	120	163		
75th:		92	125	187		
Mean:		78.8	116.7	170.1		

Other Clinical Science

Community Health

	Instructor	Assistant Professor	Associate Professor	Professor	Chief	Chair
Count:	4	35	13	36	2	3
25th:		81	120	145		
Median:		93	133	164		
75th:		108	151	229		
Mean:		97.3	138.3	184.8		

Emergency Medicine

	Instructor	Assistant Professor	Associate Professor	Professor	Chief	Chair
Count:	1	15	4	4	0	0
25th:		68				
Median:		93				
75th:		150				
Mean:		127.0				

Family Medicine

	Instructor	Assistant Professor	Associate Professor	Professor	Chief	Chair
Count:	2	33	21	14	1	1
25th:		85	88	130		
Median:		93	102	144		
75th:		100	120	157		
Mean:		95.5	106.9	145.0		

Neurology

	Instructor	Assistant Professor	Associate Professor	Professor	Chief	Chair
Count:	45	122	57	45	1	0
25th:	59	75	102	142		
Median:	66	89	122	168		
75th:	86	108	154	197		
Mean:	75.0	93.2	134.0	173.2		

TABLE 28 Summary Statistics on Medical School Faculty Compensation for Northeastern Region
Ph.D. or Other Doctoral Degree, Clinical Science Departments/Specialties
Total Compensation in Thousands of Dollars (continued)

Ophthalmology

	Instructor	Assistant Professor	Associate Professor	Professor	Chief	Chair
Count:	8	39	21	23	0	0
25th:	56	70	102	140		
Median:	70	85	122	171		
75th:	94	105	149	204		
Mean:	72.1	89.7	123.4	174.7		

Otolaryngology

	Instructor	Assistant Professor	Associate Professor	Professor	Chief	Chair
Count:	5	21	11	17	0	0
25th:	53	81	103	130		
Median:	70	92	117	158		
75th:	74	119	123	200		
Mean:	64.6	108.1	124.6	161.3		

Physical Medicine & Rehabilitation

	Instructor	Assistant Professor	Associate Professor	Professor	Chief	Chair
Count:	2	20	7	4	1	0
25th:		73	108			
Median:		85	134			
75th:		96	190			
Mean:		86.9	144.3			

Preventive Medicine

	Instructor	Assistant Professor	Associate Professor	Professor	Chief	Chair
Count:	1	27	33	14	0	1
25th:		82	114	144		
Median:		91	125	174		
75th:		103	138	179		
Mean:		93.9	124.7	176.4		

Psychiatry

	Instructor	Assistant Professor	Associate Professor	Professor	Chief	Chair
Count:	80	304	175	152	5	2
25th:	66	77	104	148	193	
Median:	83	88	118	171	246	
75th:	96	103	140	211	259	
Mean:	85.3	94.1	125.2	181.6	229.8	

TABLE 28 Summary Statistics on Medical School Faculty Compensation for Northeastern Region Ph.D. or Other Doctoral Degree, Clinical Science Departments/Specialties Total Compensation in Thousands of Dollars (continued)

Other

	Instructor	Assistant Professor	Associate Professor	Professor	Chief	Chair
Count:	4	21	22	11	0	3
25th:		83	118	158		
Median:		97	129	161		
75th:		103	145	176		
Mean:		96.7	131.1	177.0		

TABLE 29 Summary Statistics on Medical School Faculty Compensation for Southern Region Ph.D. or Other Doctoral Degree, Clinical Science Departments/Specialties Total Compensation in Thousands of Dollars

CLINICAL SCIENCE - TOTAL ALL DEPARTMENTS/SPECIALTIES

	Instructor	Assistant Professor	Associate Professor	Professor	Chief	Chair
Count:	290	1,965	985	959	57	19
25th:	50	69	91	125	148	162
Median:	58	80	108	158	192	215
75th:	70	95	129	195	243	265
Mean:	62.7	86.2	114.6	166.8	199.8	219.4

Total Anesthesiology

	Instructor	Assistant Professor	Associate Professor	Professor	Chief	Chair
Count:	4	33	19	15	0	0
25th:		66	90	158		
Median:		74	114	190		
75th:		94	131	215		
Mean:		82.0	137.2	209.5		

Anesthesiology: General

	Instructor	Assistant Professor	Associate Professor	Professor	Chief	Chair
Count:	3	33	18	15	0	0
25th:		66	90	158		
Median:		74	116	190		
75th:		94	131	215		
Mean:		82.0	139.3	209.5		

Anesthesiology: Pain Management

	Instructor	Assistant Professor	Associate Professor	Professor	Chief	Chair
Count:	1	0	1	0	0	0
25th:						
Median:						
75th:						
Mean:						

Anesthesiology: Pediatric

	Instructor	Assistant Professor	Associate Professor	Professor	Chief	Chair
Count:	0	0	0	0	0	0
25th:						
Median:						
75th:						
Mean:						

TABLE 29 Summary Statistics on Medical School Faculty Compensation for Southern Region Ph.D. or Other Doctoral Degree, Clinical Science Departments/Specialties Total Compensation in Thousands of Dollars (continued)

Total Dermatology

	Instructor	Assistant Professor	Associate Professor	Professor	Chief	Chair
Count:	2	6	4	5	0	0
25th:		76		88		
Median:		80		133		
75th:		87		242		
Mean:		81.0		158.4		

Dermatology (excluding Mohs Surgery)

	Instructor	Assistant Professor	Associate Professor	Professor	Chief	Chair
Count:	2	6	4	5	0	0
25th:		76		88		
Median:		80		133		
75th:		87		242		
Mean:		81.0		158.4		

Dermatology: Mohs Surgery

	Instructor	Assistant Professor	Associate Professor	Professor	Chief	Chair
Count:	0	0	0	0	0	0
25th:						
Median:						
75th:						
Mean:						

Total Medicine

	Instructor	Assistant Professor	Associate Professor	Professor	Chief	Chair
Count:	91	490	203	160	5	2
25th:	49	65	83	115	134	
Median:	54	77	103	153	180	
75th:	64	90	120	190	202	
Mean:	56.3	80.2	104.6	159.2	170.0	

Allergy/Immunology-Med.

	Instructor	Assistant Professor	Associate Professor	Professor	Chief	Chair
Count:	1	6	2	6	0	0
25th:		61		170		
Median:		74		171		
75th:		84		194		
Mean:		74.7		176.5		

Cardiology: Total

	Instructor	Assistant Professor	Associate Professor	Professor	Chief	Chair
Count:	8	53	18	19	0	0
25th:	50	64	88	117		
Median:	57	77	112	153		
75th:	65	87	135	198		
Mean:	60.4	81.2	123.0	169.9		

Cardiology: Invasive Interventional-Med.

	Instructor	Assistant Professor	Associate Professor	Professor	Chief	Chair
Count:	0	9	2	3	0	0
25th:		58				
Median:		80				
75th:		102				
Mean:		79.1				

Cardiology: Invasive Non-interventional-Med.

	Instructor	Assistant Professor	Associate Professor	Professor	Chief	Chair
Count:	0	0	0	2	0	0
25th:						
Median:						
75th:						
Mean:						

Cardiology: Non-invasive-Med.

	Instructor	Assistant Professor	Associate Professor	Professor	Chief	Chair
Count:	8	44	16	14	0	0
25th:	50	66	87	122		
Median:	57	76	109	156		
75th:	65	86	139	188		
Mean:	60.4	81.7	122.6	160.6		

Critical/Intensive Care-Med.

	Instructor	Assistant Professor	Associate Professor	Professor	Chief	Chair
Count:	0	0	1	0	0	0
25th:						
Median:						
75th:						
Mean:						

Endocrinology-Med.

	Instructor	Assistant Professor	Associate Professor	Professor	Chief	Chair
Count:	13	50	14	9	2	0
25th:	44	60	85	124		
Median:	50	74	106	164		
75th:	53	87	114	178		
Mean:	51.7	76.0	102.0	152.8		

Gastroenterology-Med.

	Instructor	Assistant Professor	Associate Professor	Professor	Chief	Chair
Count:	6	32	11	8	0	0
25th:	48	62	77	105		
Median:	57	75	105	144		
75th:	65	85	120	184		
Mean:	57.8	74.8	100.0	150.1		

General Internal Medicine

	Instructor	Assistant Professor	Associate Professor	Professor	Chief	Chair
Count:	3	28	22	14	0	0
25th:		72	84	100		
Median:		85	114	132		
75th:		93	130	201		
Mean:		84.2	112.6	145.0		

Geriatrics-Med.

	Instructor	Assistant Professor	Associate Professor	Professor	Chief	Chair
Count:	4	31	16	18	1	0
25th:		73	92	115		
Median:		84	105	134		
75th:		93	114	176		
Mean:		84.4	104.0	162.1		

Hematology/Oncology-Med.

	Instructor	Assistant Professor	Associate Professor	Professor	Chief	Chair
Count:	20	59	30	29	0	0
25th:	50	65	80	102		
Median:	56	76	110	166		
75th:	61	90	127	193		
Mean:	55.7	78.6	106.8	165.1		

TABLE 29

Summary Statistics on Medical School Faculty Compensation for Southern Region Ph.D. or Other Doctoral Degree, Clinical Science Departments/Specialties Total Compensation in Thousands of Dollars (continued)

Hospital Medicine

	Instructor	Assistant Professor	Associate Professor	Professor	Chief	Chair
Count:	0	1	0	0	0	0
25th:						
Median:						
75th:						
Mean:						

Infectious Disease-Med.

	Instructor	Assistant Professor	Associate Professor	Professor	Chief	Chair
Count:	10	44	16	9	0	0
25th:	50	67	89	113		
Median:	54	79	101	140		
75th:	60	93	117	172		
Mean:	54.9	82.8	102.0	142.4		

Nephrology-Med.

	Instructor	Assistant Professor	Associate Professor	Professor	Chief	Chair
Count:	6	46	21	9	0	0
25th:	49	62	82	119		
Median:	53	71	89	148		
75th:	65	92	94	194		
Mean:	55.3	78.3	97.5	165.0		

Pulmonary-Med.

	Instructor	Assistant Professor	Associate Professor	Professor	Chief	Chair
Count:	6	38	15	10	0	0
25th:	42	62	87	125		
Median:	48	71	103	164		
75th:	51	80	107	191		
Mean:	48.5	74.6	99.2	165.0		

Rheumatology-Med.

	Instructor	Assistant Professor	Associate Professor	Professor	Chief	Chair
Count:	0	15	9	9	0	0
25th:		60	81	122		
Median:		64	89	153		
75th:		75	106	173		
Mean:		66.7	93.4	142.3		

TABLE 29 Summary Statistics on Medical School Faculty Compensation for Southern Region Ph.D. or Other Doctoral Degree, Clinical Science Departments/Specialties Total Compensation in Thousands of Dollars (continued)

Other Medicine

	Instructor	Assistant Professor	Associate Professor	Professor	Chief	Chair
Count:	14	87	28	20	2	2
25th:	53	72	84	109		
Median:	62	84	107	153		
75th:	65	94	120	194		
Mean:	59.1	86.5	102.6	158.6		

Total OB/GYN

	Instructor	Assistant Professor	Associate Professor	Professor	Chief	Chair
Count:	5	35	25	32	1	1
25th:	39	70	93	123		
Median:	40	89	107	147		
75th:	64	113	120	197		
Mean:	49.0	93.5	109.2	159.8		

OB/GYN: General

	Instructor	Assistant Professor	Associate Professor	Professor	Chief	Chair
Count:	1	8	11	14	0	0
25th:		71	94	118		
Median:		82	105	128		
75th:		90	119	160		
Mean:		80.0	108.9	145.5		

OB/GYN: Gynecologic Oncology

	Instructor	Assistant Professor	Associate Professor	Professor	Chief	Chair
Count:	0	1	1	1	0	0
25th:						
Median:						
75th:						
Mean:						

OB/GYN: Maternal & Fetal

	Instructor	Assistant Professor	Associate Professor	Professor	Chief	Chair
Count:	0	4	1	3	0	0
25th:						
Median:						
75th:						
Mean:						

TABLE 29 Summary Statistics on Medical School Faculty Compensation for Southern Region Ph.D. or Other Doctoral Degree, Clinical Science Departments/Specialties Total Compensation in Thousands of Dollars (continued)

OB/GYN: Reproductive Endocrinology

	Instructor	Assistant Professor	Associate Professor	Professor	Chief	Chair
Count:	1	12	5	3	0	1
25th:		59	95			
Median:		122	120			
75th:		142	143			
Mean:		106.7	119.0			

OB/GYN: Other OB/GYN

	Instructor	Assistant Professor	Associate Professor	Professor	Chief	Chair
Count:	3	10	7	11	1	0
25th:		76	90	115		
Median:		89	110	172		
75th:		112	119	198		
Mean:		90.8	107.6	160.1		

Total Pathology

	Instructor	Assistant Professor	Associate Professor	Professor	Chief	Chair
Count:	26	126	94	158	3	0
25th:	47	63	100	135		
Median:	53	83	117	163		
75th:	70	100	141	193		
Mean:	60.0	87.2	122.5	167.1		

Pathology: Anatomic

	Instructor	Assistant Professor	Associate Professor	Professor	Chief	Chair
Count:	4	13	19	17	0	0
25th:		80	104	139		
Median:		94	120	165		
75th:		105	135	180		
Mean:		96.8	121.5	161.1		

Pathology: Clinical

	Instructor	Assistant Professor	Associate Professor	Professor	Chief	Chair
Count:	6	26	34	53	0	0
25th:	49	73	116	131		
Median:	53	90	135	162		
75th:	70	117	159	184		
Mean:	60.5	101.5	133.6	164.9		

TABLE 29 Summary Statistics on Medical School Faculty Compensation for Southern Region Ph.D. or Other Doctoral Degree, Clinical Science Departments/Specialties Total Compensation in Thousands of Dollars (continued)

Pathology: Other Pathology

	Instructor	Assistant Professor	Associate Professor	Professor	Chief	Chair
Count:	16	87	41	88	3	0
25th:	47	62	91	136		
Median:	52	74	110	161		
75th:	69	94	122	199		
Mean:	58.3	81.5	113.7	169.5		

Total Pediatrics

	Instructor	Assistant Professor	Associate Professor	Professor	Chief	Chair
Count:	36	250	120	108	5	1
25th:	56	71	89	124	159	
Median:	61	82	105	150	214	
75th:	80	92	120	192	237	
Mean:	67.1	83.8	107.7	162.4	201.0	

Adolescent Medicine

	Instructor	Assistant Professor	Associate Professor	Professor	Chief	Chair
Count:	0	4	3	1	0	0
25th:						
Median:						
75th:						
Mean:						

Allergy/Immunology-Peds.

	Instructor	Assistant Professor	Associate Professor	Professor	Chief	Chair
Count:	0	3	3	1	0	0
25th:						
Median:						
75th:						
Mean:						

Child & Adolescent Psychiatry

	Instructor	Assistant Professor	Associate Professor	Professor	Chief	Chair
Count:	2	23	7	11	0	0
25th:		70	72	100		
Median:		79	97	128		
75th:		89	108	168		
Mean:		79.4	103.9	138.3		

TABLE 29 Summary Statistics on Medical School Faculty Compensation for Southern Region Ph.D. or Other Doctoral Degree, Clinical Science Departments/Specialties Total Compensation in Thousands of Dollars (continued)

Critical/Intensive Care-Peds.

	Instructor	Assistant Professor	Associate Professor	Professor	Chief	Chair
Count:	3	1	0	1	0	0
25th:						
Median:						
75th:						
Mean:						

Emergency Medicine-Peds.

	Instructor	Assistant Professor	Associate Professor	Professor	Chief	Chair
Count:	0	1	1	0	0	0
25th:						
Median:						
75th:						
Mean:						

Endocrinology-Peds.

	Instructor	Assistant Professor	Associate Professor	Professor	Chief	Chair
Count:	3	9	2	3	0	0
25th:		59				
Median:		79				
75th:		90				
Mean:		79.9				

Gastroenterology-Peds.

	Instructor	Assistant Professor	Associate Professor	Professor	Chief	Chair
Count:	2	3	2	2	0	0
25th:						
Median:						
75th:						
Mean:						

General Pediatrics

	Instructor	Assistant Professor	Associate Professor	Professor	Chief	Chair
Count:	1	7	9	8	0	0
25th:		62	89	93		
Median:		77	109	137		
75th:		85	118	153		
Mean:		74.1	108.0	130.8		

Genetics-Peds.

	Instructor	Assistant Professor	Associate Professor	Professor	Chief	Chair
Count:	0	12	9	12	1	0
25th:		65	80	121		
Median:		77	91	148		
75th:		84	103	198		
Mean:		76.5	92.7	165.6		

Hematology/Oncology-Peds.

	Instructor	Assistant Professor	Associate Professor	Professor	Chief	Chair
Count:	7	30	13	4	0	0
25th:	55	75	86			
Median:	85	82	110			
75th:	101	96	122			
Mean:	76.9	85.9	109.9			

Hospital Medicine-Peds.

	Instructor	Assistant Professor	Associate Professor	Professor	Chief	Chair
Count:	0	0	0	0	0	0
25th:						
Median:						
75th:						
Mean:						

Infectious Disease-Peds.

	Instructor	Assistant Professor	Associate Professor	Professor	Chief	Chair
Count:	4	13	6	7	0	0
25th:		67	95	112		
Median:		82	106	127		
75th:		89	112	170		
Mean:		78.9	107.5	136.0		

Neonatology

	Instructor	Assistant Professor	Associate Professor	Professor	Chief	Chair
Count:	0	12	8	7	0	0
25th:		65	84	106		
Median:		68	93	154		
75th:		83	105	209		
Mean:		72.1	96.5	168.9		

TABLE 29 Summary Statistics on Medical School Faculty Compensation for Southern Region
Ph.D. or Other Doctoral Degree, Clinical Science Departments/Specialties
Total Compensation in Thousands of Dollars (continued)

Nephrology-Peds.

	Instructor	Assistant Professor	Associate Professor	Professor	Chief	Chair
Count:	0	4	0	1	0	0
25th:						
Median:						
75th:						
Mean:						

Neurology-Peds.

	Instructor	Assistant Professor	Associate Professor	Professor	Chief	Chair
Count:	2	10	2	5	0	0
25th:		70		114		
Median:		86		178		
75th:		100		236		
Mean:		82.8		175.4		

Pediatric Cardiology

	Instructor	Assistant Professor	Associate Professor	Professor	Chief	Chair
Count:	0	6	1	0	0	0
25th:		60				
Median:		75				
75th:		95				
Mean:		87.3				

Pulmonary-Peds.

	Instructor	Assistant Professor	Associate Professor	Professor	Chief	Chair
Count:	1	6	6	0	0	0
25th:		59	79			
Median:		74	90			
75th:		90	144			
Mean:		73.8	107.8			

Rheumatology-Peds.

	Instructor	Assistant Professor	Associate Professor	Professor	Chief	Chair
Count:	0	1	0	0	0	0
25th:						
Median:						
75th:						
Mean:						

TABLE 29 Summary Statistics on Medical School Faculty Compensation for Southern Region Ph.D. or Other Doctoral Degree, Clinical Science Departments/Specialties Total Compensation in Thousands of Dollars (continued)

Other Pediatrics

	Instructor	Assistant Professor	Associate Professor	Professor	Chief	Chair
Count:	11	105	48	45	4	1
25th:	56	76	96	131		
Median:	61	85	111	158		
75th:	74	97	122	193		
Mean:	64.4	88.4	109.9	172.8		

Total Radiology

	Instructor	Assistant Professor	Associate Professor	Professor	Chief	Chair
Count:	24	206	113	74	12	2
25th:	54	83	112	158	199	
Median:	61	102	143	190	225	
75th:	76	134	175	232	275	
Mean:	69.7	111.8	147.7	200.3	242.9	

Diagnostic Radiology: Total

	Instructor	Assistant Professor	Associate Professor	Professor	Chief	Chair
Count:	3	32	24	18	3	0
25th:		79	105	148		
Median:		95	130	178		
75th:		103	149	228		
Mean:		107.3	128.7	206.9		

Diagnostic Radiology: Interventional

	Instructor	Assistant Professor	Associate Professor	Professor	Chief	Chair
Count:	1	1	0	0	0	0
25th:						
Median:						
75th:						
Mean:						

Diagnostic Radiology: Non-interventional

	Instructor	Assistant Professor	Associate Professor	Professor	Chief	Chair
Count:	2	31	24	18	3	0
25th:		77	105	148		
Median:		94	130	178		
75th:		101	149	228		
Mean:		102.5	128.7	206.9		

Summary Statistics on Medical School Faculty Compensation for Southern Region Ph.D. or Other Doctoral Degree, Clinical Science Departments/Specialties Total Compensation in Thousands of Dollars (continued)

Nuclear Medicine

	Instructor	Assistant Professor	Associate Professor	Professor	Chief	Chair
Count:	0	3	3	4	0	0
25th:						
Median:						
75th:						
Mean:						

Radiation Oncology

	Instructor	Assistant Professor	Associate Professor	Professor	Chief	Chair
Count:	14	102	43	29	8	0
25th:	55	88	160	185	213	
Median:	57	130	175	206	248	
75th:	80	150	202	253	312	
Mean:	73.2	122.0	175.4	217.3	262.1	

Other Radiology

	Instructor	Assistant Professor	Associate Professor	Professor	Chief	Chair
Count:	7	69	43	23	1	2
25th:	52	80	111	150		
Median:	59	95	131	178		
75th:	75	109	144	221		
Mean:	61.0	99.5	132.3	182.0		

Total Surgery

	Instructor	Assistant Professor	Associate Professor	Professor	Chief	Chair
Count:	28	167	65	84	6	2
25th:	50	65	90	125	285	
Median:	55	75	108	160	312	
75th:	68	95	125	202	325	
Mean:	61.2	86.8	112.1	173.2	276.7	

General Surgery

	Instructor	Assistant Professor	Associate Professor	Professor	Chief	Chair
Count:	8	27	8	19	0	0
25th:	50	65	89	103		
Median:	53	85	105	160		
75th:	61	105	118	201		
Mean:	58.5	88.3	111.3	168.7		

Summary Statistics on Medical School Faculty Compensation for Southern Region Ph.D. or Other Doctoral Degree, Clinical Science Departments/Specialties Total Compensation in Thousands of Dollars (continued)

Neurosurgery

	Instructor	Assistant Professor	Associate Professor	Professor	Chief	Chair
Count:	1	37	15	15	1	1
25th:		59	89	129		
Median:		75	105	143		
75th:		93	133	208		
Mean:		100.7	118.7	178.2		

Orthopaedic Surgery

	Instructor	Assistant Professor	Associate Professor	Professor	Chief	Chair
Count:	5	23	9	10	1	0
25th:	55	72	84	125		
Median:	56	83	90	139		
75th:	65	115	101	189		
Mean:	59.0	94.0	93.4	151.7		

Pediatric Surgery

	Instructor	Assistant Professor	Associate Professor	Professor	Chief	Chair
Count:	2	5	1	0	0	0
25th:		64				
Median:		70				
75th:		90				
Mean:		75.4				

Plastic Surgery

	Instructor	Assistant Professor	Associate Professor	Professor	Chief	Chair
Count:	0	3	3	4	0	0
25th:						
Median:						
75th:						
Mean:						

Surgical Oncology

	Instructor	Assistant Professor	Associate Professor	Professor	Chief	Chair
Count:	0	6	3	1	0	0
25th:		73				
Median:		86				
75th:		100				
Mean:		84.7				

TABLE 29 Summary Statistics on Medical School Faculty Compensation for Southern Region Ph.D. or Other Doctoral Degree, Clinical Science Departments/Specialties Total Compensation in Thousands of Dollars (continued)

Thoracic & Cardiovascular Surgery

	Instructor	Assistant Professor	Associate Professor	Professor	Chief	Chair
Count:	1	4	2	5	0	0
25th:				108		
Median:				160		
75th:				186		
Mean:				149.4		

Transplant Surgery

	Instructor	Assistant Professor	Associate Professor	Professor	Chief	Chair
Count:	4	9	5	6	0	1
25th:		60	115	177		
Median:		72	124	183		
75th:		91	159	300		
Mean:		74.9	134.2	224.5		

Trauma/Critical Care Surgery

	Instructor	Assistant Professor	Associate Professor	Professor	Chief	Chair
Count:	1	9	2	4	0	0
25th:		60				
Median:		67				
75th:		79				
Mean:		69.1				

Urology

	Instructor	Assistant Professor	Associate Professor	Professor	Chief	Chair
Count:	2	20	4	12	0	0
25th:		57		147		
Median:		68		160		
75th:		93		192		
Mean:		75.6		172.5		

Vascular Surgery

	Instructor	Assistant Professor	Associate Professor	Professor	Chief	Chair
Count:	1	2	1	1	0	0
25th:						
Median:						
75th:						
Mean:						

TABLE 29 Summary Statistics on Medical School Faculty Compensation for Southern Region Ph.D. or Other Doctoral Degree, Clinical Science Departments/Specialties Total Compensation in Thousands of Dollars (continued)

Other Surgery

	Instructor	Assistant Professor	Associate Professor	Professor	Chief	Chair
Count:	3	22	12	7	4	0
25th:		72	88	161		
Median:		88	96	190		
75th:		98	117	264		
Mean:		86.3	103.9	199.4		

Other Clinical Science

Community Health

	Instructor	Assistant Professor	Associate Professor	Professor	Chief	Chair
Count:	3	33	37	16	4	3
25th:		81	96	153		
Median:		87	105	176		
75th:		98	119	202		
Mean:		89.7	111.6	177.2		

Emergency Medicine

	Instructor	Assistant Professor	Associate Professor	Professor	Chief	Chair
Count:	2	4	4	3	1	0
25th:						
Median:						
75th:						
Mean:						

Family Medicine

	Instructor	Assistant Professor	Associate Professor	Professor	Chief	Chair
Count:	9	59	30	35	3	0
25th:	64	70	87	96		
Median:	73	80	104	121		
75th:	80	97	113	165		
Mean:	71.4	85.4	102.0	130.9		

Neurology

	Instructor	Assistant Professor	Associate Professor	Professor	Chief	Chair
Count:	13	67	18	27	3	0
25th:	47	64	71	132		
Median:	55	80	95	155		
75th:	62	95	105	188		
Mean:	56.5	83.2	96.3	162.3		

TABLE 29 Summary Statistics on Medical School Faculty Compensation for Southern Region Ph.D. or Other Doctoral Degree, Clinical Science Departments/Specialties Total Compensation in Thousands of Dollars (continued)

Ophthalmology

	Instructor	Assistant Professor	Associate Professor	Professor	Chief	Chair
Count:	9	52	37	29	0	0
25th:	46	63	89	136		
Median:	53	80	108	171		
75th:	100	97	121	202		
Mean:	70.4	81.9	110.0	171.1		

Otolaryngology

	Instructor	Assistant Professor	Associate Professor	Professor	Chief	Chair
Count:	4	26	20	14	2	0
25th:		69	93	159		
Median:		76	102	169		
75th:		83	111	193		
Mean:		77.4	107.4	175.3		

Physical Medicine & Rehabilitation

	Instructor	Assistant Professor	Associate Professor	Professor	Chief	Chair
Count:	12	53	30	11	1	3
25th:	66	75	94	114		
Median:	70	82	99	150		
75th:	74	93	117	159		
Mean:	73.8	87.7	106.3	141.7		

Preventive Medicine

	Instructor	Assistant Professor	Associate Professor	Professor	Chief	Chair
Count:	0	20	21	19	1	3
25th:		73	100	120		
Median:		84	105	155		
75th:		90	118	198		
Mean:		82.6	110.2	185.3		

Psychiatry

	Instructor	Assistant Professor	Associate Professor	Professor	Chief	Chair
Count:	17	305	133	150	10	1
25th:	52	70	92	127	122	
Median:	59	78	105	155	156	
75th:	76	89	127	189	178	
Mean:	63.6	82.1	112.5	161.3	160.2	

TABLE 29

Summary Statistics on Medical School Faculty Compensation for Southern Region Ph.D. or Other Doctoral Degree, Clinical Science Departments/Specialties Total Compensation in Thousands of Dollars (continued)

Other

	Instructor	Assistant Professor	Associate Professor	Professor	Chief	Chair
Count:	5	33	12	19	0	1
25th:	70	68	89	105		
Median:	70	76	107	150		
75th:	86	91	118	198		
Mean:	76.4	78.8	107.0	163.3		

TABLE 30 Summary Statistics on Medical School Faculty Compensation for Midwestern Region Ph.D. or Other Doctoral Degree, Clinical Science Departments/Specialties Total Compensation in Thousands of Dollars

CLINICAL SCIENCE - TOTAL ALL DEPARTMENTS/SPECIALTIES

	Instructor	Assistant Professor	Associate Professor	Professor	Chief	Chair
Count:	180	1,386	794	800	24	11
25th:	54	74	98	131	186	180
Median:	64	87	116	160	206	247
75th:	79	101	140	200	299	279
Mean:	71.8	92.0	123.1	169.1	230.6	250.3

Total Anesthesiology

	Instructor	Assistant Professor	Associate Professor	Professor	Chief	Chair
Count:	6	16	13	22	0	0
25th:	50	79	84	130		
Median:	68	82	88	149		
75th:	77	100	125	188		
Mean:	74.2	84.8	98.5	156.3		

Anesthesiology: General

	Instructor	Assistant Professor	Associate Professor	Professor	Chief	Chair
Count:	6	15	13	22	0	0
25th:	50	79	84	130		
Median:	68	82	88	149		
75th:	77	102	125	188		
Mean:	74.2	85.1	98.5	156.3		

Anesthesiology: Pain Management

	Instructor	Assistant Professor	Associate Professor	Professor	Chief	Chair
Count:	0	1	0	0	0	0
25th:						
Median:						
75th:						
Mean:						

Anesthesiology: Pediatric

	Instructor	Assistant Professor	Associate Professor	Professor	Chief	Chair
Count:	0	0	0	0	0	0
25th:						
Median:						
75th:						
Mean:						

TABLE 30 Summary Statistics on Medical School Faculty Compensation for Midwestern Region Ph.D. or Other Doctoral Degree, Clinical Science Departments/Specialties Total Compensation in Thousands of Dollars (continued)

Total Dermatology

	Instructor	Assistant Professor	Associate Professor	Professor	Chief	Chair
Count:	0	18	4	11	0	0
25th:		82		117		
Median:		87		159		
75th:		91		185		
Mean:		87.7		159.6		

Dermatology (excluding Mohs Surgery)

	Instructor	Assistant Professor	Associate Professor	Professor	Chief	Chair
Count:	0	18	4	11	0	0
25th:		82		117		
Median:		87		159		
75th:		91		185		
Mean:		87.7		159.6		

Dermatology: Mohs Surgery

	Instructor	Assistant Professor	Associate Professor	Professor	Chief	Chair
Count:	0	0	0	0	0	0
25th:						
Median:						
75th:						
Mean:						

Total Medicine

	Instructor	Assistant Professor	Associate Professor	Professor	Chief	Chair
Count:	41	292	146	113	5	1
25th:	51	65	98	130	171	
Median:	58	82	117	153	197	
75th:	66	96	140	188	284	
Mean:	58.8	82.7	121.0	164.2	221.4	

Allergy/Immunology-Med.

	Instructor	Assistant Professor	Associate Professor	Professor	Chief	Chair
Count:	0	10	6	7	1	0
25th:		92	133	148		
Median:		105	140	186		
75th:		123	143	230		
Mean:		108.1	139.8	186.1		

TABLE 30 Summary Statistics on Medical School Faculty Compensation for Midwestern Region Ph.D. or Other Doctoral Degree, Clinical Science Departments/Specialties Total Compensation in Thousands of Dollars (continued)

Cardiology: Total

	Instructor	Assistant Professor	Associate Professor	Professor	Chief	Chair
Count:	4	37	22	12	0	0
25th:		64	91	128		
Median:		76	115	156		
75th:		97	135	179		
Mean:		81.9	114.6	157.9		

Cardiology: Invasive Interventional-Med.

	Instructor	Assistant Professor	Associate Professor	Professor	Chief	Chair
Count:	0	7	7	2	0	0
25th:		65	86			
Median:		84	130			
75th:		120	145			
Mean:		91.3	117.7			

Cardiology: Invasive Non-interventional-Med.

	Instructor	Assistant Professor	Associate Professor	Professor	Chief	Chair
Count:	1	0	0	0	0	0
25th:						
Median:						
75th:						
Mean:						

Cardiology: Non-invasive-Med.

	Instructor	Assistant Professor	Associate Professor	Professor	Chief	Chair
Count:	3	30	15	10	0	0
25th:		63	92	122		
Median:		75	112	154		
75th:		92	135	164		
Mean:		79.7	113.1	154.6		

Critical/Intensive Care-Med.

	Instructor	Assistant Professor	Associate Professor	Professor	Chief	Chair
Count:	0	0	0	0	0	0
25th:						
Median:						
75th:						
Mean:						

Summary Statistics on Medical School Faculty Compensation for Midwestern Region Ph.D. or Other Doctoral Degree, Clinical Science Departments/Specialties Total Compensation in Thousands of Dollars (continued)

Endocrinology-Med.

	Instructor	Assistant Professor	Associate Professor	Professor	Chief	Chair
Count:	2	18	12	15	0	0
25th:		55	91	117		
Median:		62	111	149		
75th:		86	122	187		
Mean:		70.7	108.1	153.1		

Gastroenterology-Med.

	Instructor	Assistant Professor	Associate Professor	Professor	Chief	Chair
Count:	5	23	13	8	0	0
25th:	47	61	104	133		
Median:	51	84	120	156		
75th:	76	96	146	180		
Mean:	59.2	80.3	123.1	159.8		

General Internal Medicine

	Instructor	Assistant Professor	Associate Professor	Professor	Chief	Chair
Count:	2	27	18	14	0	0
25th:		65	105	113		
Median:		85	115	135		
75th:		100	134	167		
Mean:		84.1	124.1	147.4		

Geriatrics-Med.

	Instructor	Assistant Professor	Associate Professor	Professor	Chief	Chair
Count:	4	16	5	2	0	0
25th:		65	95			
Median:		79	96			
75th:		87	170			
Mean:		79.1	125.2			

Hematology/Oncology-Med.

	Instructor	Assistant Professor	Associate Professor	Professor	Chief	Chair
Count:	12	41	17	19	0	0
25th:	51	69	111	135		
Median:	56	81	137	157		
75th:	63	95	149	225		
Mean:	56.5	81.5	129.9	181.7		

TABLE 30 Summary Statistics on Medical School Faculty Compensation for Midwestern Region Ph.D. or Other Doctoral Degree, Clinical Science Departments/Specialties Total Compensation in Thousands of Dollars (continued)

Hospital Medicine

	Instructor	Assistant Professor	Associate Professor	Professor	Chief	Chair
Count:	0	0	0	0	0	0
25th:						
Median:						
75th:						
Mean:						

Infectious Disease-Med.

	Instructor	Assistant Professor	Associate Professor	Professor	Chief	Chair
Count:	3	15	7	10	0	0
25th:		76	73	129		
Median:		91	96	147		
75th:		109	104	159		
Mean:		91.5	89.4	143.1		

Nephrology-Med.

	Instructor	Assistant Professor	Associate Professor	Professor	Chief	Chair
Count:	0	12	10	6	0	0
25th:		58	84	109		
Median:		71	89	135		
75th:		92	114	142		
Mean:		77.1	95.1	133.8		

Pulmonary-Med.

	Instructor	Assistant Professor	Associate Professor	Professor	Chief	Chair
Count:	3	39	13	6	0	0
25th:		64	98	121		
Median:		76	129	173		
75th:		87	160	184		
Mean:		78.9	127.7	165.7		

Rheumatology-Med.

	Instructor	Assistant Professor	Associate Professor	Professor	Chief	Chair
Count:	0	17	5	5	0	0
25th:		56	104	124		
Median:		82	114	138		
75th:		98	202	158		
Mean:		82.8	145.2	140.2		

Other Medicine

	Instructor	Assistant Professor	Associate Professor	Professor	Chief	Chair
Count:	6	37	18	9	4	1
25th:	55	73	102	176		
Median:	64	88	115	200		
75th:	66	101	140	246		
Mean:	62.3	88.4	132.4	219.2		

Total OB/GYN

	Instructor	Assistant Professor	Associate Professor	Professor	Chief	Chair
Count:	2	32	25	24	1	0
25th:		71	95	138		
Median:		82	106	161		
75th:		90	122	198		
Mean:		84.3	122.2	166.4		

OB/GYN: General

	Instructor	Assistant Professor	Associate Professor	Professor	Chief	Chair
Count:	1	16	13	10	0	0
25th:		80	101	160		
Median:		86	115	188		
75th:		90	188	217		
Mean:		91.2	138.4	187.8		

OB/GYN: Gynecologic Oncology

	Instructor	Assistant Professor	Associate Professor	Professor	Chief	Chair
Count:	1	0	0	4	0	0
25th:						
Median:						
75th:						
Mean:						

OB/GYN: Maternal & Fetal

	Instructor	Assistant Professor	Associate Professor	Professor	Chief	Chair
Count:	0	1	0	1	0	0
25th:						
Median:						
75th:						
Mean:						

TABLE 30 Summary Statistics on Medical School Faculty Compensation for Midwestern Region Ph.D. or Other Doctoral Degree, Clinical Science Departments/Specialties Total Compensation in Thousands of Dollars (continued)

OB/GYN: Reproductive Endocrinology

	Instructor	Assistant Professor	Associate Professor	Professor	Chief	Chair
Count:	0	3	2	3	0	0
25th:						
Median:						
75th:						
Mean:						

OB/GYN: Other OB/GYN

	Instructor	Assistant Professor	Associate Professor	Professor	Chief	Chair
Count:	0	12	10	6	1	0
25th:		64	87	99		
Median:		75	97	127		
75th:		85	106	142		
Mean:		76.3	98.2	121.8		

Total Pathology

	Instructor	Assistant Professor	Associate Professor	Professor	Chief	Chair
Count:	25	123	85	101	1	0
25th:	50	78	107	134		
Median:	62	96	124	166		
75th:	77	118	150	210		
Mean:	65.2	103.6	129.6	178.2		

Pathology: Anatomic

	Instructor	Assistant Professor	Associate Professor	Professor	Chief	Chair
Count:	1	23	12	20	0	0
25th:		143	116	131		
Median:		165	190	165		
75th:		190	192	211		
Mean:		157.4	164.5	184.5		

Pathology: Clinical

	Instructor	Assistant Professor	Associate Professor	Professor	Chief	Chair
Count:	9	31	20	25	0	0
25th:	47	71	117	152		
Median:	70	97	140	181		
75th:	80	107	168	219		
Mean:	65.7	98.7	138.5	191.9		

TABLE 30 Summary Statistics on Medical School Faculty Compensation for Midwestern Region Ph.D. or Other Doctoral Degree, Clinical Science Departments/Specialties Total Compensation in Thousands of Dollars (continued)

Pathology: Other Pathology

	Instructor	Assistant Professor	Associate Professor	Professor	Chief	Chair
Count:	15	69	53	56	1	0
25th:	50	72	100	129		
Median:	62	90	114	164		
75th:	75	101	137	200		
Mean:	65.5	87.8	118.4	169.8		

Total Pediatrics

	Instructor	Assistant Professor	Associate Professor	Professor	Chief	Chair
Count:	18	258	120	99	9	1
25th:	66	77	107	137	197	
Median:	78	87	120	174	296	
75th:	104	101	139	205	325	
Mean:	84.4	90.9	121.7	171.8	278.1	

Adolescent Medicine

	Instructor	Assistant Professor	Associate Professor	Professor	Chief	Chair
Count:	0	1	0	1	0	0
25th:						
Median:						
75th:						
Mean:						

Allergy/Immunology-Peds.

	Instructor	Assistant Professor	Associate Professor	Professor	Chief	Chair
Count:	0	6	3	0	0	0
25th:		75				
Median:		81				
75th:		95				
Mean:		83.7				

Child & Adolescent Psychiatry

	Instructor	Assistant Professor	Associate Professor	Professor	Chief	Chair
Count:	1	33	20	10	1	0
25th:		78	101	152		
Median:		85	116	192		
75th:		92	139	226		
Mean:		92.0	117.4	187.2		

Critical/Intensive Care-Peds.

	Instructor	Assistant Professor	Associate Professor	Professor	Chief	Chair
Count:	0	1	1	1	0	0
25th:						
Median:						
75th:						
Mean:						

Emergency Medicine-Peds.

	Instructor	Assistant Professor	Associate Professor	Professor	Chief	Chair
Count:	0	2	0	0	0	0
25th:						
Median:						
75th:						
Mean:						

Endocrinology-Peds.

	Instructor	Assistant Professor	Associate Professor	Professor	Chief	Chair
Count:	0	3	0	3	0	0
25th:						
Median:						
75th:						
Mean:						

Gastroenterology-Peds.

	Instructor	Assistant Professor	Associate Professor	Professor	Chief	Chair
Count:	1	7	2	0	0	0
25th:		72				
Median:		86				
75th:		100				
Mean:		86.0				

General Pediatrics

	Instructor	Assistant Professor	Associate Professor	Professor	Chief	Chair
Count:	1	29	10	14	0	1
25th:		69	104	142		
Median:		81	115	170		
75th:		107	131	187		
Mean:		89.3	119.4	164.8		

TABLE 30 Summary Statistics on Medical School Faculty Compensation for Midwestern Region Ph.D. or Other Doctoral Degree, Clinical Science Departments/Specialties Total Compensation in Thousands of Dollars (continued)

Genetics-Peds.

	Instructor	Assistant Professor	Associate Professor	Professor	Chief	Chair
Count:	1	6	9	2	0	0
25th:		83	96			
Median:		88	117			
75th:		103	141			
Mean:		91.7	117.2			

Hematology/Oncology-Peds.

	Instructor	Assistant Professor	Associate Professor	Professor	Chief	Chair
Count:	0	23	9	7	0	0
25th:		77	111	146		
Median:		90	132	202		
75th:		96	143	205		
Mean:		85.8	126.4	191.4		

Hospital Medicine-Peds.

	Instructor	Assistant Professor	Associate Professor	Professor	Chief	Chair
Count:	0	0	0	0	0	0
25th:						
Median:						
75th:						
Mean:						

Infectious Disease-Peds.

	Instructor	Assistant Professor	Associate Professor	Professor	Chief	Chair
Count:	3	5	1	1	0	0
25th:		74				
Median:		83				
75th:		102				
Mean:		87.0				

Neonatology

	Instructor	Assistant Professor	Associate Professor	Professor	Chief	Chair
Count:	4	8	5	5	0	0
25th:		73	130	184		
Median:		86	141	200		
75th:		98	144	224		
Mean:		86.4	137.6	203.0		

TABLE 30 Summary Statistics on Medical School Faculty Compensation for Midwestern Region Ph.D. or Other Doctoral Degree, Clinical Science Departments/Specialties Total Compensation in Thousands of Dollars (continued)

Nephrology-Peds.

	Instructor	Assistant Professor	Associate Professor	Professor	Chief	Chair
Count:	0	1	0	0	0	0
25th:						
Median:						
75th:						
Mean:						

Neurology-Peds.

	Instructor	Assistant Professor	Associate Professor	Professor	Chief	Chair
Count:	0	6	3	2	0	0
25th:		71				
Median:		76				
75th:		78				
Mean:		74.5				

Pediatric Cardiology

	Instructor	Assistant Professor	Associate Professor	Professor	Chief	Chair
Count:	2	3	3	5	0	0
25th:				128		
Median:				144		
75th:				231		
Mean:				172.4		

Pulmonary-Peds.

	Instructor	Assistant Professor	Associate Professor	Professor	Chief	Chair
Count:	0	11	2	2	0	0
25th:		79				
Median:		82				
75th:		96				
Mean:		84.2				

Rheumatology-Peds.

	Instructor	Assistant Professor	Associate Professor	Professor	Chief	Chair
Count:	0	1	1	1	0	0
25th:						
Median:						
75th:						
Mean:						

TABLE 30 Summary Statistics on Medical School Faculty Compensation for Midwestern Region Ph.D. or Other Doctoral Degree, Clinical Science Departments/Specialties Total Compensation in Thousands of Dollars (continued)

Other Pediatrics

	Instructor	Assistant Professor	Associate Professor	Professor	Chief	Chair
Count:	5	112	51	45	8	0
25th:	66	82	112	130	206	
Median:	86	93	125	156	300	
75th:	97	104	133	210	325	
Mean:	82.4	94.2	125.9	167.6	289.0	

Total Radiology

	Instructor	Assistant Professor	Associate Professor	Professor	Chief	Chair
Count:	34	107	100	85	3	1
25th:	58	87	107	160		
Median:	67	111	136	187		
75th:	126	172	179	217		
Mean:	92.1	129.0	151.6	195.2		

Diagnostic Radiology: Total

	Instructor	Assistant Professor	Associate Professor	Professor	Chief	Chair
Count:	15	17	20	19	0	0
25th:	55	80	106	147		
Median:	58	92	128	181		
75th:	64	102	157	205		
Mean:	63.4	95.3	146.7	181.5		

Diagnostic Radiology: Interventional

	Instructor	Assistant Professor	Associate Professor	Professor	Chief	Chair
Count:	1	0	1	1	0	0
25th:						
Median:						
75th:						
Mean:						

Diagnostic Radiology: Non-interventional

	Instructor	Assistant Professor	Associate Professor	Professor	Chief	Chair
Count:	14	17	19	18	0	0
25th:	56	80	106	174		
Median:	58	92	128	183		
75th:	64	102	151	205		
Mean:	64.7	95.3	143.4	183.5		

TABLE 30 Summary Statistics on Medical School Faculty Compensation for Midwestern Region Ph.D. or Other Doctoral Degree, Clinical Science Departments/Specialties Total Compensation in Thousands of Dollars (continued)

Nuclear Medicine

	Instructor	Assistant Professor	Associate Professor	Professor	Chief	Chair
Count:	0	0	1	2	0	0
25th:						
Median:						
75th:						
Mean:						

Radiation Oncology

	Instructor	Assistant Professor	Associate Professor	Professor	Chief	Chair
Count:	15	50	31	33	2	0
25th:	84	103	105	168		
Median:	130	146	168	200		
75th:	152	186	252	249		
Mean:	122.9	150.0	177.3	203.2		

Other Radiology

	Instructor	Assistant Professor	Associate Professor	Professor	Chief	Chair
Count:	4	40	48	31	1	1
25th:		84	112	145		
Median:		102	132	187		
75th:		146	161	212		
Mean:		117.0	137.4	191.7		

Total Surgery

	Instructor	Assistant Professor	Associate Professor	Professor	Chief	Chair
Count:	12	93	50	53	3	0
25th:	50	66	103	130		
Median:	57	85	117	167		
75th:	80	98	136	217		
Mean:	64.6	86.2	120.2	176.7		

General Surgery

	Instructor	Assistant Professor	Associate Professor	Professor	Chief	Chair
Count:	2	16	14	12	2	0
25th:		66	101	126		
Median:		80	111	163		
75th:		98	142	232		
Mean:		85.5	120.4	172.2		

TABLE 30 Summary Statistics on Medical School Faculty Compensation for Midwestern Region Ph.D. or Other Doctoral Degree, Clinical Science Departments/Specialties Total Compensation in Thousands of Dollars (continued)

Neurosurgery

	Instructor	Assistant Professor	Associate Professor	Professor	Chief	Chair
Count:	2	16	5	4	0	0
25th:		75	114			
Median:		86	134			
75th:		93	169			
Mean:		85.3	139.8			

Orthopaedic Surgery

	Instructor	Assistant Professor	Associate Professor	Professor	Chief	Chair
Count:	4	20	12	12	0	0
25th:		64	98	142		
Median:		81	108	190		
75th:		94	135	208		
Mean:		86.1	115.4	181.4		

Pediatric Surgery

	Instructor	Assistant Professor	Associate Professor	Professor	Chief	Chair
Count:	1	2	1	0	0	0
25th:						
Median:						
75th:						
Mean:						

Plastic Surgery

	Instructor	Assistant Professor	Associate Professor	Professor	Chief	Chair
Count:	0	4	0	1	0	0
25th:						
Median:						
75th:						
Mean:						

Surgical Oncology

	Instructor	Assistant Professor	Associate Professor	Professor	Chief	Chair
Count:	0	4	0	0	0	0
25th:						
Median:						
75th:						
Mean:						

TABLE 30 Summary Statistics on Medical School Faculty Compensation for Midwestern Region
Ph.D. or Other Doctoral Degree, Clinical Science Departments/Specialties
Total Compensation in Thousands of Dollars (continued)

Thoracic & Cardiovascular Surgery

	Instructor	Assistant Professor	Associate Professor	Professor	Chief	Chair
Count:	0	3	5	4	0	0
25th:			89			
Median:			124			
75th:			142			
Mean:			117.2			

Transplant Surgery

	Instructor	Assistant Professor	Associate Professor	Professor	Chief	Chair
Count:	3	6	3	5	0	0
25th:		93		146		
Median:		97		186		
75th:		103		313		
Mean:		100.0		220.4		

Trauma/Critical Care Surgery

	Instructor	Assistant Professor	Associate Professor	Professor	Chief	Chair
Count:	0	0	0	0	0	0
25th:						
Median:						
75th:						
Mean:						

Urology

	Instructor	Assistant Professor	Associate Professor	Professor	Chief	Chair
Count:	0	6	6	8	0	0
25th:		70	101	106		
Median:		86	115	134		
75th:		112	137	178		
Mean:		88.7	115.2	138.8		

Vascular Surgery

	Instructor	Assistant Professor	Associate Professor	Professor	Chief	Chair
Count:	0	2	0	1	0	0
25th:						
Median:						
75th:						
Mean:						

Summary Statistics on Medical School Faculty Compensation for Midwestern Region Ph.D. or Other Doctoral Degree, Clinical Science Departments/Specialties Total Compensation in Thousands of Dollars (continued)

Other Surgery

	Instructor	Assistant Professor	Associate Professor	Professor	Chief	Chair
Count:	0	14	4	6	1	0
25th:		80		126		
Median:		92		158		
75th:		100		192		
Mean:		90.9		179.2		

Other Clinical Science

Community Health

	Instructor	Assistant Professor	Associate Professor	Professor	Chief	Chair
Count:	2	27	11	14	0	0
25th:		72	80	116		
Median:		80	88	140		
75th:		96	108	155		
Mean:		84.6	96.2	139.7		

Emergency Medicine

	Instructor	Assistant Professor	Associate Professor	Professor	Chief	Chair
Count:	0	5	2	3	0	0
25th:		59				
Median:		63				
75th:		215				
Mean:		122.0				

Family Medicine

	Instructor	Assistant Professor	Associate Professor	Professor	Chief	Chair
Count:	3	46	33	25	0	2
25th:		77	97	109		
Median:		91	107	123		
75th:		98	127	155		
Mean:		89.6	113.5	127.6		

Neurology

	Instructor	Assistant Professor	Associate Professor	Professor	Chief	Chair
Count:	10	51	22	24	0	1
25th:	43	67	93	126		
Median:	50	82	114	173		
75th:	60	98	127	206		
Mean:	52.7	82.8	114.3	172.7		

TABLE 30 Summary Statistics on Medical School Faculty Compensation for Midwestern Region Ph.D. or Other Doctoral Degree, Clinical Science Departments/Specialties Total Compensation in Thousands of Dollars (continued)

Ophthalmology

	Instructor	Assistant Professor	Associate Professor	Professor	Chief	Chair
Count:	1	34	17	44	0	0
25th:		70	90	129		
Median:		79	109	145		
75th:		87	132	173		
Mean:		85.8	114.8	158.1		

Otolaryngology

	Instructor	Assistant Professor	Associate Professor	Professor	Chief	Chair
Count:	1	21	18	25	1	0
25th:		71	79	110		
Median:		84	96	139		
75th:		96	126	179		
Mean:		84.8	107.2	145.9		

Physical Medicine & Rehabilitation

	Instructor	Assistant Professor	Associate Professor	Professor	Chief	Chair
Count:	6	41	28	15	0	2
25th:	74	78	94	119		
Median:	79	86	103	127		
75th:	87	91	134	151		
Mean:	78.2	85.7	111.7	138.1		

Preventive Medicine

	Instructor	Assistant Professor	Associate Professor	Professor	Chief	Chair
Count:	1	41	12	16	0	1
25th:		85	118	152		
Median:		92	124	166		
75th:		100	153	197		
Mean:		90.1	132.4	177.9		

Psychiatry

	Instructor	Assistant Professor	Associate Professor	Professor	Chief	Chair
Count:	17	147	75	88	0	0
25th:	66	76	89	129		
Median:	68	87	106	158		
75th:	81	104	138	192		
Mean:	75.5	92.4	113.8	163.9		

TABLE 30

Summary Statistics on Medical School Faculty Compensation for Midwestern Region Ph.D. or Other Doctoral Degree, Clinical Science Departments/Specialties Total Compensation in Thousands of Dollars (continued)

Other

	Instructor	Assistant Professor	Associate Professor	Professor	Chief	Chair
Count:	1	34	33	38	1	2
25th:		71	92	136		
Median:		84	106	163		
75th:		97	119	213		
Mean:		87.0	109.7	179.0		

TABLE 31

Summary Statistics on Medical School Faculty Compensation for Western Region Ph.D. or Other Doctoral Degree, Clinical Science Departments/Specialties Total Compensation in Thousands of Dollars

CLINICAL SCIENCE - TOTAL ALL DEPARTMENTS/SPECIALTIES

	Instructor	Assistant Professor	Associate Professor	Professor	Chief	Chair
Count:	110	885	581	735	19	6
25th:	62	80	99	146	150	169
Median:	73	90	117	180	225	174
75th:	85	106	143	224	298	235
Mean:	77.0	96.8	124.9	192.9	230.7	240.8

Total Anesthesiology

	Instructor	Assistant Professor	Associate Professor	Professor	Chief	Chair
Count:	4	29	13	18	0	0
25th:		80	115	162		
Median:		90	142	186		
75th:		107	173	235		
Mean:		106.8	158.0	199.9		

Anesthesiology: General

	Instructor	Assistant Professor	Associate Professor	Professor	Chief	Chair
Count:	3	22	12	13	0	0
25th:		78	122	158		
Median:		91	143	193		
75th:		122	173	237		
Mean:		112.0	162.2	204.4		

Anesthesiology: Pain Management

	Instructor	Assistant Professor	Associate Professor	Professor	Chief	Chair
Count:	0	5	1	4	0	0
25th:		84				
Median:		88				
75th:		104				
Mean:		92.4				

Anesthesiology: Pediatric

	Instructor	Assistant Professor	Associate Professor	Professor	Chief	Chair
Count:	1	2	0	1	0	0
25th:						
Median:						
75th:						
Mean:						

TABLE 31 Summary Statistics on Medical School Faculty Compensation for Western Region Ph.D. or Other Doctoral Degree, Clinical Science Departments/Specialties Total Compensation in Thousands of Dollars (continued)

Total Dermatology

	Instructor	Assistant Professor	Associate Professor	Professor	Chief	Chair
Count:	5	9	4	6	1	0
25th:	49	80		135		
Median:	54	96		152		
75th:	58	104		165		
Mean:	53.4	94.8		171.8		

Dermatology (excluding Mohs Surgery)

	Instructor	Assistant Professor	Associate Professor	Professor	Chief	Chair
Count:	5	9	4	4	1	0
25th:	49	80				
Median:	54	96				
75th:	58	104				
Mean:	53.4	94.8				

Dermatology: Mohs Surgery

	Instructor	Assistant Professor	Associate Professor	Professor	Chief	Chair
Count:	0	0	0	2	0	0
25th:						
Median:						
75th:						
Mean:						

Total Medicine

	Instructor	Assistant Professor	Associate Professor	Professor	Chief	Chair
Count:	28	199	120	116	2	0
25th:	60	75	100	147		
Median:	66	86	115	176		
75th:	75	101	145	219		
Mean:	68.5	89.9	123.3	191.1		

Allergy/Immunology-Med.

	Instructor	Assistant Professor	Associate Professor	Professor	Chief	Chair
Count:	3	2	2	2	0	0
25th:						
Median:						
75th:						
Mean:						

TABLE 31 Summary Statistics on Medical School Faculty Compensation for Western Region Ph.D. or Other Doctoral Degree, Clinical Science Departments/Specialties Total Compensation in Thousands of Dollars (continued)

Cardiology: Total

	Instructor	Assistant Professor	Associate Professor	Professor	Chief	Chair
Count:	3	13	11	17	0	0
25th:		79	100	133		
Median:		87	112	158		
75th:		96	180	205		
Mean:		85.2	127.0	175.1		

Cardiology: Invasive Interventional-Med.

	Instructor	Assistant Professor	Associate Professor	Professor	Chief	Chair
Count:	0	0	0	0	0	0
25th:						
Median:						
75th:						
Mean:						

Cardiology: Invasive Non-interventional-Med.

	Instructor	Assistant Professor	Associate Professor	Professor	Chief	Chair
Count:	0	0	0	0	0	0
25th:						
Median:						
75th:						
Mean:						

Cardiology: Non-invasive-Med.

	Instructor	Assistant Professor	Associate Professor	Professor	Chief	Chair
Count:	3	13	11	17	0	0
25th:		79	100	133		
Median:		87	112	158		
75th:		96	180	205		
Mean:		85.2	127.0	175.1		

Critical/Intensive Care-Med.

	Instructor	Assistant Professor	Associate Professor	Professor	Chief	Chair
Count:	1	0	0	0	0	0
25th:						
Median:						
75th:						
Mean:						

TABLE 31 Summary Statistics on Medical School Faculty Compensation for Western Region Ph.D. or Other Doctoral Degree, Clinical Science Departments/Specialties Total Compensation in Thousands of Dollars (continued)

Endocrinology-Med.

	Instructor	Assistant Professor	Associate Professor	Professor	Chief	Chair
Count:	2	22	15	10	0	0
25th:		70	89	147		
Median:		78	100	160		
75th:		85	130	198		
Mean:		76.9	111.9	175.0		

Gastroenterology-Med.

	Instructor	Assistant Professor	Associate Professor	Professor	Chief	Chair
Count:	0	11	8	8	0	0
25th:		85	101	181		
Median:		86	114	222		
75th:		95	130	304		
Mean:		88.0	119.5	251.1		

General Internal Medicine

	Instructor	Assistant Professor	Associate Professor	Professor	Chief	Chair
Count:	1	23	17	16	0	0
25th:		67	105	174		
Median:		90	135	196		
75th:		115	159	238		
Mean:		93.7	134.0	214.1		

Geriatrics-Med.

	Instructor	Assistant Professor	Associate Professor	Professor	Chief	Chair
Count:	0	9	5	5	0	0
25th:		79	95	165		
Median:		86	104	200		
75th:		106	194	271		
Mean:		99.0	136.2	214.4		

Hematology/Oncology-Med.

	Instructor	Assistant Professor	Associate Professor	Professor	Chief	Chair
Count:	3	25	13	18	0	0
25th:		72	94	116		
Median:		80	111	167		
75th:		95	126	250		
Mean:		83.0	113.2	194.9		

TABLE 31 Summary Statistics on Medical School Faculty Compensation for Western Region Ph.D. or Other Doctoral Degree, Clinical Science Departments/Specialties Total Compensation in Thousands of Dollars (continued)

Hospital Medicine

	Instructor	Assistant Professor	Associate Professor	Professor	Chief	Chair
Count:	0	0	0	0	0	0
25th:						
Median:						
75th:						
Mean:						

Infectious Disease-Med.

	Instructor	Assistant Professor	Associate Professor	Professor	Chief	Chair
Count:	5	16	4	6	1	0
25th:	54	83		126		
Median:	54	99		187		
75th:	63	111		267		
Mean:	57.4	95.8		203.3		

Nephrology-Med.

	Instructor	Assistant Professor	Associate Professor	Professor	Chief	Chair
Count:	1	9	4	2	0	0
25th:		81				
Median:		96				
75th:		111				
Mean:		95.2				

Pulmonary-Med.

	Instructor	Assistant Professor	Associate Professor	Professor	Chief	Chair
Count:	2	13	5	9	0	0
25th:		61	89	139		
Median:		82	98	150		
75th:		101	118	181		
Mean:		83.6	102.0	159.0		

Rheumatology-Med.

	Instructor	Assistant Professor	Associate Professor	Professor	Chief	Chair
Count:	2	8	2	6	0	0
25th:		80		162		
Median:		83		170		
75th:		89		179		
Mean:		86.0		176.0		

TABLE 31 Summary Statistics on Medical School Faculty Compensation for Western Region Ph.D. or Other Doctoral Degree, Clinical Science Departments/Specialties Total Compensation in Thousands of Dollars (continued)

Other Medicine

	Instructor	Assistant Professor	Associate Professor	Professor	Chief	Chair
Count:	5	48	34	17	1	0
25th:	64	81	113	144		
Median:	80	97	129	181		
75th:	91	113	159	214		
Mean:	77.8	97.2	132.8	180.0		

Total OB/GYN

	Instructor	Assistant Professor	Associate Professor	Professor	Chief	Chair
Count:	2	18	14	19	0	0
25th:		90	115	136		
Median:		101	128	191		
75th:		117	140	230		
Mean:		101.8	141.8	195.8		

OB/GYN: General

	Instructor	Assistant Professor	Associate Professor	Professor	Chief	Chair
Count:	0	1	4	4	0	0
25th:						
Median:						
75th:						
Mean:						

OB/GYN: Gynecologic Oncology

	Instructor	Assistant Professor	Associate Professor	Professor	Chief	Chair
Count:	0	0	0	1	0	0
25th:						
Median:						
75th:						
Mean:						

OB/GYN: Maternal & Fetal

	Instructor	Assistant Professor	Associate Professor	Professor	Chief	Chair
Count:	1	1	2	0	0	0
25th:						
Median:						
75th:						
Mean:						

TABLE 31 Summary Statistics on Medical School Faculty Compensation for Western Region Ph.D. or Other Doctoral Degree, Clinical Science Departments/Specialties Total Compensation in Thousands of Dollars (continued)

OB/GYN: Reproductive Endocrinology

	Instructor	Assistant Professor	Associate Professor	Professor	Chief	Chair
Count:	0	9	2	10	0	0
25th:		99		156		
Median:		117		210		
75th:		126		288		
Mean:		114.7		216.7		

OB/GYN: Other OB/GYN

	Instructor	Assistant Professor	Associate Professor	Professor	Chief	Chair
Count:	1	7	6	4	0	0
25th:		81	116			
Median:		94	130			
75th:		100	140			
Mean:		92.4	127.0			

Total Pathology

	Instructor	Assistant Professor	Associate Professor	Professor	Chief	Chair
Count:	5	76	46	79	3	0
25th:	62	80	100	142		
Median:	80	94	115	178		
75th:	88	120	156	233		
Mean:	75.8	102.1	129.4	194.2		

Pathology: Anatomic

	Instructor	Assistant Professor	Associate Professor	Professor	Chief	Chair
Count:	0	13	4	6	0	0
25th:		85		155		
Median:		94		201		
75th:		119		252		
Mean:		108.9		211.2		

Pathology: Clinical

	Instructor	Assistant Professor	Associate Professor	Professor	Chief	Chair
Count:	1	18	15	22	3	0
25th:		102	119	150		
Median:		111	150	236		
75th:		147	169	276		
Mean:		126.1	155.3	236.8		

TABLE 31 Summary Statistics on Medical School Faculty Compensation for Western Region Ph.D. or Other Doctoral Degree, Clinical Science Departments/Specialties Total Compensation in Thousands of Dollars (continued)

Pathology: Other Pathology

	Instructor	Assistant Professor	Associate Professor	Professor	Chief	Chair
Count:	4	45	27	51	0	0
25th:		69	94	137		
Median:		85	104	164		
75th:		97	116	206		
Mean:		90.5	111.6	173.9		

Total Pediatrics

	Instructor	Assistant Professor	Associate Professor	Professor	Chief	Chair
Count:	24	95	54	56	3	0
25th:	72	79	94	140		
Median:	77	89	107	170		
75th:	90	98	130	211		
Mean:	79.4	89.4	114.7	179.7		

Adolescent Medicine

	Instructor	Assistant Professor	Associate Professor	Professor	Chief	Chair
Count:	0	1	0	0	0	0
25th:						
Median:						
75th:						
Mean:						

Allergy/Immunology-Peds.

	Instructor	Assistant Professor	Associate Professor	Professor	Chief	Chair
Count:	0	0	1	1	0	0
25th:						
Median:						
75th:						
Mean:						

Child & Adolescent Psychiatry

	Instructor	Assistant Professor	Associate Professor	Professor	Chief	Chair
Count:	2	2	3	11	0	0
25th:				119		
Median:				190		
75th:				228		
Mean:				185.6		

TABLE 31 Summary Statistics on Medical School Faculty Compensation for Western Region Ph.D. or Other Doctoral Degree, Clinical Science Departments/Specialties Total Compensation in Thousands of Dollars (continued)

Critical/Intensive Care-Peds.

	Instructor	Assistant Professor	Associate Professor	Professor	Chief	Chair
Count:	3	4	2	2	0	0
25th:						
Median:						
75th:						
Mean:						

Emergency Medicine-Peds.

	Instructor	Assistant Professor	Associate Professor	Professor	Chief	Chair
Count:	1	0	0	0	0	0
25th:						
Median:						
75th:						
Mean:						

Endocrinology-Peds.

	Instructor	Assistant Professor	Associate Professor	Professor	Chief	Chair
Count:	1	3	2	1	0	0
25th:						
Median:						
75th:						
Mean:						

Gastroenterology-Peds.

	Instructor	Assistant Professor	Associate Professor	Professor	Chief	Chair
Count:	1	1	3	0	0	0
25th:						
Median:						
75th:						
Mean:						

General Pediatrics

	Instructor	Assistant Professor	Associate Professor	Professor	Chief	Chair
Count:	11	31	11	8	1	0
25th:	52	85	96	145		
Median:	72	90	104	170		
75th:	89	100	117	226		
Mean:	73.0	95.6	107.7	181.3		

TABLE 31 Summary Statistics on Medical School Faculty Compensation for Western Region Ph.D. or Other Doctoral Degree, Clinical Science Departments/Specialties Total Compensation in Thousands of Dollars (continued)

Genetics-Peds.

	Instructor	Assistant Professor	Associate Professor	Professor	Chief	Chair
Count:	1	11	5	5	0	0
25th:		75	98	122		
Median:		88	115	141		
75th:		98	121	212		
Mean:		90.7	110.6	161.6		

Hematology/Oncology-Peds.

	Instructor	Assistant Professor	Associate Professor	Professor	Chief	Chair
Count:	0	2	4	3	0	0
25th:						
Median:						
75th:						
Mean:						

Hospital Medicine-Peds.

	Instructor	Assistant Professor	Associate Professor	Professor	Chief	Chair
Count:	0	0	0	0	0	0
25th:						
Median:						
75th:						
Mean:						

Infectious Disease-Peds.

	Instructor	Assistant Professor	Associate Professor	Professor	Chief	Chair
Count:	0	4	2	2	0	0
25th:						
Median:						
75th:						
Mean:						

Neonatology

	Instructor	Assistant Professor	Associate Professor	Professor	Chief	Chair
Count:	1	6	4	6	0	0
25th:		81		114		
Median:		83		179		
75th:		105		198		
Mean:		93.5		161.0		

TABLE 31 Summary Statistics on Medical School Faculty Compensation for Western Region Ph.D. or Other Doctoral Degree, Clinical Science Departments/Specialties Total Compensation in Thousands of Dollars (continued)

Nephrology-Peds.

	Instructor	Assistant Professor	Associate Professor	Professor	Chief	Chair
Count:	0	1	0	0	0	0
25th:						
Median:						
75th:						
Mean:						

Neurology-Peds.

	Instructor	Assistant Professor	Associate Professor	Professor	Chief	Chair
Count:	2	4	1	1	0	0
25th:						
Median:						
75th:						
Mean:						

Pediatric Cardiology

	Instructor	Assistant Professor	Associate Professor	Professor	Chief	Chair
Count:	0	1	2	1	0	0
25th:						
Median:						
75th:						
Mean:						

Pulmonary-Peds.

	Instructor	Assistant Professor	Associate Professor	Professor	Chief	Chair
Count:	0	1	1	4	0	0
25th:						
Median:						
75th:						
Mean:						

Rheumatology-Peds.

	Instructor	Assistant Professor	Associate Professor	Professor	Chief	Chair
Count:	0	0	0	0	0	0
25th:						
Median:						
75th:						
Mean:						

Summary Statistics on Medical School Faculty Compensation for Western Region Ph.D. or Other Doctoral Degree, Clinical Science Departments/Specialties Total Compensation in Thousands of Dollars (continued)

Other Pediatrics

	Instructor	Assistant Professor	Associate Professor	Professor	Chief	Chair
Count:	1	23	13	11	2	0
25th:		67	91	122		
Median:		83	99	185		
75th:		95	140	219		
Mean:		81.5	116.0	181.8		

Total Radiology

	Instructor	Assistant Professor	Associate Professor	Professor	Chief	Chair
Count:	9	87	48	78	7	0
25th:	73	88	118	166	214	
Median:	110	101	139	199	240	
75th:	114	134	180	240	298	
Mean:	95.3	116.9	150.6	205.8	240.1	

Diagnostic Radiology: Total

	Instructor	Assistant Professor	Associate Professor	Professor	Chief	Chair
Count:	2	34	20	38	1	0
25th:		85	118	163		
Median:		92	133	186		
75th:		103	160	240		
Mean:		107.4	141.3	203.9		

Diagnostic Radiology: Interventional

	Instructor	Assistant Professor	Associate Professor	Professor	Chief	Chair
Count:	0	3	0	2	0	0
25th:						
Median:						
75th:						
Mean:						

Diagnostic Radiology: Non-interventional

	Instructor	Assistant Professor	Associate Professor	Professor	Chief	Chair
Count:	2	31	20	36	1	0
25th:		88	118	163		
Median:		92	133	182		
75th:		103	160	236		
Mean:		107.4	141.3	202.4		

TABLE 31 Summary Statistics on Medical School Faculty Compensation for Western Region Ph.D. or Other Doctoral Degree, Clinical Science Departments/Specialties Total Compensation in Thousands of Dollars (continued)

Nuclear Medicine

	Instructor	Assistant Professor	Associate Professor	Professor	Chief	Chair
Count:	1	0	0	3	1	0
25th:						
Median:						
75th:						
Mean:						

Radiation Oncology

	Instructor	Assistant Professor	Associate Professor	Professor	Chief	Chair
Count:	4	32	17	19	4	0
25th:		125	118	201		
Median:		134	175	210		
75th:		160	208	242		
Mean:		144.3	170.9	228.9		

Other Radiology

	Instructor	Assistant Professor	Associate Professor	Professor	Chief	Chair
Count:	2	21	11	18	1	0
25th:		83	110	135		
Median:		90	123	169		
75th:		97	147	202		
Mean:		90.7	136.1	175.7		

Total Surgery

	Instructor	Assistant Professor	Associate Professor	Professor	Chief	Chair
Count:	10	60	56	88	0	0
25th:	68	76	104	141		
Median:	86	86	121	183		
75th:	130	98	136	219		
Mean:	92.2	94.1	124.7	194.9		

General Surgery

	Instructor	Assistant Professor	Associate Professor	Professor	Chief	Chair
Count:	2	9	4	7	0	0
25th:		78		150		
Median:		90		160		
75th:		146		210		
Mean:		107.6		177.7		

TABLE 31 Summary Statistics on Medical School Faculty Compensation for Western Region Ph.D. or Other Doctoral Degree, Clinical Science Departments/Specialties Total Compensation in Thousands of Dollars (continued)

Neurosurgery

	Instructor	Assistant Professor	Associate Professor	Professor	Chief	Chair
Count:	3	14	11	28	0	0
25th:		80	114	157		
Median:		88	125	195		
75th:		95	138	215		
Mean:		90.6	126.4	197.4		

Orthopaedic Surgery

	Instructor	Assistant Professor	Associate Professor	Professor	Chief	Chair
Count:	1	12	18	24	0	0
25th:		74	93	122		
Median:		84	108	169		
75th:		92	134	201		
Mean:		96.8	116.8	173.1		

Pediatric Surgery

	Instructor	Assistant Professor	Associate Professor	Professor	Chief	Chair
Count:	1	3	2	0	0	0
25th:						
Median:						
75th:						
Mean:						

Plastic Surgery

	Instructor	Assistant Professor	Associate Professor	Professor	Chief	Chair
Count:	0	0	0	0	0	0
25th:						
Median:						
75th:						
Mean:						

Surgical Oncology

	Instructor	Assistant Professor	Associate Professor	Professor	Chief	Chair
Count:	0	5	1	0	0	0
25th:		64				
Median:		74				
75th:		86				
Mean:		74.4				

TABLE 31 Summary Statistics on Medical School Faculty Compensation for Western Region Ph.D. or Other Doctoral Degree, Clinical Science Departments/Specialties Total Compensation in Thousands of Dollars (continued)

Thoracic & Cardiovascular Surgery

	Instructor	Assistant Professor	Associate Professor	Professor	Chief	Chair
Count:	1	5	3	5	0	0
25th:		74		116		
Median:		85		149		
75th:		98		173		
Mean:		85.6		145.2		

Transplant Surgery

	Instructor	Assistant Professor	Associate Professor	Professor	Chief	Chair
Count:	0	2	2	4	0	0
25th:						
Median:						
75th:						
Mean:						

Trauma/Critical Care Surgery

	Instructor	Assistant Professor	Associate Professor	Professor	Chief	Chair
Count:	0	1	1	3	0	0
25th:						
Median:						
75th:						
Mean:						

Urology

	Instructor	Assistant Professor	Associate Professor	Professor	Chief	Chair
Count:	0	5	8	8	0	0
25th:		80	114	161		
Median:		95	124	179		
75th:		122	136	221		
Mean:		99.6	127.5	196.4		

Vascular Surgery

	Instructor	Assistant Professor	Associate Professor	Professor	Chief	Chair
Count:	1	1	2	0	0	0
25th:						
Median:						
75th:						
Mean:						

TABLE 31 Summary Statistics on Medical School Faculty Compensation for Western Region Ph.D. or Other Doctoral Degree, Clinical Science Departments/Specialties Total Compensation in Thousands of Dollars (continued)

Other Surgery

	Instructor	Assistant Professor	Associate Professor	Professor	Chief	Chair
Count:	1	3	4	9	0	0
25th:				105		
Median:				224		
75th:				351		
Mean:				255.6		

Other Clinical Science

Community Health

	Instructor	Assistant Professor	Associate Professor	Professor	Chief	Chair
Count:	0	17	9	11	0	1
25th:		85	101	143		
Median:		99	135	163		
75th:		116	153	204		
Mean:		103.1	136.4	168.7		

Emergency Medicine

	Instructor	Assistant Professor	Associate Professor	Professor	Chief	Chair
Count:	0	2	3	1	0	0
25th:						
Median:						
75th:						
Mean:						

Family Medicine

	Instructor	Assistant Professor	Associate Professor	Professor	Chief	Chair
Count:	1	25	11	16	0	1
25th:		67	88	127		
Median:		82	122	155		
75th:		88	155	179		
Mean:		84.7	123.4	164.1		

Neurology

	Instructor	Assistant Professor	Associate Professor	Professor	Chief	Chair
Count:	4	55	29	32	0	0
25th:		86	94	163		
Median:		102	105	199		
75th:		121	133	283		
Mean:		105.4	111.5	242.6		

TABLE 31 Summary Statistics on Medical School Faculty Compensation for Western Region Ph.D. or Other Doctoral Degree, Clinical Science Departments/Specialties Total Compensation in Thousands of Dollars (continued)

Ophthalmology

	Instructor	Assistant Professor	Associate Professor	Professor	Chief	Chair
Count:	1	14	21	30	0	0
25th:		74	103	158		
Median:		81	115	199		
75th:		130	132	245		
Mean:		100.8	117.5	192.1		

Otolaryngology

	Instructor	Assistant Professor	Associate Professor	Professor	Chief	Chair
Count:	0	12	13	21	0	0
25th:		80	91	137		
Median:		87	100	190		
75th:		90	113	213		
Mean:		85.9	103.9	183.1		

Physical Medicine & Rehabilitation

	Instructor	Assistant Professor	Associate Professor	Professor	Chief	Chair
Count:	4	22	33	17	1	1
25th:		75	88	110		
Median:		82	93	120		
75th:		88	100	129		
Mean:		81.5	96.6	121.2		

Preventive Medicine

	Instructor	Assistant Professor	Associate Professor	Professor	Chief	Chair
Count:	3	38	20	27	0	1
25th:		92	133	173		
Median:		99	144	189		
75th:		105	155	197		
Mean:		99.1	145.6	191.1		

Psychiatry

	Instructor	Assistant Professor	Associate Professor	Professor	Chief	Chair
Count:	10	125	85	119	1	0
25th:	67	80	101	148		
Median:	71	90	117	189		
75th:	79	106	144	230		
Mean:	70.2	94.6	123.9	195.4		

TABLE 31

Summary Statistics on Medical School Faculty Compensation for Western Region Ph.D. or Other Doctoral Degree, Clinical Science Departments/Specialties Total Compensation in Thousands of Dollars (continued)

Other

	Instructor	Assistant Professor	Associate Professor	Professor	Chief	Chair
Count:	0	2	2	1	1	2
25th:						
Median:						
75th:						
Mean:						

TABLE 32 Change in Mean and Median Total Compensation By Department/Specialty Faculty with an M.D. or Equivalent Degree: Combined Assistant, Associate, and Professor Ranks 2010-2011 through 2008-2009

($ in thousands)

DEPARTMENT/SPECIALTY	2010-2011 Mean	2010-2011 Median	2009-2010 Mean	2009-2010 Median	2008-2009 Mean	2008-2009 Median	% Change 2009-2010 to 2010-2011 Mean	% Change 2009-2010 to 2010-2011 Median
TOTAL BASIC SCIENCE	**150.6**	**140**	**146.6**	**135**	**144.5**	**132**	**2.7**	**3.7**
Anatomy	104.4	89	102.1	87	110.0	93	2.3	2.3
Biochemistry	130.8	119	131.7	121	131.6	112	-0.7	-1.7
Bioethics/Medical Humanities	155.5	177	**	**	143.3	151	**	**
Biomedical Informatics	188.3	170	184.1	175	172.6	153	2.3	-2.9
Biostatistics	163.1	152	153.0	137	149.6	127	6.6	10.9
Genetics	158.3	153	159.4	149	156.2	146	-0.7	2.7
Microbiology	150.3	141	155.1	146	149.5	139	-3.1	-3.4
Molecular & Cellular Biology	161.2	142	155.2	137	154.9	137	3.9	3.6
Neurosciences	156.2	142	149.3	134	142.7	120	4.6	6.0
Pharmacology	152.6	148	151.3	142	144.9	139	0.9	4.2
Physiology	146.0	141	141.7	140	132.3	120	3.0	0.7
Other Basic Sciences	154.3	137	139.0	125	147.6	127	11.0	9.6
TOTAL CLINICAL SCIENCE	**262.5**	**229**	**254.9**	**222**	**245.6**	**214**	**3.0**	**3.2**
Total Anesthesiology	**325.8**	**322**	**319.8**	**316**	**313.3**	**308**	**1.9**	**1.9**
Anesthesiology: General	324.6	322	319.2	316	313.5	307	1.7	1.9
Anesthesiology: Pain Management	319.0	312	306.0	300	292.6	289	4.2	4.0
Anesthesiology: Pediatric	338.3	335	331.5	329	322.4	320	2.1	1.8
Total Dermatology	**343.2**	**286**	**332.5**	**277**	**316.3**	**256**	**3.2**	**3.2**
Dermatology (excluding Mohs Surgery)	311.9	269	307.0	261	292.7	246	1.6	3.1
Dermatology: Mohs Surgery	544.6	460	542.3	463	498.5	376	0.4	-0.6
Total Medicine	**229.5**	**205**	**223.4**	**200**	**214.5**	**193**	**2.7**	**2.5**
Allergy/Immunology-Med.	193.2	183	191.2	183	181.3	171	1.0	0.0
Cardiology: Total	**315.7**	**285**	**306.8**	**275**	**295.3**	**270**	**2.9**	**3.6**
Cardiology: Invasive Interventional-Med.	379.0	349	365.0	333	353.4	324	3.8	4.8
Cardiology: Invasive Non-interventional-Med.	328.8	304	313.6	281	291.5	261	4.8	8.2
Cardiology: Non-invasive-Med.	275.0	257	267.6	250	260.3	249	2.8	2.8
Critical/Intensive Care-Med.	249.3	227	252.5	226	232.4	216	-1.3	0.4
Endocrinology-Med.	185.7	173	181.8	170	179.1	168	2.1	1.8
Gastroenterology-Med.	288.0	266	277.9	257	264.3	247	3.6	3.5
General Internal Medicine	194.7	178	188.8	172	179.8	167	3.1	3.5
Geriatrics-Med.	178.3	170	171.1	165	163.1	156	4.2	3.0
Hematology/Oncology-Med.	246.2	226	240.1	220	230.3	214	2.5	2.7
Hospital Medicine	193.3	188	192.5	182	174.3	169	0.4	3.3
Infectious Disease-Med.	177.7	165	174.6	162	169.7	160	1.8	1.9
Nephrology-Med.	205.0	195	202.0	189	195.8	185	1.5	3.2
Pulmonary-Med.	219.5	206	213.5	200	204.5	192	2.8	3.0
Rheumatology-Med.	182.6	170	177.8	166	173.6	160	2.7	2.4
Other Medicine	220.5	207	211.6	192	211.7	194	4.2	7.8

** Indicates that fewer than 10 faculty were reported.

TABLE 32 Change in Mean and Median Total Compensation By Department/Specialty Faculty with an M.D. or Equivalent Degree: Combined Assistant, Associate, and Professor Ranks 2010-2011 through 2008-2009

($ in thousands)

DEPARTMENT/SPECIALTY	2010-2011 Mean	2010-2011 Median	2009-2010 Mean	2009-2010 Median	2008-2009 Mean	2008-2009 Median	% Change 2009-2010 to 2010-2011 Mean	% Change 2009-2010 to 2010-2011 Median
Total OB/GYN	**283.4**	**252**	**275.4**	**242**	**262.6**	**234**	**2.9**	**4.1**
OB/GYN: General	252.0	231	243.5	223	235.6	220	3.5	3.6
OB/GYN: Gynecologic Oncology	333.5	292	329.4	291	315.0	288	1.2	0.3
OB/GYN: Maternal & Fetal	322.1	302	313.5	287	311.4	282	2.7	5.2
OB/GYN: Reproductive Endocrinology	375.2	264	376.1	257	317.2	248	-0.2	2.7
OB/GYN: Other OB/GYN	244.9	222	235.9	206	217.4	195	3.8	7.8
Total Pathology	**230.1**	**217**	**223.9**	**210**	**216.6**	**205**	**2.8**	**3.3**
Pathology: Anatomic	240.7	226	231.4	214	228.7	213	4.0	5.6
Pathology: Clinical	229.0	216	227.0	214	220.1	207	0.9	0.9
Pathology: Other Pathology	208.5	196	203.5	196	187.2	180	2.5	0.0
Total Pediatrics	**192.4**	**178**	**190.3**	**174**	**184.7**	**170**	**1.1**	**2.3**
Adolescent Medicine	155.4	145	149.1	141	147.4	139	4.2	2.8
Allergy/Immunology-Peds.	183.3	162	178.7	157	176.2	160	2.6	3.2
Child & Adolescent Psychiatry	195.5	185	186.3	177	178.0	166	4.9	4.5
Critical/Intensive Care-Peds.	228.8	218	220.2	207	208.9	198	3.9	5.3
Emergency Medicine-Peds.	201.4	195	194.3	187	192.4	187	3.7	4.3
Endocrinology-Peds.	160.1	149	153.7	144	153.2	143	4.2	3.5
Gastroenterology-Peds.	200.1	185	193.5	180	188.5	177	3.4	2.8
General Pediatrics	171.5	154	168.9	153	175.1	157	1.5	0.7
Genetics-Peds.	162.6	153	160.9	150	157.1	148	1.1	2.0
Hematology/Oncology-Peds.	179.1	164	181.9	164	169.3	155	-1.5	0.0
Hospital Medicine-Peds.	160.1	149	158.0	148	144.8	138	1.3	0.7
Infectious Disease-Peds.	164.0	147	160.9	145	159.7	146	1.9	1.4
Neonatology	230.2	216	226.5	214	224.5	209	1.6	0.9
Nephrology-Peds.	173.4	162	168.3	159	163.8	155	3.0	1.9
Neurology-Peds.	185.2	178	179.1	171	174.3	167	3.4	4.1
Pediatric Cardiology	241.6	225	247.5	223	230.8	216	-2.4	0.9
Pulmonary-Peds.	181.1	167	180.9	168	181.7	170	0.1	-0.6
Rheumatology-Peds.	163.0	156	158.7	147	154.5	146	2.7	6.1
Other Pediatrics	193.7	170	197.6	165	175.8	160	-2.0	3.0
Total Radiology	**358.7**	**347**	**353.9**	**341**	**341.4**	**334**	**1.4**	**1.8**
Diagnostic Radiology: Total	**358.4**	**346**	**353.9**	**340**	**343.1**	**336**	**1.3**	**1.8**
Diagnostic Radiology: Interventional	408.8	400	390.2	378	373.9	364	4.8	5.8
Diagnostic Radiology: Non-interventional	344.6	334	342.7	333	333.0	327	0.6	0.3
Nuclear Medicine	328.0	315	322.8	306	314.2	306	1.6	2.9
Radiation Oncology	359.3	352	350.9	339	333.7	326	2.4	3.8
Other Radiology	372.4	365	376.5	375	354.6	352	-1.1	-2.7

** Indicates that fewer than 10 faculty were reported.

TABLE 32

Change in Mean and Median Total Compensation By Department/Specialty Faculty with an M.D. or Equivalent Degree: Combined Assistant, Associate, and Professor Ranks 2010-2011 through 2008-2009

($ in thousands)

DEPARTMENT/SPECIALTY	2010-2011 Mean	2010-2011 Median	2009-2010 Mean	2009-2010 Median	2008-2009 Mean	2008-2009 Median	% Change 2009-2010 to 2010-2011 Mean	% Change 2009-2010 to 2010-2011 Median
Total Surgery	**402.4**	**355**	**384.8**	**345**	**366.8**	**329**	**4.6**	**2.9**
General Surgery	318.1	300	308.8	286	299.3	280	3.0	4.9
Neurosurgery	545.2	468	521.1	455	485.3	448	4.6	2.9
Orthopaedic Surgery	457.6	412	438.0	403	419.4	389	4.5	2.2
Pediatric Surgery	422.6	412	403.8	380	385.1	364	4.7	8.4
Plastic Surgery	402.0	346	360.2	324	346.0	322	11.6	6.8
Surgical Oncology	300.0	271	299.9	271	286.4	268	0.0	0.0
Thoracic & Cardiovascular Surgery	481.2	425	456.9	404	439.2	381	5.3	5.2
Transplant Surgery	384.7	350	370.5	335	350.5	325	3.8	4.5
Trauma/Critical Care Surgery	326.1	313	308.7	300	309.1	291	5.6	4.3
Urology	347.3	319	332.5	315	320.2	310	4.5	1.3
Vascular Surgery	360.6	330	353.1	322	339.2	307	2.1	2.5
Other Surgery	311.0	279	307.4	263	281.7	243	1.2	6.1
Other Clinical Science								
Community Health	174.3	161	170.1	161	165.5	161	2.5	0.0
Emergency Medicine	246.8	238	237.6	228	230.4	223	3.9	4.4
Family Medicine	174.8	168	168.4	164	165.7	161	3.8	2.4
Neurology	194.9	182	189.9	177	184.0	173	2.6	2.8
Ophthalmology	273.2	238	261.5	229	256.9	229	4.5	3.9
Otolaryngology	333.5	300	331.8	288	308.8	282	0.5	4.2
Physical Medicine & Rehabilitation	206.3	191	202.7	190	192.8	183	1.8	0.5
Preventive Medicine	182.0	176	184.4	166	179.8	165	-1.3	6.0
Psychiatry	191.0	179	186.1	175	181.3	171	2.6	2.3
Other	218.5	205	181.9	172	197.0	172	20.1	19.2

** Indicates that fewer than 10 faculty were reported.

TABLE 33

Change in Mean and Median Total Compensation By Department/Specialty Faculty with a Ph.D. or Other Doctoral Degree: Combined Assistant, Associate, and Professor Ranks 2010-2011 through 2008-2009

($ in thousands)

DEPARTMENT/SPECIALTY	2010-2011		2009-2010		2008-2009		% Change 2009-2010 to 2010-2011	
	Mean	Median	Mean	Median	Mean	Median	Mean	Median
TOTAL BASIC SCIENCE	**124.2**	**112**	**122.3**	**110**	**121.3**	**109**	**1.6**	**1.8**
Anatomy	114.5	106	112.6	104	111.9	104	1.7	1.9
Biochemistry	125.7	114	123.5	111	122.3	110	1.8	2.7
Bioethics/Medical Humanities	113.5	100	111.7	98	113.4	102	1.6	2.0
Biomedical Informatics	130.8	117	122.9	110	126.2	111	6.4	6.4
Biostatistics	131.3	116	128.5	116	126.4	113	2.2	0.0
Genetics	130.0	118	127.8	113	125.8	112	1.7	4.4
Microbiology	124.1	110	122.2	108	121.8	107	1.6	1.9
Molecular & Cellular Biology	124.1	112	123.2	110	120.6	108	0.7	1.8
Neurosciences	125.5	112	123.2	110	123.0	109	1.9	1.8
Pharmacology	123.6	111	122.4	110	120.8	109	1.0	0.9
Physiology	123.2	114	122.0	112	122.1	111	1.0	1.8
Other Basic Sciences	124.5	110	122.3	107	122.4	108	1.8	2.8
TOTAL CLINICAL SCIENCE	**123.4**	**107**	**120.7**	**105**	**119.4**	**104**	**2.2**	**1.9**
Total Anesthesiology	**142.2**	**120**	**134.0**	**116**	**134.3**	**113**	**6.1**	**3.4**
Anesthesiology: General	142.8	120	135.7	120	133.9	117	5.2	0.0
Anesthesiology: Pain Management	128.8	108	115.3	100	123.5	102	11.7	8.0
Anesthesiology: Pediatric	**	**	**	**	**	**	**	**
Total Dermatology	**125.1**	**104**	**118.9**	**101**	**120.9**	**103**	**5.2**	**3.0**
Dermatology (excluding Mohs Surgery)	124.3	103	118.7	101	120.4	103	4.7	2.0
Dermatology: Mohs Surgery	**	**	**	**	**	**	**	**
Total Medicine	**112.2**	**98**	**110.6**	**97**	**108.7**	**94**	**1.4**	**1.0**
Allergy/Immunology-Med.	124.6	119	125.0	123	119.0	109	-0.3	-3.3
Cardiology: Total	**113.6**	**97**	**113.4**	**100**	**111.0**	**98**	**0.2**	**-3.0**
Cardiology: Invasive Interventional-Med.	114.3	116	107.4	100	114.2	118	6.4	16.0
Cardiology: Invasive Non-interventional-Med.	**	**	**	**	**	**	**	**
Cardiology: Non-invasive-Med.	112.4	96	113.6	97	110.5	95	-1.1	-1.0
Critical/Intensive Care-Med.	**	**	**	**	**	**	**	**
Endocrinology-Med.	104.4	93	104.3	90	104.8	90	0.1	3.3
Gastroenterology-Med.	111.7	96	110.1	94	109.4	94	1.5	2.1
General Internal Medicine	126.0	111	121.2	108	119.3	105	4.0	2.8
Geriatrics-Med.	112.0	98	115.4	101	111.8	96	-2.9	-3.0
Hematology/Oncology-Med.	116.5	98	114.4	98	112.3	95	1.8	0.0
Hospital Medicine	**	**	**	**	**	**	**	**
Infectious Disease-Med.	107.4	95	105.7	92	102.9	90	1.6	3.3
Nephrology-Med.	98.1	88	98.9	84	97.3	84	-0.8	4.8
Pulmonary-Med.	101.4	87	102.4	89	100.3	89	-1.0	-2.2
Rheumatology-Med.	108.3	92	102.8	89	99.9	91	5.4	3.4
Other Medicine	113.4	100	110.3	99	109.1	97	2.8	1.0

** Indicates that fewer than ten faculty were reported.

TABLE 33

Change in Mean and Median Total Compensation By Department/Specialty Faculty with a Ph.D. or Other Doctoral Degree: Combined Assistant, Associate, and Professor Ranks 2010-2011 through 2008-2009

($ in thousands)

DEPARTMENT/SPECIALTY	2010-2011		2009-2010		2008-2009		% Change 2009-2010 to 2010-2011	
	Mean	Median	Mean	Median	Mean	Median	Mean	Median
Total OB/GYN	**129.4**	**112**	**126.1**	**109**	**122.4**	**108**	**2.6**	**2.8**
OB/GYN: General	131.4	117	129.0	112	123.2	110	1.9	4.5
OB/GYN: Gynecologic Oncology	140.9	133	130.2	112	**	**	8.2	18.8
OB/GYN: Maternal & Fetal	128.6	109	152.4	135	128.3	130	-15.6	-19.3
OB/GYN: Reproductive Endocrinology	152.8	128	146.1	126	141.1	126	4.6	1.6
OB/GYN: Other OB/GYN	114.5	102	110.3	99	105.9	94	3.8	3.0
Total Pathology	**136.6**	**127**	**132.7**	**123**	**130.8**	**120**	**2.9**	**3.3**
Pathology: Anatomic	146.2	139	136.7	127	137.1	125	6.9	9.4
Pathology: Clinical	151.6	142	145.7	136	144.7	136	4.0	4.4
Pathology: Other Pathology	127.5	115	124.7	113	122.5	112	2.2	1.8
Total Pediatrics	**114.7**	**100**	**111.1**	**99**	**110.5**	**98**	**3.2**	**1.0**
Adolescent Medicine	101.6	87	98.6	89	102.5	88	3.0	-2.2
Allergy/Immunology-Peds.	94.6	91	98.8	92	93.4	91	-4.3	-1.1
Child & Adolescent Psychiatry	118.0	100	112.7	99	110.3	98	4.7	1.0
Critical/Intensive Care-Peds.	120.2	110	119.9	108	115.3	110	0.3	1.9
Emergency Medicine-Peds.	**	**	**	**	**	**	**	**
Endocrinology-Peds.	102.6	85	96.2	83	101.8	89	6.7	2.4
Gastroenterology-Peds.	118.9	101	108.8	96	102.9	85	9.3	5.2
General Pediatrics	113.5	100	107.1	101	108.1	95	6.0	-1.0
Genetics-Peds.	114.0	98	111.7	101	105.5	93	2.1	-3.0
Hematology/Oncology-Peds.	108.3	94	107.4	95	107.0	93	0.8	-1.1
Hospital Medicine-Peds.	**	**	123.2	111	**	**	**	**
Infectious Disease-Peds.	107.6	103	101.7	95	104.7	98	5.8	8.4
Neonatology	116.5	103	117.3	101	113.2	102	-0.7	2.0
Nephrology-Peds.	78.9	77	100.3	81	96.9	77	-21.3	-4.9
Neurology-Peds.	115.7	101	110.2	104	110.8	101	5.0	-2.9
Pediatric Cardiology	119.4	99	120.0	103	126.4	104	-0.5	-3.9
Pulmonary-Peds.	98.4	90	93.9	87	94.3	88	4.8	3.4
Rheumatology-Peds.	**	**	**	**	**	**	**	**
Other Pediatrics	118.5	104	114.5	100	115.5	100	3.5	4.0
Total Radiology	**148.0**	**136**	**143.8**	**133**	**143.7**	**132**	**2.9**	**2.3**
Diagnostic Radiology: Total	**144.2**	**124**	**137.0**	**119**	**136.4**	**122**	**5.3**	**4.2**
Diagnostic Radiology: Interventional	184.2	187	163.2	177	155.3	134	12.9	5.6
Diagnostic Radiology: Non-interventional	143.0	123	136.2	118	135.9	122	5.0	4.2
Nuclear Medicine	139.3	122	129.0	110	126.2	106	8.0	10.9
Radiation Oncology	163.7	159	159.7	154	159.2	153	2.5	3.2
Other Radiology	133.5	123	133.0	123	134.0	121	0.4	0.0

** Indicates that fewer than ten faculty were reported.

TABLE 33

Change in Mean and Median Total Compensation By Department/Specialty Faculty with a Ph.D. or Other Doctoral Degree: Combined Assistant, Associate, and Professor Ranks 2010-2011 through 2008-2009

($ in thousands)

DEPARTMENT/SPECIALTY	2010-2011		2009-2010		2008-2009		% Change 2009-2010 to 2010-2011	
	Mean	Median	Mean	Median	Mean	Median	Mean	Median
Total Surgery	**126.6**	**106**	**123.9**	**105**	**122.4**	**104**	**2.2**	**1.0**
General Surgery	125.3	106	125.3	105	117.3	104	0.0	1.0
Neurosurgery	133.3	105	126.6	107	124.1	107	5.3	-1.9
Orthopaedic Surgery	132.2	107	130.9	110	131.0	108	0.9	-2.7
Pediatric Surgery	81.5	78	88.7	80	100.6	78	-8.1	-2.5
Plastic Surgery	112.7	99	119.8	105	106.3	103	-5.9	-5.7
Surgical Oncology	106.0	96	95.8	85	96.0	89	10.6	12.9
Thoracic & Cardiovascular Surgery	115.7	105	120.7	107	111.9	104	-4.1	-1.9
Transplant Surgery	145.4	120	132.6	109	133.8	112	9.7	10.1
Trauma/Critical Care Surgery	113.3	88	123.6	93	122.6	103	-8.3	-5.4
Urology	122.6	113	121.0	110	122.0	107	1.3	2.7
Vascular Surgery	116.6	107	108.4	94	108.0	100	7.6	13.8
Other Surgery	125.7	104	120.7	102	125.0	102	4.1	2.0
Other Clinical Science								
Community Health	123.2	108	119.8	107	120.4	108	2.8	0.9
Emergency Medicine	136.2	131	125.8	117	127.1	125	8.3	12.0
Family Medicine	107.1	99	105.5	99	106.7	98	1.5	0.0
Neurology	120.5	104	118.0	100	113.2	97	2.1	4.0
Ophthalmology	124.3	111	120.5	109	119.0	110	3.2	1.8
Otolaryngology	121.4	105	122.2	107	120.2	107	-0.7	-1.9
Physical Medicine & Rehabilitation	101.9	93	99.8	91	98.8	92	2.1	2.2
Preventive Medicine	127.0	112	125.8	113	124.1	110	1.0	-0.9
Psychiatry	120.8	105	119.3	104	117.4	103	1.3	1.0
Other	121.6	109	117.6	104	121.4	102	3.4	4.8

** Indicates that fewer than ten faculty were reported.

AAMC

Tomorrow's Doctors, Tomorrow's Cures

My Resources | My Account | Logout

2011 AAMC Faculty Salary Survey

Medical School:

Welcome to the 2011 AAMC Faculty Salary Survey (FSS). You may provide your faculty compensation data through one or both of the following methods:

- Online Data Entry - compensation data is entered manually for each faculty member in department/specialty-specific data entry screens.
- Salary File Upload - compensation data is uploaded as tab-delimited text files. Complete instructions for creating tab-delimited files from your Excel or Access files can be accessed from the Table of Contents page.
  Departmental Users may upload data files for their assigned departments/specialties only.

What's New This Year?

Two medical schools have been invited to participate in the Faculty Salary Survey for the first time:
Florida Atlantic University College of Medicine and Cooper Medical School of Rowan University.

Continue

2011-055

AAMC

Tomorrow's Doctors, Tomorrow's Cures

My Resources | My Account | Logout

2011 AAMC Faculty Salary Survey

Medical School:

Table of Contents

- Review the "Instructions and Definitions" section before entering or uploading salary data.
- View the "FAQs" to see answers to the most frequently asked questions about completing the survey.
- Use the "Add Departmental User Role" link below to create roles which have access to only those departments/specialties you assign.
- Use the "View/Edit Departmental User Roles" link to view departmental user roles and access codes, edit a department/specialty list, or delete a role.
- Use the "Online Data Entry/Department Listing" link to add/update/view individual salary data by department/specialty.
- Click the "File Upload Tool" link to view upload instructions and to upload salary data as a tab-delimited text file. *Departmental Users may upload salary survey files for their assigned departments/specialties only.*
- Use the "Salary File Upload History" section to review file uploads and/or delete uploaded files.
- Click the "Update Contact Information" link to modify your contact information.

It is not necessary to complete your survey in one visit; all data entered or uploaded is saved and may be edited on future visits. When you are completely finished and have reviewed your entries for completeness and accuracy, click the "Submit Completed Survey" button below or in the file upload tool. Once you have clicked the "Submit Completed Survey" button, you will be able to view your data, but you will no longer be able to edit the data. The deadline for submitting data to the Faculty Salary Survey is **October 14, 2011**. If you need any assistance, please contact Fan Zhang at fzhang@aamc.org, 202-862-6133.

Note: Departmental Users will not see the "Add Departmental User Role" link, the "View/Edit Departmental User Roles" link, or the "Submit Completed Survey" button. The final submission of the Faculty Salary Survey must be completed by the institution's main user.

Survey Sections

Instructions and Definitions - **Please read before completing the survey.**

FAQs

Add Departmental User Role

View/Edit Departmental User Roles

Online Data Entry/Department Listing

File Upload Tool, File Upload Instructions, and AAMC Codes

Salary File Upload History

Update Contact Information

Update Faculty ID Choice

Submit Completed Survey

(Please do not click this button until you have reviewed your entries and are certain you are finished with the survey.)

2011-055

2011 AAMC Faculty Salary Survey

Medical School:

Instructions and Definitions

Table of Contents

Each faculty record must include complete information for faculty rank, degree, and all compensation components.

Include:

a. Only 12-month salaries for **full-time paid** faculty, chairs, and chiefs by department or division of major appointment for fiscal year 2010-2011, which at many institutions may correspond to the period of July 1, 2010 to June 30, 2011. In general, report individuals who would be considered full-time faculty for LCME reporting purposes. Nine-month salaries should be converted by multiplying compensation by 1.22 (11/9).
b. Full salary of faculty on sabbatical leave.
c. All full-time research faculty regardless of tenure status.
d. Employee retirement contributions as part of a salary reduction program.
e. Full-time faculty members who received all or part of their compensation from affiliated institutions, except those who received 100 percent of their compensation from the Veterans Administration. (For faculty who received less than 100 percent of their compensation from the Veterans Administration, report the VA compensation in the Fixed Salary column.)
f. All sources of income (for example, income from the medical school and affiliated institutions).
g. Center or institute directors with full-time faculty appointments whose responsibilities are similar to those of a department chair or division chief. Classify the directors as chairs or chiefs as appropriate.

Exclude:

a. Full salary for vacant positions.
b. Employer retirement contributions as part of a salary reduction program.
c. Faculty in administrative positions such as medical school dean, associate dean, or practice plan CFO, as well as center or institute directors whose responsibilities are similar to those of a dean, associate dean, or assistant dean.

Department/Specialty

When compensation is derived from more than one department or division, please report all compensation in a single department/specialty on the survey. In so far as possible, faculty should be reported in their primary department of appointment, regardless of whether the faculty member's responsibilities are typical of those in that department. For instance, faculty performing research in the emergency medicine department should be classified in emergency medicine, not in a basic science department/specialty.

Depending on the structure of your medical school, some faculty may work in specialties (e.g., Mohs Surgery) that are not formal organizational units, such as departments, divisions, or sections. Please classify faculty at the finest level of granularity possible on the survey, even if the faculty member's specialty is not a formal organizational unit at your medical school. For instance, if you do not have a separate department for Mohs Surgery, but have faculty who work primarily as Mohs surgeons in your Dermatology department, please classify those faculty under "Dermatology-Mohs Surgery."

Report a chair or chief in the department/specialty that most resembles the department or division/section of the individual. If there is no comparable department/specialty, please report the individual under the appropriate "Other" category. For example, report a "Chair of Medicine" in "Other Medicine."

Hopefully, the assignment of faculty to the AAMC departments/specialties is straightforward. However, some departments/specialties have posed problems for institutions. The following instructions provide guidance for some of these circumstances.

Anatomic Pathology: Typically, institutions report specialties such as Autopsy Pathology, Cytopathology, Forensic Pathology, and Surgical Pathology under Anatomic Pathology.

Clinical Pathology: Typically, institutions report specialties such as Chemistry/Molecular Diagnostics, Molecular Cytometry, and Transfusion Medicine under Clinical Pathology.

Ophthalmology: Please report specialties such as General/Comprehensive Ophthalmology, Corneal/Refractive Surgery, Glaucoma, Neuro-Ophthalmology, Oculoplastic/Reconstructive Surgery, Optometry, and Retinal Ophthalmology under Ophthalmology.

Pediatrics: With the exception of Pediatric Surgery, which is classified under "Surgery," and Pediatric Anesthesiology, which is classified under "Anesthesiology" in this survey, all Pediatric specialties are listed under Pediatrics. If a particular pediatric specialty at your institution is not listed in Pediatrics, please enter the compensation for the faculty members in that specialty under "Other Pediatrics."

Psychiatry: Please include specialties such as Addiction Psychiatry, Forensic Psychiatry, and Geriatric Psychiatry under Psychiatry.

Radiation Oncology: Please include Therapeutic Radiology under Radiation Oncology.

If you are unable to classify a department/specialty into one of the existing categories, please record the compensation for the faculty members in that department/specialty in the appropriate "Other" category. Include faculty members in educational support departments under "Other Basic" or "Other Clinical."

Rank

For purposes of this survey, a Chief is defined as the head of the unit just smaller than the department, while a Chair is defined as the head of the department. If a person is both a Chair and a Professor, please indicate Chair. If a person is both a Chief and a Professor, please indicate Chief.

Degree

Faculty should be classified by the degree that the faculty member holds, regardless of whether the faculty member's responsibilities are typical of those in that degree classification. For instance, a faculty member with an M.D. or equivalent degree (e.g., M.B.Ch.B) who is performing research should be classified in the M.D. or Equivalent category, not in the Ph.D. or Other Doctoral category or in the Non Doctoral category.

If Holding:	Report:
M.D. or M.D. equivalent degree (e.g., D.O., M.B.Ch.B., M.B.B.S., D.M.D., D.D.S.) but no Ph.D. or other doctoral degree	M.D. or Equivalent.
Ph.D. or other doctoral degree (e.g., Ed.D. or D.S.W.) but no M.D. or equivalent degree	Ph.D. or Other Doctoral.
M.D. or equivalent degree as well as a Ph.D. or other doctoral degree, regardless of whether the degrees were earned simultaneously	M.D. and Ph.D.
No degree or any degree other than a doctoral degree	Non Doctoral.

Compensation

The compensation reported should reflect the total amount before deductions are made for taxes and retirement set-asides. No benefits or services provided by the institution should be considered in determining compensation. All sources of income (for example, income from the medical school and affiliated institutions) should be included. Report the compensation information using the definitions listed below, *rounding to the nearest thousand.* It is necessary that the Association know that all compensation components are accounted for, even if the actual dollars are not known. Thus, the following designations should be used for each faculty member in the appropriate column where there are no dollars to report:

NA - Not Applicable. This compensation component does not apply as part of total compensation derived from teaching, patient care, and research activity.

NI - No Information. Compensation component is applicable, but amount is unknown and cannot be estimated.

0 - Zero dollars. Compensation component is applicable, but no dollars were reported.

Compensation Component Definitions

Fixed/Contractual Salary: Compensation, exclusive of fringe benefits, that was fixed at the beginning of the fiscal year and contractually obligated to the faculty member for that year assuming satisfactory performance. This component should include salary that is provided by general operating revenues, grant support, and the medical practice plan when that amount is fixed and not contingent upon medical practice billings/collections. It should also include any portion of compensation that is tied to assigned administrative duties as long as that portion is fixed at the beginning of the year.

Medical Practice Supplement: Income that was not fixed at the beginning of the fiscal year but was directly tied to the amount of medical practice earnings during the year derived from an institutionally controlled or affiliated source. *The use of NI in the Medical Practice Supplement field will cause the salary record to be excluded from published tables since total compensation cannot be derived when one or more of the compensation sources is not known.*

Bonus/Incentive Pay: Income earned by the faculty member as a result of the achievement of specific performance goals by the individual or the department or institution. Examples of bonus/incentive pay are:

- Year-end bonus from a faculty practice plan.
- Incentive earnings according to the practice plan.
- Outside earnings where limited or controlled by the institution.

Note: If the total amount derived from the medical practice plan is known, but the distribution between Medical Practice Supplement and Bonus/Incentive Pay is not, please report the total amount from the practice plan in the Medical Practice Supplement column and NA (Not Applicable) in the Bonus/Incentive Pay column. *The use of NI in the Bonus/Incentive Pay field will cause the salary record to be excluded from the published tables since total compensation cannot be derived when one or more of the compensation sources is not known.*

Uncontrolled Outside Earnings: Known but unregulated outside professional income related to the health professions (e.g., patient services income, royalties, and consulting fees). Do not report income from affiliated institutions in Uncontrolled Outside Earnings; report income from affiliated institutions in Fixed Salary, Medical Practice Supplement, and/or Bonus Pay, as appropriate. Please report a whole number, NA, or zero; NI is to be used where it is known that this outside amount is considerable, but the exact amount is not available. Our intention is to keep the use of NI to a minimum. *Beginning with the 2001 survey, the use of NI in this field will **not** cause the salary record to be excluded from the published tables.*

Table of Contents

2011-055

 [redacted]

AAMC

Tomorrow's Doctors, Tomorrow's Cures

My [redacted]urces | My Account | Logout

2011 AAMC Faculty Salary Survey

Medical School:

Add/Edit Survey

Update Faculty ID Choice | Instructions and Definitions | Department/Specialty Listing
View Current Department/Specialty | Update Decision Rules | Table of Contents

Department/Specialty - Critical/Intensive Care-Med. (0)

Select a Department/Specialty to Update

Add New Survey Entries

- Add faculty information in the blank rows below.
- If the Total Compensation includes only a Single, Fixed Salary Component, **check NA (Not Applicable) to prefill the three Supplemental Income fields**.
- Report dollars rounded to the nearest thousand (e.g., $36,600 would be reported as 37).
- Click the "Add New Survey Entries" button to save the entries to the database.
- After you have added entries for a department, an Update/Delete section will be displayed in the lower half of this page.
- Underlined column headings link to definitions.
- The drop-down box at the top of this page can be used to move quickly to another department/specialty.

Report dollars rounded to nearest thousand.

Entry	Faculty ID	Rank	Degree	Fixed Salary	NA	Supplemental Income: Medical Practice Supp.	Supplemental Income: Bonus/ Incentive Pay	Supplemental Income: Uncontr. Outside Earnings	Total Comp.
#1		Select a Rank	Select a Degree		☐				
#2		Select a Rank	Select a Degree		☐				
#3		Select a Rank	Select a Degree		☐				
#4		Select a Rank	Select a Degree		☐				
#5		Select a Rank	Select a Degree		☐				
#6		Select a Rank	Select a Degree		☐				
#7		Select a Rank	Select a Degree		☐				
#8		Select a Rank	Select a Degree		☐				
#9		Select a Rank	Select a Degree		☐				
#10		Select a Rank	Select a Degree		☐				

Add New Survey Entries | Clear Form

2011-055